WHITE, POOR AND ANGRY

To Rachel Stewart

White, Poor and Angry
White working class families in Johannesburg

LIS LANGE
Council on Higher Education
South Africa

LONDON AND NEW YORK

First published 2003 by Ashgate Publishing

Reissued 2018 by Routledge
2 Park Square, Milton Park, Abingdon, Oxon OX14 4RN
711 Third Avenue, New York, NY 10017, USA

Routledge is an imprint of the Taylor & Francis Group, an informa business

Copyright © Lis Lange 2003

Lis Lange has asserted her right under the Copyright, Designs and Patents Act, 1988, to be identified as author of this work.

All rights reserved. No part of this book may be reprinted or reproduced or utilised in any form or by any electronic, mechanical, or other means, now known or hereafter invented, including photocopying and recording, or in any information storage or retrieval system, without permission in writing from the publishers.

Notice:
Product or corporate names may be trademarks or registered trademarks, and are used only for identification and explanation without intent to infringe.

Publisher's Note
The publisher has gone to great lengths to ensure the quality of this reprint but points out that some imperfections in the original copies may be apparent.

Disclaimer
The publisher has made every effort to trace copyright holders and welcomes correspondence from those they have been unable to contact.

A Library of Congress record exists under LC control number: 2002032691

ISBN 13: 978-1-138-72667-3 (hbk)
ISBN 13: 978-1-138-72666-6 (pbk)
ISBN 13: 978-1-315-19099-0 (ebk)

Contents

List of Tables		*vi*
Preface		*vii*
1	Class Experience, Class Consciousness and White Working Class Identity in South African Historiography	1
2	The Emergence of the South African White Working Class in Johannesburg, 1890-1906	9
3	The Political Economy of White Working Class Housing in Johannesburg, 1890-1906	39
4	White Working Class Housing and the Emergence of the Urban Problem in Johannesburg, 1907-1922	75
5	White Workers' Daily Life in Johannesburg, 1890-1922	101
6	The Ideological Construction of the Poor White Problem, 1890-1922	133
7	The Making of the White Working Class in Johannesburg, 1890-1922	165
Bibliography		*173*
Index		*183*

List of Tables

2.1	White population of greater Johannesburg	12
2.2	Conjugal condition of the white population in Johannesburg	12
2.3	Number of white families in Johannesburg	12
2.4	Number of white males and females by place of birth	14
2.5	Percentage of English and Afrikaner by occupation, 1890-1906	19
3.1	Number and types of buildings, 1890	51
3.2	Population by wards 1896	53
3.3	Occupations by wards 1896	54
4.1	Population of Johannesburg, 1904-1921	84
6.1	Numbers of poor whites in the Union of South Africa, 1917	141

Preface

Had it not been for Abebe Zegeye and, indirectly, Robert Kriger, this book would have never been published. My thanks to both of them for their timely intervention.

Almost four years have gone by since I finished my thesis. In the intervening years my life has changed so much that I am in many senses a different person from the one who wrote the thesis. This change has at least two consequences. On the one hand, although the basic argument of the book does not differ from what I wrote in the thesis, there are some marked differences in the theorization of both the problem and of the historian's work. On the other hand, my intellectual and personal debt has both increased and diversified.

I am as ever in debt to the organizations that funded my research at different stages of the approximately seven years I took to complete my PhD. These are the Anglo American and De Beer's Chairman's Fund, the Oppenheimer Memorial Trust, the International Federation of University Women and the SEPHIS project of the University of Rotterdam. To all of them goes my sincere gratitude for their support.

The University of the Witwatersand provided me with a senior bursary for several years but fundamentally gave me the opportunity to work with Charles van Onselen who was for seven years my supervisor. Although I never had any doubt about how privileged I was for the opportunity to work with a historian-craftsman of van Onselen's stature, it is only with hindsight that I realize how much he moulded me. He was endlessly patient but also endlessly demanding. I am deeply grateful for his unmitigated search and demand for excellence, his rigour and his brutal intellectual discipline. Not so long ago I met a philosopher-cum-viola player who mentioned that before starting to play a piece he would listen to the best available recording to learn how it should sound. In similar fashion prior to writing any of the chapters of this book, as with the thesis previously, I read and re-read Charles van Onselen's books. Needless to say that knowing how history should sound does not mean for a second that this book so sounds. Simply, I have tried.

One of the reasons why I did not publish this book earlier was because I did not have the time to work on it. For four years I stopped, at least in practice, being a historian so as to take part in a project aimed at reconfiguring the production and funding of research in the social sciences and humanities in South Africa. The stimulating intellectual environment of the Centre for Science Development opened for me new areas of inquiry and different ways of looking at academic work, research and society. I am especially grateful to Prem Naidoo, who not only taught me the profound meaning of development and its value for individuals and societies but also gave me his friendship and his trust. Mala Singh has to assume responsibility for having re-ignited the theoretical and philosophical flame in me. Her demand for rigour can only be measured by her intellectual integrity and generosity with her ideas. Working with her is a tall order amply compensated by the gift of her friendship.

Through both Mala Singh and Prem Naidoo I met a group of people who make critical intellectual engagement a way of living, and who influence my life and my thinking by the way they live and think. Among them, I owe a particularly large personal and intellectual debt to Enver Motala.

Jutta Van Dalsen has freed me from myself enough to be able to write without too much fear.

Rachel Stewart has given me the rootedness necessary to grow and the love and companionship to make life worth living. She and ten year-old Puleng have had to bear the brunt of my obsession with this book, not to mention in Rachel's case the editing of the chapters. To both of them go my love and my gratitude.

Thanks are due to Verso Books for permission to quote from D. Roediger's *Towards the Abolition of Whiteness*, and to Johns Hopkins University Press for permission to quote from H. White's *The Content of the Form*.

Chapter 1

Class Experience, Class Consciousness and White Working Class Identity in South African Historiography

The Anglo-Boer War, latterly referred to as the South African War, like all nationalistic and colonial wars was a fundamental episode in the construction of the identity of the people at war. In the years leading to the war, during it and immediately afterwards, British and Afrikaner cultures, experiences and traditions as well as political interests and ideologies were at work to define the identity and behaviour of the enemy, and therefore the nature and limits of the political and social interactions between the warring factions.

The book's historical narrative starts on the eve of the South African War with the questions raised by a story of the baptism of two children. In 1898, a year before the outbreak of the South African War, William Kirby, a self-employed cab owner who lived in Fordsburg with his wife, Elizabeth, and two children, asked his colleague, Stefanus van Niekerk, to be godparent to his third child, a boy, who was to be baptized in the Anglican Church of the neighbourhood, the Church of Christ. Stefanus, who also lived in Fordsburg, accepted the honour and a few years later, in 1903, he and his wife Phoebe had their own child baptized in the same church.

Here was an English working class family, the Kirbys, sealing a relationship with an Afrikaner family, the van Niekerks, through the baptism of one of their children. At the same time, there was an Afrikaner family stepping outside that which history and common sense tell about Afrikaner folk and religion to have their child baptized in the Anglican Church. Why did the Kirbys choose Stefanus van Niekerk as godparent to their child instead of choosing an Englishman? Was this exceptional? Why did Stefanus accept? Why, finally, did the van Niekerks have their own child baptized in the Anglican Church instead of in the Dutch Reformed Church? In historiographical terms this book takes the example of these two families to raise questions about the interactions between the two distinct national elements that constituted the South African white working class; about the role of the churches in developing a sense of belonging and identity among immigrant people in the city, whether they came from abroad or from the countryside; about the elements of day-to-day life that made possible social interaction that seemingly went beyond and indeed defied, at least in part, nationalistic politics.

This book looks into different aspects of the history of the white working class in Johannesburg between 1890 and 1922 to try to answer these questions in the light of the events of the 1922 Rand Revolt, a major mining strike during which working class solidarity transcended the divisions between workers of Afrikaner and British descent, and workers' actions spilled beyond the borders of the workplace into the working class neighbourhoods in the west of the city, eliciting support from some non-mining workers.

These questions suggest a series of theoretical, analytical and methodological issues for reflection. At the theoretical level the definition, nature, and explicative value of concepts such as class, class consciousness, identity and experience become a fundamental historiographic problem. At the analytical level the competing, contested and hard-to-reconcile strands of thought, such as, crassly put, Marxism and Postmodernism, seem to highlight the complexity of a topic that was thought fairly straightforward 20 or 30 years ago. Finally, at the methodological level, and in whichever way the concepts of class and identity, and their theoretical derivations, intersect with different analytical frameworks, there is the issue of the value of the historical sources and of the narrative that enacts the historical "findings" for the reader.

In the 1960s and 1970s South African historiography of the white working class showed little interest in the theoretical engagement with the conceptual instruments of the métier. For most historians, whether on the left or not, class was both a social reality and a useful and necessary analytical tool that need not to be interrogated. The origins of the South African white working class were explained through the process of dispossession of rural labourers and the arrival of members of a fully fledged working class from overseas whose modes of organization and political responses were consistent with their experiences of working class organization in Britain.[1] And while the role of race in both the organization of the colonial society and in defining the social and political behaviour of the working class was duly noted, no theoretical elaboration was offered to explain how the sense of belonging to a class overlapped and/or interacted with that of belonging to a racial group. The preoccupation with the organizations of the working class as well as with its leaders rather than with the workers themselves was based on the assumption that workers' lives were shaped largely by their conditions of employment.[2]

The universe of workers' lives was even further removed from the 1970s Marxist-structuralist writings on the white working class, which, however, did much to explain the class position of the South African white working class in relation to its place in society and its relative access to the state in a racially organized society.[3]

In the same way that South African historians' and social scientists' understanding of the state was influenced by the explicative and political power of the writings of Althusser, Poulantzas and other theorists of the state, social history as proposed by Williams, Hobsbawm, Hill, and Thompson, to name only British historians, had an enormous appeal for a generation of South African historians, who found in the 'history from below' a way to write a more comprehensive and nuanced history of the white working class and, at the same time, to illuminate the South African political present in the 1980s. It has been said aptly that social history writing in South Africa, and not just in relation to the white working class, took two narrative forms, the one based on culturalist notions of class and the other located within the politics of nationalism.[4] These strands produced some remarkable research. Indeed, social history contributed greatly in broadening the subject of history and in connecting the material with the ideological and the cultural with the political as layers of meaning or rather causality that needed to be brought together in a textured narrative capable of "reconstructing" the past for the reader. Outstanding in this regard are the chapters on white working class culture in van Onselen's studies on the Witwatersrand.[5]

A fundamental element in the understanding of working class culture as described by social historians was the differentiation between class experience and class consciousness proposed by Thompson in his *Making of the English Working Class*. While class experience derives from workers' position in the relations of production and helps them to articulate an identity of interests as different from those of other social classes, class consciousness is the cultural expression of this class experience through values, institutions, traditions, etc.[6] This proposition solved, at least in part, the issue of what to look for at the methodological level when trying to establish the process of the making of a working class while it simultaneously purged a good deal of historical writing on the left from a teleological and simplistic view of the working class.

However, as grand historical narratives were contested in their theoretical and methodological validity, class became too broad and undetermined a concept to deal with the reality of subaltern groups' lives and their cultural or political expressions. Social historians turn to 'community' as a more manageable and somewhat more "real" term to deal with the complex and more subtle problems of identity formation and the ways in which it relates to different forms of class consciousness. One of the most substantive theorizations of the usage of community as a historical or sociological analytical category comes from Bozzoli's *Class, Community and Conflict*.[7] Whether communities were invented as part of bourgeoisie's projects as Anderson proposed[8] or became manifest social entities, as Stedman Jones saw it in the case of the English working class,[9] the investigation of the process of identity formation in specific communities, and of the manner in which concrete communities interact with class, have produced interesting interpretations of the South African past.[10] Bozzoli's recommendation to combine into one approach the understanding of communities as produced with that of communities as real and interacting with classes, enabling a more nuanced and complex explanation of social processes, seems to have echoed with those interested in gendered history.[11]

At the general methodological level social historians not only rescued the voices of the subaltern groups through skilful readings of written sources, they also incorporated their actual voices through the use of oral testimony. Oral history became a tool that connected past and present politically at the same time that it established the link between the individual and the collective.[12]

A different form of investigation of the individual and the collective memory was attempted by historians and social scientists who were concerned about the nature, value and practical force of ideology and intellectual discourse. Saul Dubow, with his work on the intellectual history and ideological underpinnings of racism, and Adam Ashford, with his book on the role of commissions of enquiry in discourse formation, made valuable contributions to the broadening of historical enquiry to the realm of words, discourse and ideology.[13]

As Foucault, Derrida, Deleuze and Guatari, Homi Bhaba and many others helped in effecting the linguistic and postcolonial turn in the production of social sciences (and humanities) in South Africa, grand historical narratives were replaced by the stories of the local and of the individual; the history of class and community were replaced by the stories of the inbetweeness and the otherness. Aided by the political moment, the question for identity - racial, cultural, political, sexual, literary - gained currency among social scientists with very different results in terms of academic output.[14]

In the context of postcolonial writing race ceased to be defined simply in terms of the constitutive elements of colonial discourse and was given all the force of a product of a 'race science'. Writings on race start by asserting that there is no such a thing as Black 'race'. This revisiting of the theorizations of race and its implications at the societal and individual level is far from being limited to the oppressed groups in colonial situations. A revision of whiteness from a radical political perspective has been under way for a while, especially in the US.[15] This revision, which hinges on the critique of the assumption that white is not a race, makes two important contributions to the study of the white working class in racially organized societies. Firstly, it suggests that ignoring white as a race is to naturalize its hegemony. Second, it proposes that in analyzing working class behaviour historians and sociologist have to do away with the idea that workers "view the world objectively through their class experience in one part of their brain, and subjectively through the distorting filter of race in another".[16] Race among the American white working class, as much as among its South African counterpart, was/is a constitutive element of workers' experience of themselves and of the others and in this sense is as indispensable in understanding workers' politics and lives as class itself. In recent elaborations on the issue of race and its political effect, it has been argued that race can be seen as "common sense made juridical" and therefore translated in a series of apparatus and technologies that govern peoples' lives.[17] Despite the historical distance between apartheid South Africa and the Union of South Africa, race in the 1910s was certainly about governability, but, interestingly, not so much of the Black 'race' as of the white. As will be argued in this book, this made sense in the specific historical context of early twentieth century South Africa.

The impact of different strands of post-structuralism on historical writing has been felt particularly at the methodological level. The displacement of the subject has questioned fundamentally the value of narrative and has brought about a salutary scrutiny of the supposedly unproblematic relation between individual and collective memory, between memory and truth, between narrative and the historian/writer, all of which has highlighted the tensions that exist between conversational narrative and dramatic monologue, especially in the terrain of oral history.[18]

When this is translated to the terrain of a history based on written sources, and, in the case of working class history, of sources that only reflect the voices of the subjects indirectly, the issue of the tension between conversational narrative and dramatic monologue becomes even more daunting. Who does the narrative represent: the workers themselves; that which the middle classes, the government, the church thought of the workers; or the historical imagination of the writer?

Moreover, the contemporary trend of inspecting individual lives so as to make sense of historicized (racial) subjectivities, which proceeds with an almost psychoanalytical perspective to interpret its subject, poses a methodological conundrum in the case of collective subjects.[19]

This book sits slightly uncomfortably in the midst of these trends because most of its interpretative framework is based on the reality of social classes whose existence is largely conditioned by the material circumstances in which they live, and on the notion that while individuals have personal experiences of those circumstances which are, contradictorily, expressed in both cultural and political terms, most individuals make sense of their experiences in a social community of meaning. But neither community nor identity are ahistorical or mere processes undergone by the individual as such.

In this book the analysis of the development of white workers' identity and sense of community in Johannesburg between 1890 and 1922 takes into account that a sense of community is not a precondition for the existence of a class but a process the constitutive elements of which need to be identified, explained and put in relation with each other. Thus, the chapters of this book are organized around a rather conventional idea of historical narration. Chapter 2 examines the process of formation of the white working class from a demographic perspective and focuses on the role that family had in social and cultural reproduction. Chapters 3 and 4 examine the ways in which economic processes, social developments and racially defined colonial culture conditioned the political economy of working class housing. Chapter 5 analyzes the ways in which individuals' daily experiences made possible the development of a sense of community in the working class neighbourhoods of Johannesburg. Chapter 6 focuses on the construction of the poor white problem and the role it played in defining the relations between the white working class and the state. Finally, Chapter 7 reflects on the construction of working class identity as a historical process and on the role that historical narrative has in its reconstruction.

This narrative of the life of white workers in Johannesburg between 1890 and 1922 is based on the painful weaving together of information and snatches of "real life" as it appears through church records, government documents, travellers' accounts, newspapers, street directories, old pictures, police records, court cases, etc. The evidence was patchy and so is the result. The reader would be good enough to treat this book as if it were a picture from the Impressionist school and to apply the usual caution of looking at it with enough distance for the image not to become blurred.

Notes

[1] Simons, H.J. and Simons, R.E., *Class and Colour in South Africa, 1850-1950* (Harmondsworth 1969). Hereafter *Class and Colour in South Africa*.

[2] Katz, E., *A Trade Union Aristocracy: A History of White Workers in the Transvaal and the General Strike of 1913* (Johannesburg 1976); Katz, E., 'Miners by Default: Afrikaners and the Gold Mining Industry Before Union', *The South African Journal of Economic History*, 6, 1, 1991, pp. 61-80; Katz, E., *The White Death: Silicosis on the Witwatersrand Mines, 1886-1910* (Johannesburg 1994); Hirson, B. and Williams, G.A., *The Delegate for Africa: David Ivon Jones, 1883-1924* (London 1995); Roux, E., *S.P. Bunting: A Political Biography* (Bellville 1993), Roux, E. and Roux, W., *Rebel Pity: The Life of Eddie Roux* (London 1970) and Cope, R.K., *Comrade Bill: The Life and Times of W. Andrews, Workers' Leader* (Cape Town 1943).

[3] Johnstone, F.A., *Class, Race and Gold: A Study of Class Relations and Racial Discrimination in South Africa* (London 1976). Hereafter *Class, Race and Gold*; Davies, R. H., *Capital, State and White Labour in South Africa 1900-1960: A Historical Materialist Analysis of Class*

    Formation and Class Relations (Brighton 1979). Hereafter *Capital, State and White Labour*.
4   Minkley, G. and Rasool, C., 'Orality, Memory and Social History in South Africa' in S. Nuttall and C. Coetzee, *Negotiating the Past. The Making of Memory in South Africa* (Oxford 1998), p. 92. Hereafter Minkley and Rasool, *Orality*.
5   Van Onselen, C., *Studies in the Social and Economic History of the Witwatersrand, 1886-1914*, volume 1, *New Babylon*; volume 2, *New Nineveh* (Johannesburg 1982), 'The World the Mine Owners Made: Social Themes in the Economic Transformation of the Witwatersrand, 1886-1914', volume 1, *New Babylon*, p. 5; and p. 8, p. 18, p. 22, p. 27, p. 30, p. 31 and p. 32. See also 'Prostitutes and Proletarians, 1886-1914', volume 1, *New Babylon*, pp. 103-62; 'The Witches of Suburbia: Domestic Service on the Witwatersrand, 1890-1914', pp. 1-73; and 'The Main Reef Road into the Working Class: Proletarianisation, Unemployment and Class Consciousness amongst Johannesburg's Afrikaner Poor, 1886-1914', pp. 111-70, volume 2, *New Nineveh*.
6   Thompson, E.P., *The Making of the English Working Class* (Harmondsworth 1968), pp.9-10.
7   Bozzoli, B., 'Class, Community and Ideology in the Evolution of South African Society', in Bozzoli, B. (ed.), *Class, Community and Conflict: South African Perspectives* (Johannesburg 1987).
8   Giliomee, H., and Adam H., *The Rise and Crisis of Afrikaner Power* (Cape Town 1979); Hofmeyr, I., 'Building a Nation from Words: Afrikaans Language, Literature and Ethnicity, 1902-1924', in Marks, S. and Trapido, S. (eds.) *The Politics of Race, Class and Nationalism in Twentieth Century South Africa* (London 1987), pp. 95-123; O'Meara, D., *Volkskapitalisme: Class, Capital and Ideology in the Development of Afrikaner Nationalism, 1932-1948* (Cambridge 1983).
9   Stedman-Jones, G., *Language of Class: Studies on English Working Class History, 1832-1982* (Cambridge 1983); Cumber, J.T., *Working Class Community in Industrial America: Work, Leisure and Struggle in Two Cities, 1880-1930* (Connecticut 1979).
10 Amongst the essays collected by Bozzoli those that dealt specifically with the white working class are Mantzaris, E.A., 'Radical Community: The Yiddish-speaking Branch of the International Socialist League, 1818-1920'; Brink, E., Maar'n klomp "factory" meide: Afrikaner Family and Community on the Witwatersrand during the 1920s; Clynick, T., 'Community Politics on the Lichtenburg Alluvial Diamond Fields, 1926-1929' and Witz, L., 'A Case of Schizophrenia: The Rise and Fall of the Independent Labour Party'.
11 Brink, E., 'Man-made Women: Gender, Class and the Ideology of the Volksmoeder' in Walker, C. (ed.), *Women and Gender in Southern Africa to 1945* (London 1990) pp. 273-92; Berger, I., *Threads of Solidarity: Women in South African Industry, 1900-1980* (London 1992); du Toit, M., 'Women, Welfare and the Nurturing of Afrikaner Nationalism: A Social History of the Afrikaanse Christelike Vroue Vereeniging, c. 1870-1939', Ph.D. thesis, University of Cape Town, 1996. To this category also belongs the collection of essays on poor whites edited by Robert Morell, *White But Poor: Essays on the History of Poor Whites in South Africa, 1880-1949* (Pretoria 1995).
12 Witz, L., *Write Your Own History* (Johannesburg 1988) and 'The "Write Your Own History" Project', *Radical History Review* 47 (7).
13 Dubow, S., 'Race, Civilisation and Culture: The Elaboration of Segregationist Discourse in the Inter-war Years' in Marks, S. and Trapido, S. (eds.), *The Politics of Race, Class and Nationalism in Twentieth Century South Africa* (London 1987) and *Illicit Marriage: Scientific Racism in South Africa* (Cambridge 1995); Ashforth, A., *The Politics of Official Discourse in Twentieth Century South Africa* (New York 1990).

14 See the volumes published by Kwela Books in the collection Social Identities South African Series.
15 Roediger, D., *The Wages of Whiteness: Race and the Making of the American Working Class* (London 1991), and *Towards the Abolition of Whiteness* (London 1994). Hereafter, Roediger, *Abolition*.
16 Roediger, *Abolition*, p. 9-10.
17 See D. Possel's paper, "What is a name? Racial Categorisations under Apartheid and their Afterlife", presented at the conference 'The Burden of Race? 'Whiteness' and 'Blackness' in Modern South Africa', History Workshop and Wits Institute for Social and Economic Research, University of the Witwatersrand, Johannesburg 5-8 July 2001.
18 Minkley and Rasool, *Orality*, p. 99.
19 See S. Nuttall's paper, "Subjectivities of Whiteness", presented at the conference 'The Burden of Race? "Whiteness" and "Blackness" in Modern South Africa', History Workshop and Wits Institute for Social and Economic Research, University of the Witwatersrand, Johannesburg 5-8 July 2001. Although this kind of writing, that reads and analyses authors through their writings, is at first sight more compatible with Lacanian approaches, it often ends up in a sad simplification of issues and, no less worrying, of the subjects themselves.

Chapter 2

The Emergence of the South African White Working Class in Johannesburg, 1890-1906

Introduction

The history of the Witwatersrand is to a large extent the history of the gold mining industry. The area, which stretches for 40 miles from Springs in the east to Krugersdorp in the west, has the city of Johannesburg as its economic centre. The city's claim to fame was the discovery of goldfields in 1886, which determined that its prosperity, and certainly that of its inhabitants, was bound to the booms and slumps of the mining industry. The gold of the Witwatersrand attracted large numbers of people to the area and determined their settlement patterns, drawing class boundaries along the geography of the city. Because the reef that constituted the Witwatersrand ran from east to west and dipped southwards, the working class neighbourhoods developed east and west of the town centre in close proximity to the mines. Similarly, the boarding houses and bars frequented by the mostly single British, Australian and American miners were concentrated in the neighbourhoods of Jeppestown (1889) and Belgravia in the east and Fordsburg (1888) and Vrededorp (1892) in the west.

The geology of the reef did more than determine the geography of class of Johannesburg, it also determined the history of the gold mining industry in South Africa from the point of view of both technology and labour. The gold deposits of the Rand were extremely regular but contained low-grade ore. This was compounded by the fact that the reef ran deep under the surface. Thus since 1889 the history of the mining industry can be explained through a series of economic, social, political and technological strategies designed to profitably recover gold from the reef. In 1889 it became clear that the success of the industry depended on its transformation into a capital and labour intensive operation. In that year the Chamber of Mines replaced the Diggers' Committee as the representative of the gold mining industry's interests. Between 1890 and 1891, the Chamber of Mines faced the first crisis in the industry: the gold found in the deep reef did not respond to the existing technology of mercury amalgamation. The introduction of the MacArthur-Forrest process solved this aspect of the problem[1] but availability of technology was only part of the answer to the 1890-1 crisis. The industry needed both capital and a change in its organizational structure to respond more adequately to the uncertainties of deep level mining. This was the origin of the group system that dominated the Rand throughout the twentieth century. The groups were established through the amalgamation of individual mines and were based on the creation of a pool of financial and managerial expertise. Five mining groups dominated the mining industry on the Rand. The London-based financial house of Wernher, Beit and Company and its Johannesburg representatives, Eckstein and Company, created Rand Mines Limited in 1893 and Central Mining Investment Corporation in 1905. Together these firms controlled 37 per cent of the gold produced on the Rand between 1902 and 1913. The second group of importance was Consolidated Goldfields, founded by Cecil Rhodes and Charles Rudd, which controlled 11 per cent of the Rand's gold during the same period. Finally, three other groups - the Barnato family's Johannesburg Consolidated Investment, Joseph Robinson, and George Farrar and Associates - controlled about 20 per cent. The amalgamation of mines that started in the early 1890s renewed confidence in the market and created the financial climate for what was called the 'Kaffir boom' of 1895.[2]

The development of the deep level mines changed the nature of the mining industry on the Rand in many senses. Fundamental in this regard was the realization that the gold industry, contrary to initial impression, constituted a long-term investment. This implied a radical transformation in the mining industry's approach to both state and labour. The intervention of the state was necessary on three counts: to reduce the costs of transport, foodstuff and dynamite; to guarantee an adequate supply of cheap African labour; and to reduce the high cost of living in Johannesburg so that overseas miners and artisans could be enticed to settle on the Rand.

Despite the mining companies' need for state support and the benefits the state could accrue from the gold industry the relations between the mine owners and the government of the South African Republic were far from easy. While the mining industry saw the government of President Paul Kruger (1882-1900) as obstructive and uncooperative, Kruger was rightly suspicious of Britain's intentions towards the Transvaal and deeply protective of the republic's independence from the colonial power. These tensions lay at the origin of the Jameson Raid. Otto Beit,[3] Lionel Phillips[4] and George Farrar[5] together with Cecil Rhodes[6] plotted and supported, with the tacit approval of the Secretary of State for the Colonies, Joseph Chamberlain, a military expedition led by Dr. L. S. Jameson which, on 31 December 1895, attempted, unsuccessfully, to overthrow Kruger's government. The failure of the raid created a sense of instability that caused the mining industry to slide into a financial crisis that lasted until 1898.

Whatever efforts the Kruger government made to satisfy the mine magnates' demands, such as the development of a more efficient recruitment of black workers, they fell short of fulfilling the industry's needs.[7] British interest in the Witwatersrand goldfields, which by 1898 produced 27 per cent of the world's gold, was important enough for the British Empire to wage a colonial war against the Boer republics between 1899 and 1902.[8]

The military incorporation of the Transvaal into the British Empire after the war had to be transformed into a political, social and economic reality. Sir Alfred Milner was the man chosen for this task. A man with a brilliant career in the colonial service and an enthusiastic advocate of the Empire, his appointment as British High Commissioner for South Africa in 1897 and, in the aftermath of the war, as Governor of the Transvaal (1902-1905), gave him the ideal opportunity to lay the foundations of a colonial state in the economic and socio-political spheres. The political and economic interests of the newly incorporated colony coincided with particular clarity when it came to the issue of the white labour force. Skilled British workers were as necessary to the development of the mining industry as they were to guarantee the British character of the Transvaal at the political level.

Thus, from the point of view of the social history of the white working class, the 17 years that separate the beginning of deep level mining from the concession of Responsible Government to the Transvaal were formative years. It was during the reconstruction period, 1902-1906, that the issue of the stabilization of the white working class on the Witwatersrand through the settlement of working class families acquired particular importance.[9] By 1907, when the Transvaal gained new political status through the granting of Responsible Government, the main trends of Johannesburg's white working class demography were established and the first elective government's concern shifted from workers' stabilization to other aspects of the social reproduction of the white working class.

White Working Class Families in Johannesburg, 1890-1901

Ten years after the proclamation of Johannesburg's public diggings in 1886, the first census of the city, focused on the area within a three-mile radius of Market Square, indicated that the total white population was 39,454 persons. The city's male population heavily outnumbered the female (Table 2.1) while in terms of conjugal status, there were more single men than women in Johannesburg (Table 2.2).

Table 2.1 White population of greater Johannesburg[10]

Year	Males		Females		Children		Total
	Numb	%	Numb	%	Numb	%	
1896	20,169	51.12	9,208	23.34	10,077	25.54	39,454
1904	40,846	51.58	21,515	27.17	20,458	21.24	82,819

Table 2.2 Conjugal condition of the white population in Johannesburg

	Married				Single			
	Males		Females		Males		Females	
	Numb	%	Numb	%	Numb	%	Numb	%
1896	8,421	41.7	5,624	61.0	11,748	58.2	3,584	38.9
1904	17,929	43.9	14,371	66.8	22,917	56.1	7,144	33.2

According to the census, slightly less than half of the population of Johannesburg was married. This included married people who were not living with their husbands or wives, and also widows and widowers. The actual proportion of families living in Johannesburg was estimated on the assumption that for every married woman living in the city there was a married man (Table 2.3).[11]

Table 2.3 Number of white families in Johannesburg

Census	Males	Females	Families	%
1896	8,421	5,624	5,624	66.79
1904	17,929	14,371	14,371	80.16

The remainder represented the married men who did not have their families with them, the latter presumably overseas. Thus, on the basis of the 1896 Census it is possible to estimate that about 66 per cent of the married male population of Johannesburg had settled their families in the city. Although these calculations are rather crude, they provide an indication of the relative importance of families in the city.

The rapid economic development of the Witwatersrand in the age of cheap steamship travel had made Johannesburg the destination of Russians, Germans, Hollanders, Norwegians, Italians, the French and the Swiss, not to mention the ubiquitous Britons, Americans and Australians, all in search of better opportunities.[12] But despite the significant presence of foreigners in the city, most of its population had been born in the subcontinent.

By 1896 (Table 2.4) the proportion of men born in the United Kingdom (46.25 per cent) was less than the proportion of men born in the two British colonies (36.03 per cent) and in the Boer republics (27.11 per cent). The great majority of the female population (73.71 per cent) was born in the subcontinent. Only 26.30 per cent of the females living in Johannesburg were British by birth.

The influx of foreigners, particularly the British, attracted by the gold mines had been gaining momentum through 1893-4, and 1895 saw the largest number of skilled mine workers coming into the Witwatersrand. As British workers arrived in the Transvaal, bringing their experience to bear on the transition of the gold industry into a deep-mining one, the relations between the Randlords and the Kruger Government were deteriorating. The mine owners organized their political opposition to Kruger in the Reform Committee and galvanized British discontent with Kruger's government around the franchise issue.[13] Kruger's dislike and mistrust of the British population in the Transvaal, called *Uitlanders* in Afrikaans, i.e. outlanders, was hardly surprising. Not only had Britain annexed the Transvaal in 1877 but despite having been repelled by Boer forces in 1881 it insisted on being considered a paramount power in the region.

It was against this background that the Jameson Raid took place in 1895. Disastrous as the raid was from a military and political perspective, not to mention the economic uncertainty it caused, it seems to have had some effect because by 1897 the government of the South African Republic had set up a commission of enquiry into the mining industry.

The Industrial Commission of Enquiry gave the mine magnates the opportunity to put the needs of the gold industry before the government. The argument was fairly simply: deep-level mining implied a far greater investment of capital which needed to be compensated by reductions in the costs of production. The Randlords proposed that the government intervene to guarantee lower costs of both dynamite and transport, to constitute a centralized structure for the recruitment of cheap African labour, and that it take the necessary measures to encourage the settlement of British miners on the Witwatersrand.

Table 2.4 Number of white males and females by place of birth[a]

		CENSUS 1896			1904		
		Numb	% of total males	% of total females	Numb	% of total males	% of total females
Transvaal	Male	2,543	13.71		6,561	17.19	
	Female	2,269		18.59	6,520		25.04
Orange Free State	Male	632	3.41		1,119	2.93	
	Female	665		5.45	1,205		5.63
Cape Colony	Male	6,188	33.37		7,517	19.70	
	Female	5,653		46.31	7,966		30.59
Natal	Male	494	2.66		895	2.35	
	Female	410		3.36	950		3.65
UK	Male	8,687	46.85		22,070	57.83	
	Female	3,211		26.30	9,400		36.10
Total	Male	18,544	100.00		38,162	100.00	
	Female	12,208		100.00	26,041		100.00

a) The table only reflects the places of birth that are relevant for this study.

According to mine managers, engineers and the workers themselves the main issue conspiring against the settlement of experienced miners in the area was the high cost of living in Johannesburg. It was accepted during the enquiry that approximately 54 per cent of the mine workers were single, and that, of the 46 per cent who were married, only 13 per cent had their families with them. These figures underlined, according to the mine owners, the fact that the Rand was regarded only as a temporary source of high wages and that the aim of these workers was to make as much money as possible and then go back home.[14]

The lure of the money to be made on the Witwatersrand gold mines, however, was not enough to counteract the deterrent effect that the prevalence of silicosis, the lung disease caused by the inhalation of silica particles in underground work, had on prospective immigrants.[15]

Despite this and the fact that the high cost of living on the Rand continued to be a problem well into the 1910s, the slow amelioration of working conditions in the mines and new confidence in the future of the gold mining industry did induce mine workers to settle on the Rand. By 1902 the number of married miners with resident families had increased to 20 per cent and in 1912 it reached 42 per cent.[16]

In the years prior to the South African War married men who lived in the city with their families had to pay the rent of a cottage or rooms in a boarding house. The cost of accommodation represented between 26 per cent and 39 per cent of a miner's wage, which was approximately £23 per month. Accommodation expenses were only the beginning. Men had to feed and clothe their families, educate their children and provide in case of illness. In this context family size was an element to reckon with. The £23 that a miner could earn monthly was not nearly enough to support a family of six – a wife and four children. Besides the difficulties of keeping a family in Johannesburg it was not always easy to raise the money to pay for a steamship fare to South Africa. A third class ticket from England to the Cape cost 16 guineas in 1897; once the price of the railway fare from Cape Town to Johannesburg was added the cost of the voyage amounted to £21 4s 9d.[17] This was probably the reason why workers tended to delay bringing out their families until they were established. According to R. Barrow's evidence to the 1897 commission of enquiry, this was precisely the case. He came out to the colony by himself in 1887 and worked for six months for De Beers' in the Kimberley diamond mines. After this he moved to the Transvaal, where he was employed on the mines as a carpenter but it took him until 1893 to feel established enough to bring his family over from Lancashire.[18]

Apart from these British married workers with their families based overseas, there were those single men who decided to settle in the Transvaal and married Afrikaner women. The presence of working class families on the Rand became evident after the outbreak of the South African War. In September 1899, Kruger appointed the *Rust en Orde Kommissie* to govern the Rand during the war. Amongst the functions of the commission was the granting of Johannesburg residence permits to the local population. An analysis of these permits showed that by 1899 there were quite a number of British workers married to Republican women. All the families listed by the *Rust en Orde Kommissie* wanted to stay on the Rand despite the outbreak of the war and the fact that some of the men were unemployed.[19]

Since Johannesburg was a mining town mine workers constituted a large part of its population, but they were not the only white workers on the Rand.[20] The economic development of the city, especially in terms of construction and transport, offered employment to large numbers of people who had fled locusts and rinderpest in the countryside and were in search of higher wages or a better life. But not every newcomer was equally well equipped to withstand the fluctuations of the Rand economy.

By the early 1890s economic crises had taken their toll and destitute white working class families could be seen in the poorer neighbourhoods of the city. And although destitution did not in general have a dramatic turn, dramatic episodes sometimes happened. On 11 October 1890, *The Star* published an account of George Muller's suicide. Muller was an Afrikaner mason who had started his working life in the Cape. Following the discovery of diamonds he moved with his family to Kimberley. In 1886, along with thousands of other hopefuls, Muller headed for the South African Republic to try his luck on the Rand. Once in Johannesburg he could not get work as a mason and did odd jobs for a year until, probably as a consequence of the economic crisis of 1890, he was completely out of work. Father of six children and sick, George Muller committed suicide in Fordsburg on 10 October 1890.[21]

The life of the very poor and destitute in the years before the Jameson Raid was especially difficult since Johannesburg did not offer many charitable institutions for the assistance of the unemployed. The more fortunate found some relief in casual employment as barmen, waiters or billiard markers while others were reduced to vagrancy or petty crime.[22] During the 1890s Johannesburg the middle classes were kept informed of the happenings in the city's underworld by the stories in the *The Star* and *Standard and Diggers' News*.[23] Colonial Victorians' interest in the effects of poverty, as with their counterparts back 'home', was not mere curiosity, but was firmly rooted in the desire to moralize poverty and the poor. A good example of this was the growing involvement of private institutions such as the Present Help League, established in 1895 by the mine magnate Lionel Phillips, and churches in alleviating indigency. The concern about destitution became more acute when in the context of the prosperity of 1895, the railway link between Johannesburg and Cape Town (1893) and Delagoa Bay (1895) increased the number of immigrant workers coming from overseas. The Church of England had been actively involved in the diocese of Johannesburg since 1892. Under the pastoral direction of Rev. John Darragh, the church expanded its activities from St. Mary's Cathedral in central Johannesburg to the ever-growing mining suburbs in the south-east like City and Suburban, in the south-west, like Ferreirastown, and to Brickfields, the poverty-stricken area south of the railway line.

The naturalistic view of poverty and degeneration characteristic of 'enlightened' Victorians was not necessarily shared by the Anglican Church. A mining town exposed to the fluctuations of gold production and populated by large numbers of men who were either single or lived as bachelors, was, in the opinion of the Church, an environment conducive to sinful lives.

Working class culture in early 1890s Johannesburg revolved around drinking and prostitution.[24] The large numbers of prostitutes, who entertained the workers (but not only them) and scandalized the middle classes, arrived in the city in the early 1890s after fleeing the enactment of the 1885 Contagious Disease Act in Cape Town, Port Elizabeth and Kimberley.[25] By 1896 it seems that approximately 1,000 prostitutes, the majority of them southern African-born, worked in Johannesburg. They settled right in the heart of Johannesburg between Bree Street in the north, Anderson Street in the south, Kruis Street in the east and Sauer Street in the west, in the area named, following deeply-seated cultural stereotypes, 'Frenchfontein'. The lack of discretion of the ladies, who, it is said, called out to prospective customers from their windows, did not sit well with Victorian mores.

Into this state of things arrived in the city two Anglican missionaries in September 1894 to hold a series of special services at St. Mary's. Fathers Osborne and Simeon preached to men and women separately, making the indissolubility of marriage the centre of their sermons. Invoking the very appealing idea for the British community that "an Englishman's home is his castle", the priests called for the defence of family values against "external enemies", which were probably best embodied by the bars and brothels that had mushroomed in late nineteenth century Johannesburg.[26]

Johannesburg's white workers, however, seemed to have other concerns in the years before the South African War. Far more important for the working men, especially for those who had their families with them, was how to cope with the fluctuations of the Rand economy. Nevertheless, the booms and slumps of the economy did not affect all trades equally. While men employed in the building or in the mining industries were more exposed to economic shifts, those breadwinners employed in the service and commercial sectors were comparatively more protected.

Two images of working class life emerge from the analysis of the baptismal records of 2,290 families[27] in the working class parishes of the Anglican Church,[28] which was, according to the 1896 Census of Johannesburg, one of the most important denominations among the city's population. One shows a certain correlation between trade of the father, size of the family and the effect of economic crisis on families. The other suggests that attendance at the Anglican Church was defined by more complex social and cultural experiences than language and nationality.

Table 2.5 shows the trades of the breadwinners of the families identified in the baptismal records and the proportion of families headed by English and Afrikaner males in 23 different trades during this period.[29] Between 1890 and 1901 144 miners had their children baptized in the Anglican Church.[30] Unsurprisingly, given the origins of the city, mining and mining-related employment such as cyanider, amalgamator and platelayer constituted the single most frequent category of employment in the baptismal records. In most cases the male breadwinner in these families was British. British men married to Afrikaner women represented approximately 10 per cent of the mining families in the records.

The stories of three mining families stick out in the historical reconstruction: the Bayleys, the Heughs and the Isaacs. Lennox and Isabelle Bayley got married in 1897. In 1899 when the couple had their first child, a boy, they were living in the centre of town and Lennox was employed in the mining industry. Lennox seemed to have been luckier than some of his colleagues since he managed to keep his job in the mines despite the outbreak of the South African War. However, the family moved from central Johannesburg to the married quarters in City and Suburban mine. Two of the Bayleys' children were born during this period, a girl in 1900 and a boy in 1903. On 24 September 1905 when Lennox and Isabelle registered their fourth child, a baby girl, in the Anglican Church, the family had left subsidized mining accommodation in City and Suburban for a more expensive, and probably bigger, house in the western working class suburb of Fordsburg, where 15 months later the Bayleys had their fifth child, a boy.[31]

When Samuel Heugh married Rosa Cox in September 1889 he was employed as a coachman. During the 11 years that followed the birth of their first child in 1893, the lives of the Heughs were punctuated by moves between the west and east of the city, from Fordsburg to Jeppestown. By the mid-1890s Samuel had changed jobs and was working on the mines as a platelayer. Between 1895 and 1896 Samuel and Rosa had two sons. In 1899, at the time of the birth of their second daughter, Samuel was still employed on the mines. The Boer occupation of Johannesburg immediately after the outbreak of the war imposed a halt on most mining operations. Samuel did not have many options at the time: he could either join the unemployed mine workers in town or follow the British troops. Whatever it was, by 1904, when his and Rose's fifth child was born, Samuel had left the mines and was earning much less as an unskilled labourer on the railways.[32]

Charles and Jane Isaacs lived for three years in Marshallstown, south of the city centre. At the time of the birth of their first child, in 1895, Charles was a miner. By 1896-7, when Charles and Jane had two more children baptized, economic recession had hit the family, Charles had left the mines, probably retrenched, and was working as a cab driver, a particularly dicey occupation at the time since the extension of the horse-drawn tram line by 25 per cent had halved the number of cabbies in the city.[33]

Table 2.5 Percentage of English and Afrikaner by occupation, 1890-1906

TRADE	TOTAL	BRITISH	AFRIKAN.	%[a]
Miner	218	88.07	11.92	26.60
Platelayer	11	72.72	27.27	54.54
Eng.driv.	104	82.69	17.30	33.65
Amalgamat.	30	93.33	6.66	43.33
Mechanic	31	93.33	6.46	29.03
Cyanider	7	85.71	14.28	14.28
Blacksmith	92	76.08	23.92	26.08
Carpenter	196	84.69	15.30	20.91
Mason	129	79.06	20.93	33.33
Bricklayer	81	87.65	12.34	32.09
Painter	46	76.08	23.91	28.26
Cab owner	31	64.51	35.48	22.58
Cab driver	68	80.00	20.00	20.58
Coachman	64	62.50	37.50	26.50
Driver	108	58.33	41.66	18.75
Coach builder	9	55.55	44.44	44.44
Groom	38	71.05	28.94	28.94
Railway	29	75.86	24.13	17.25
Policeman	55	41.81	58.18	23.13
Barman	48	95.83	4.17	28.85
Cook	32	73.80	26.19	28.57
Labourer	42	73.80	26.19	28.57

a) Percentage of families reconstructed by trade.

Construction was the second most frequent occupation of the breadwinners in the families registered in the baptismal records of the Anglican Church. The construction industry was a source of employment for people with very different skills. From the late 1880s former Afrikaner tenant farmers (*bywoners*) who had moved to the city after the discovery of gold had found in the small-scale production of bricks a moderately profitable enterprise to which they could apply their skills. In late 1887 President Kruger authorized Afrikaner brickmakers to settle on the south-west *spruit* of the Braamfontein farm, recently acquired by the government, to manufacture bricks using the clay deposits in the area. Between 1891 and 1896 brickmakers benefited from the town's first building boom. This period of prosperity in the building trade also favoured skilled workers such as plasterers, bricklayers and builders who saw their trades flourish. Nevertheless, the 1896-7 economic crisis and the outbreak of the war in 1899 were a setback to most of these workers. But while all building trades were adversely affected by the crisis, the lot of the self-employed brickmakers was made worse by an independent development: the introduction of the capitalist production of bricks in the early 1890s.[34]

Brickmaking has been regarded as chiefly an Afrikaner trade. Nevertheless, half of the brickmaker families who had their children baptized in the Anglican Church between 1890 and 1901 were English and lived in Brickfields.[35] Amongst the brickmakers, as in most other trades, there was a small, if significant, proportion (16 per cent) of British men married to Afrikaner women and Afrikaner men married to British women.

Some of the bricklayer families constitute an example of upward social mobility. That was the case of William and Maria Muller, both Afrikaners, who had their first child in Brickfields in 1893. In the next seven years in which they lived in Brickfields they had three more children, two girls and a boy. In 1901, at the time of the baptism of their fourth daughter, the Mullers were living at 20 De Beer Street, Braamfontein, a better and more expensive neighbourhood, north of the railway line.[36]

It was not uncommon that brickmakers exchanged self-employment for positions as employee brickmakers on the mines. In most of these cases they moved with their families to subsidized accommodation on mine property. Henry Bates married an Afrikaner woman, Maria, with whom he had three daughters. While in 1894 Henry was a self-employed brickmaker, the next two births found him working for Spes Bona Mine.[37] In other cases general recession combined with the fluctuations of the trade to make social mobility impossible. In this context each new birth might have acted as a burden on the economy of the family. This was the case for George and Ellen Coleman. Their first child was born in 1896, at the end of the building boom that started in 1891, while they were living in Fordsburg. Eleven months later, in the context of the economic crisis of 1896-7, their second child was born and they had to move to the slum-like Malay Location south of Vrededorp in the west of the city, which, following the logic of the racially organized colony, had been designated for the settlement of so called Cape Malays and Cape coloured people.[38]

The fortunes of the more skilled workers within the building trade, such as bricklayers, masons, builders, plasterers and painters, were not very different.[39] The size of the family more often than not acted as an obstacle to economic mobility. A typical case was that of the Roses, who started their family in the mid-1880s. Benjamin and Minnie Rose lived in central Johannesburg for eight years during which time they had four children, two girls and two boys, with Benjamin alternatively employed as bricklayer or mason. But when in 1894 their fifth child was born, they were also living in the Malay Location, where they had their sixth and, it seems, last child.[40]

Construction was not the only economic activity to provide opportunities for self-employment to Johannesburg's newly urbanized population; the transport industry also offered an alternative to full proletarianization for many Afrikaners who had fled the countryside. Between the late 1880s and the early 1900s many Afrikaner newcomers made use of their rural skills in the transport riding business. Although the 1896 Census of Johannesburg shows only 53 transport riders in the city, during its heyday transport riding provided employment for thousands of poor *burghers*.[41] This occupation was particularly viable in the years prior to the extension of the railway link from the coastal cities to the Rand (1892-5) when transport riders ensured the flow of food and machinery to the mining industry.

At the same time the growth of Johannesburg made the development of a system of urban transport a pressing necessity. Under the protection of Kruger's republican government, owner-drivers of cabs started a business which at least until 1896 created jobs for the less fortunate cab drivers. The census indicated that amongst Johannesburg's working population there were 83 cab owners and 692 cab drivers. Although these jobs were largely taken up by Afrikaners, they were by no means alone in the transport business. It also provided employment for a fair number of Jews, coloured Muslims, so-called Malays, and English workers who were trying to find their feet in Johannesburg.

Until the early 1900s self-employment as transport rider or owner-driver of cabs acted as an alternative to full proletarianization. Thus, transport rider, cab owner, cab driver and coachman were more than urban occupations. They represented different strategies of survival for both the newly urbanized and the unemployed overseas worker.

Between 1892 and 1898 Edward and Jane Murphy had five children, three girls and two boys. During four of these six years Edward worked as a cab driver living alternatively in central Johannesburg, in close proximity to Market Square and not far away from Fordsburg where most stables were located, and Brickfields. By 1896 the rising prices of horses and forage, due to the rinderpest coupled with the extension of the horse-drawn tram line in the city by City & Suburban Transport Company,[42] had put many cabbies out of business. In this context it is hardly surprising that when the Murphys baptized their fifth child in 1898 Edward had changed jobs. He was a miner.[43] It is quite probable that Murphy was a miner by trade who, due to the crises of the industry, in 1890-1 and 1896-7, had found it very difficult to get a job on the mines. In this case the transport industry protected the Murphy family from the consequences of unemployment.

William and Anna Culvert started their family on the eve of the South African War. William was employed as a coachman in 1898 when his first daughter was born and the family was living in Fordsburg. The following year he was a labourer in Ferreira Deep with his wife and two children living with him on the mine's property. The war interrupted mining operations and we lose track of the Culverts until 1903, when they had their third child, and William reappears with his job as a labourer in Ferreira Deep. Four years and a son later, the Culverts had moved from Ferreira to Rietfontein in the East Rand where their fifth child was born while William was employed as a labourer.[44]

There were times, however, when the escape routes of the working class did function in a more comprehensive way and, with time, some drivers became cab proprietors. John Morkel, son of an Afrikaner family, married Catherine, from England, sometime between 1892 and 1895. In May 1895, when they registered in the Anglican Church the birth of their first daughter, the Morkels lived in Brickfields and John was a driver. There is no reason to doubt that John's family enjoyed the buoyant period for the cabbies trade between 1892 and 1895. In 1897 they moved to Fordsburg where they lived until at least 1899. They had two more children and John kept his job as cab driver. The recession in the trade in 1896 and the war itself must have made it difficult to support a family of four. Nevertheless, during the British occupation of Johannesburg in 1900, and especially with the return of the civilian population to the city, there was again a brief period of prosperity for the cabbies. It was then that John managed to leap into independence, becoming a cab proprietor. The timing for this move was not very good because an electric tram service for Johannesburg was among the plans of the new municipal administration. The demand for transport to serve the cross-town routes offset generalized unemployment among the cabbies, but the falling numbers of licensed cab drivers in the city between 1904 and 1906 indicates that the heyday of this occupation was over.[45]

Between 1904 and 1906, the year when the first tram started working, the Morkels, who were now living, like other cabbies, in Vrededorp, had two more children baptized in the Anglican Church, in 1904 and 1906.[46]

During the late 1890s work as a member of the South African Republic's police force (*ZARP*) was an alternative to unemployment for poor *burghers*.[47]

The life of Bernard Shultz is a good illustration of this. Bernard was a policeman for two years, 1895 and 1896. During this period he had two children by his wife, Catherine, and they moved from Jeppestown to the north-eastern suburb of Troyeville. In 1897, at the time of the birth of their third daughter, Shultz left the police force for a job as a cab driver, which he kept until 1899, the year of the birth of his first son. If the war did not put Bernard out of work, at least it narrowed the market for urban transport - all this assuming that he did not follow the Boer troops. Whether he went to fight the war or stayed behind, there are no more records of the Shultz family until 1903. Only in 1903, when Bernard had his fourth daughter baptized, do we learn that he was now a mechanic living in Norwood. Two years later, when the Shultzes had their second son baptized, Bernard had gone back to Troyeville and was working as a handyman.[48]

The racial division of the labour market characteristic of the colonial world made the life of unskilled white workers particularly difficult. Ideological as well as economic reasons dictated that unskilled jobs were the almost exclusive preserve of African labourers. Not only was unskilled labour regarded as a non-white occupation but when whites were actually employed in these jobs the wages they got were higher than the pittance received by their black counterparts, and were therefore not economical for their employers.

Most of the labourers who had their children baptized in the Anglican Church were employed on the mines and with time some were promoted to miners. Such was the case of Harry Abrahams who worked for two years as a labourer in the Langlaagte mine and finally found work as a miner in Roodeport on the west Rand.[49] The progressive job fragmentation that was taking place on the gold mines since the 1890s opened more opportunities for employment to men less trained than the overseas "all round" miners or the artisans.[50] This process, which paved the way for the entrance of newly urbanized Afrikaners into the industry, might have also helped unskilled British workers to find employment on the mines. An attraction that a job on the mines had for unskilled workers was probably accommodation, as at least in some cases they lived with their families in the mines' married quarters, as was the case with the Bayley family.

Labourers often changed from one unskilled job to another, living in Fordsburg, Vrededorp or Brickfields. Andrew and Elizabeth Lopson had three children between 1895 and 1899. Each birth was accompanied by a change of job: from labourer to painter in 1896 and from painter to brickmaker in 1899. These changes were coupled with moves from Fordsburg to Brickfields and back to Fordsburg.[51]

While family size, father's trade and economic fluctuations combined in different ways to decide the fortunes of working class families in Johannesburg, family formation was by no means a direct consequence of economic calculation. Emotional, cultural and historical elements had a fundamental part in the constitution of families.[52]

Amongst each of the 23 different trades of the workers whose children were baptized as Anglicans (Table 2.5) there was a small but significant proportion of families with one British and one Afrikaner parent. More importantly there was a comparatively large number of Afrikaner families who had their children baptized in the Anglican Church. Why this happened and the influence that this phenomenon had on shaping (class) identity amongst white workers in Johannesburg constitutes one of the central issues of this book.

The charitable and educational centres that the Anglican Church established in Johannesburg functioned along non-denominational and non-ethnic lines. Particularly in the period before the South African War when, with the exception of very minor state involvement, there were no institutions devoted to alleviating urban poverty or to providing education to the children of the poor, the Anglican Church played a much needed role in the city. The church's awareness of the fact that poverty in the city was practically untouched by any charitable agency "partly because it has little or no household claim on any religious body",[53] was made evident in 1895 at the time of the creation of a shelter for destitute white people, the Johannesburg Home. This approach of the Anglican Church to social problems might explain, for example, the fostering of close links with poor Afrikaner families living in Brickfields.[54]

Nevertheless, the fact that Afrikaner families actually embraced the Anglican faith cannot be explained exclusively through the church's attitude towards the poor. More complex and deeper social processes were at play among the late nineteenth century white population of the Transvaal. The process of proletarianization that was under way in the countryside was loosening the ties between the religious authority of the Dutch Reformed Church and the *bywoners*. By the 1890s the process of capitalist transformation of the countryside had sharpened the already extant class divisions amongst the Boer population on the Highveld. Fencing, decimation of game and the introduction of the railways served to create a class "which was already in transition to lumpenproletariat status".[55] Class cleavages within rural society influenced the type of allegiance the *bywoners* were prepared to demonstrate to the Boer state in either of the two republics both before and during the South African War.[56]

During the years immediately prior to the war the Afrikaner poor showed Kruger's government that their class and political consciousness was not necessarily, or exclusively, defined on ethnic or nationalistic terms.[57] And after the outbreak of the South African War a significant number of Boers either refused to heed the call up or else actively collaborated with the imperial troops.[58]

Religion had played and important cohesive role in Afrikaner rural society. The undermining of patriarchal authority which accompanied the movement of entire families to the city, or even of only the younger generation, served also to weaken the links between the Dutch Reformed Church and its congregants.[59] The Dutch Reformed Church had been present in Johannesburg since 1885.[60] The first community centre was established in Langlaagte, west of Fordsburg, in 1886, and by 1891 there were Dutch churches in Fordsburg, and in two other towns on the west Rand, Maraisburg and Florida. The total Johannesburg congregation that year amounted to 2,300 members. By 1896, Fordsburg's Dutch Reformed Church congregation brought together less than a quarter of the South African-born population of Fordsburg. By 1895 the church's ministers were complaining about the difficulty in keeping congregations together. The poor spiritual life of the newly urbanized Afrikaner was blamed for decreasing attendance at services in Fordsburg, Jeppestown and Langlaagte and for the decline in the practice of religion at home.[61] Towards the end of the 1890s the Dutch Reformed Church's concern with the withering of Afrikaner family spirituality was aggravated by the realization that Afrikaner women constituted the majority of the army of 1,500 prostitutes who settled in Johannesburg after 1895.[62] This seemed the final proof of the decline of the Afrikaner family.

While economic transformation played its part in weakening family and community ties amongst urbanized Afrikaners, the South African War not only accentuated ongoing social cleavages, it also added political divisions. The existence of *bittereinders*, Afrikaners not prepared to surrender, and *hensoppers*, those Afrikaners ready to capitulate, was yet another indication of the cracks in the community.[63]

The comparatively high proportion of Afrikaner families who baptized their children in the Anglican Church between 1890 and 1906 - which coincides almost perfectly with the occupational groups and neighbourhoods of the recently urbanized Afrikaners - suggest that Afrikaner 'ethnicity' was not that strong amongst the poor Boers and, most importantly, it demonstrates that people's political and religious attitudes cannot be simply read off their 'ethnic' identity. According to the Dutch Reformed Church councils, the Anglicization of urbanized Afrikaners between 1902 and 1909 was manifested in the fact that they were having their children baptized in the Anglican Church.[64]

The records of the Anglican Church indicate that among the working class families who had their children baptized (Table 2.5) 51.85 per cent of the families of brickmakers were Afrikaner, and so were 41.66 per cent of the drivers'; 37.50 per cent of the coachmen's; 44.44 per cent of the coach-builders' and 35.48 per cent of the families of the cab owners; and that families constituted by one Afrikaner and one British parent were not infrequent. Most of these families lived in Brickfields, Vrededorp and Fordsburg. All of this seems to suggest that national distinctions among white workers, especially among the very poor, were superseded by the common experience of the hazards of living in such places.

White Working Class Families in Johannesburg, 1902-1906: The Immigration Policy of the Reconstruction Administration

After the imperial victory of 1901 secured British control of the gold of the Witwatersrand, the colonial administration of the Transvaal was expected to reform the state in such a way that it achieved capitalist accumulation based on the gold mining industry.[65] In this regard it was not a coincidence that the tasks of social engineering that Milner and his team of young Oxford graduates, the so-called kindergarten, were going to undertake were in many aspects a response to the suggestions put by the Randlords before the Industrial Commission of Enquiry of 1897.[66]

Milner's intention to make South Africa into "a strong and effective link in the imperial chain" implied a grand political design in which the recently incorporated Transvaal was a key piece. Whatever the degree of optimism of Milner's collaborators they all knew that the task would not be easy. The newly appointed Town Clerk of Johannesburg put it very eloquently in 1901:

> It is not as if you have a half finished painting to complete, or a clean canvas to paint. It is rather as if you have a dirty torn canvas to clean and mend before you can begin painting at all.[67]

Milner's project to convert the Transvaal into a British colony was predicated on the demographic predominance of British population in the colony.[68] Achieving this depended on offsetting the current predominance of Boer population through an active immigration policy that encouraged British families to settle in the South African colony. Milner's policy was consistent with the metropolitan attempt to keep emigration within the Empire[69] as well as with the social imperialists' view of the colonies as a safety valve for the social problems in the metropolis, such as unemployment, crowded conditions in working class tenements and dissatisfaction amongst the popular classes.[70]

Milner's immigration policy, particularly in its relation to the reproduction of the white working class, addressed as much a political-ideological problem as an economic one.[71] While immigration of British subjects in general was regarded as the strategy to guarantee imperial dominance in the area, the encouragement of the immigration of British women was meant to secure the ethnic reproduction of the British community, particularly of its working class component.[72]

And the issue of the immigration of women was both urgent and important. If the mining industry[73] and the general promises of a better life in the Transvaal managed to attract a British industrial, commercial and rural population to the colony, the problem remained of the small number of British women among the Transvaal population. Not only was there a general, as the administrators used to put it, "racial" unevenness amongst the Transvaal population, but there was also an imbalance of the sexes which urgently needed to be corrected if the government were to prevent British workers marrying Afrikaner women who were, in the words of the head of the Immigration Department, Basil Williams, "lazy, unprogressive and incredibly dirty".[74] The risks of the conversion of Briton into Boer through marriage and the ominous implications this had for the future of the Empire were not to be trifled with.

As Milner himself put it in 1903, South Africa could only be maintained "by maintaining this strength of British sentiment and by increasing the numbers of British people".[75] And if the final goal were the reproduction of the working class through the agency of the nuclear family, the immigration of single women, who would eventually marry the British workers, was as important as the immigration of whole families.

The view that made women the breeders of the imperial race converted the traditional domestic role of women into a patriotic mission. In 1900, Ellen Joyce, a member of the British Women's Emigration Association, founded in 1892, explained the importance of women emigrating to South Africa:

> The great interest in emigration centres in the future of South Africa. The responsibility of great territorial possessions is upon us, increasing the onus of selecting the right women to follow the pioneer men. The possibility of the settler marrying his own countrywomen is of Imperial as well as of family importance.[76]

In August 1902, the British administration of the Transvaal created the Women's Immigration Department under the direction of Basil Williams.[77] It liaised in London with the South African Colonisation Society - the new name for the South African Expansion Committee - which helped in the selection of British women to come to South Africa as nurses, domestics and governesses, but fundamentally as marriageable women.

The British administration in the Transvaal did not involve itself with the actual selection of intended women emigrants, but it provided assistance with both the passages by sea and by rail to bring these women to the Transvaal. It also made arrangements for the provision, at the administration's expense, of lodging in Cape Town for the women travelling north. In Johannesburg it provided accommodation for these women at 5/- per day, board and lodging included, for a month while they were looking for employment. With this purpose two houses situated on Plein Street, previously used to house the Refugee Aid Committee, were converted into a hostel for women.[78]

In 1902 an internal memorandum of the Colonial Secretary's Office made clear the idea behind the emigration of British women to South Africa. In a telegram addressed to the Secretary of State, J. Chamberlain, the Governor of the Transvaal, Sir A. Lawley, referred to the Dynamite Company's desire to "import at once 100 British girls". When a copy of the telegram reached Basil Williams' office he made it plain that "importation of British women is an unfortunate phrase in a circular which will probably become public".[79]

By 1904 correspondence between the Transvaal Immigration Office and the Colonial Secretary, P. Duncan, asserted that the office's function of facilitating the immigration of women was not solely aimed at supplying domestic servants:

> The object of the committee (Ladies Advisory Committee) is to introduce respectable persons, whether single women or families, into this Colony without regard to their particular occupation, but merely with a view to add to the permanent British element in the country.[80]

The Immigration Act of 1902, which provided the legal framework for Milner's policy, was promulgated in August 1903. Its application was the responsibility of the Medical Officer of Health of the Cape Colony. When in 1904 the first report on the working of the act was published it indicated a net increase of 28,745 persons in the population of the South African colony.[81] Although the report did not specify what proportion of the newcomers proceeded to the Transvaal there is little doubt that a large number of immigrants had the Transvaal as their final destination.

The majority of the arrivals, 64.85 per cent, travelled third class,[82] presumably workers, which seems to be confirmed by the fact that tradesman and artisan constituted the largest occupation group among the immigrants, and that 18.4 percent were presumably unemployed. Under the 'undetermined' occupational category women and children counted for 24.7 per cent of the passengers.[83] As this suggests, there were more men than women among the newcomers,[84] and, in a boost for Milner's policy, by far the most common nationality among the passengers (67.7 per cent) was British or Colonial.

In the following years the meagre results of the immigration policy as evidenced in the first report would be further thwarted by economic crisis. This was especially true of 1903 when the declining grade of the ore mined on the

Witwatersrand precipitated a new crisis in the mining industry. The strategy chosen by the mining companies to offset decreasing profit margins - exploitation of new ground and incorporation of technology - was jeopardized by a shortage of African labour, which was driving up wages.[85] The mine magnates' solution to this aspect of the crisis, the employment of Chinese indentured labour, was supported by the colonial government and in 1904 the first labourers started arriving on the Rand amidst serious opposition from the unions, who saw the importation of Chinese labourers as aggravating already serious unemployment.[86]

By 1905 the effects of the economic crisis were visible in the immigration figures. Not only was there a general decrease (43 per cent) in the total number of immigrants entering the Cape Colony but the passengers travelling third class - the category covering the bulk of immigrants - diminished by 50 per cent.[87] The administration responded to these discouraging figures by transferring the application of the Immigration Act from the Medical Officer of Health of Cape Colony to the Immigration and Labour Branch of the Colonial Secretary, which was more in touch with the problems and needs of the labour market in the southern African colonies. The newly created branch was thus to deal with assisting immigration, relieving distress, and giving advice to the Government Labour Bureau.[88] At the same time a fund to aid immigration was made available through the Transvaal Parliament in July 1905. The money - £1,000 - was to help in bringing out to the colonies the wives and children of the artisans as well as domestic servants.

This last scheme provided the well-to-do colonial bourgeoisie with domestic servants while also aiding the development of a stable white working class on the Rand. However, the general type of domestic servant required by the middle and upper classes in the colony was not easily found in England.[89] This, combined with the fact that, once on the Rand, most white women servants preferred to be employed as waitresses, assistants in shops or clerical workers in offices, had a rather negative effect on at least one of the objectives of the scheme.[90] The other, the provision of wives for the British workers on the Rand, seems to have been at least partially successful as the Colonisation Society was being called a "matrimonial agency" by despondent and dissatisfied householders.

The immigration fund expected future employers and husbands to contribute half of the cost of the ticket. This measure was devised to guarantee that husbands had sufficient means to support a family and that employers were not disreputable people involved in Johannesburg's flourishing prostitution business or in international slave trafficking.[91] The scheme encouraged the immigration and settlement of the "best type of English women of this class".[92] The actual figures after six months of the establishment of the fund were hardly encouraging.

According to report of the official in charge of the Immigration and Labour Branch, C. W. Cousins, from July 1905, only 75 passages had been booked - 12 for the wives of artisans, 30 for children and 33 for domestic servants.[93] The report for the following year indicated that net immigration at the end of 1906 was negative.[94] The figures showed that 6,573 more persons left the colony than entered it.[95]

Milner's immigration policy did not yield the expected fruits. Nevertheless, in the eight years that separated the 1896 Census from the one taken in 1904 Johannesburg's population had increased dramatically. In 1904 the city had 82,839 white inhabitants. The growth of the British population, both male, from 8,687 in 1896 to 22,070 in 1904, and female, from 3,211 to 9,400, can be credited to immigration. The increase in the number of the South African-born - males from 9,767 in 1896 to 16,241 in 1904 and females from 8,997 to 16,746 - reflects the movement of rural population into the city, which was particularly intense between 1895 and 1906.

Despite the increase in the number of adult women the ratio between males and females was still unbalanced. Married people now made up more than half (51.80 per cent) of the total adult population, and the number of families actually living in Johannesburg had increased to a staggering 80.16 per cent (Tables 2.2 and 2. 3). The slight drop in the proportion of children compared with the results of the 1896 Census can be explained by the effects that the South African War had on most families.

The impact of South African-born women outnumbering all males was illustrated by George Turner, the census commissioner, in 1906 when he acknowledged that British men tended to marry colonial 'girls'.[96] With a stroke of the pen, George Turner put an end to the political expectations that the reconstruction administration had for the ethnic reproduction of Johannesburg's population. The South African-born population outnumbered the British in Johannesburg, with the granting of Responsible Government just around the corner.

Conclusion

With more than half of the population of Johannesburg married by 1904, and more than 80 per cent of it living within a six-mile radius of Market Square, there can be little doubt as to the rooted nature of the Johannesburg population. Nevertheless, the results of the settlement were far from that which the reconstruction administration had set as its goal. The gender imbalance had not been fully corrected and, even worse, the predominance of women over men in the Afrikaner population provided, almost naturally, the female companions that British men were lacking in Johannesburg.

However, the marriage between English and Afrikaner which so worried Milner cannot be seen simply as the outcome of the greater number of Afrikaners amongst the female population of Johannesburg. The history of the urbanization of the Afrikaner population in Johannesburg responded to its own internal economic, social and ideological dynamics. The movement of rural Afrikaners to Johannesburg took place in the midst of withering ethnic solidarity and progressive class differentiation in the countryside. Once in the city some of these families did not seem to be especially attached to the Dutch Reformed Church. Whether this was a consequence of their dissatisfaction with the church itself or simply a matter of pragmatic response to the more readily available help from the Anglican Church is difficult to establish. What is indisputable is that a comparatively large proportion of Afrikaner families baptized their children in the Anglican Church.

The fact that between 1890 and 1906 British workers and newly proletarianized Afrikaners largely acted against the political designs of the British administration and the admonitions of the Dutch Reformed Church has to be understood in the context of the economic and social history of the Witwatersrand. Between 1890 and 1906 British workers and newly proletarianized Afrikaners largely acted against the political designs of the British administration and the admonitions of the Dutch Reformed Church has to be understood in the context of the economic and social history of the Witwatersrand. Between 1890 and 1906 the white workers who lived in Johannesburg faxed a bloody and costly was (1899-1902); three major economic recessions related to the slumps of the mining industry (1890-1; 1896-97 and 1906-8); and the specific consequences that capitalist transformation had on their particular trades in the city. The forces of capitalist development, especially in times of crisis, stressed what British and Afrikaner workers had in common: insecurity. The booms and slumps of the economy manifested themselves in varying forms according to the combination of skills, trade, level of income and size of the family that each worker supported. But at no point did capitalist development distinguish British from Afrikaner families.

There was, in fact, very little difference between some of the experiences of the British family of Andrew and Elizabeth Lopson, and the Afrikaner family of William and Maria Muller, or that of Henry Bates and his Afrikaner wife. The Lopsons had three children, the Mullers five and the Bates four. All three families lived for some years in Brickfields, all three moved in and out of Brickfields according to their changing fortunes, and all three fathers shifted jobs at least once in the context of an economic crisis.

The slumps of the economy, the high cost of living, the poor sanitary conditions of the neighbourhoods, illness and death were some of the constitutive elements of white working class experience in Johannesburg.

During a period in which Afrikaner national identity was not clearly defined, social and economic relations in the city played an important role in fostering a working class that was not acutely divided along 'ethnic' lines. Contrary to the interpretation of some historians,[97] Afrikaner identity did not always express itself in a tightly 'ethnic' way. It is in this context that van Onselen's account of the development of class consciousness amongst the constituency of Vrededorp in the early twentieth century acquires full force. The high geographical mobility of white working class families, together with the fairly frequent job changes of their male breadwinners, brought British and Afrikaner workers closer. This closeness, which, as we will see, translated into friendships and even fictive kinship, raises several questions about the ways in which white working class identity has been both defined and theorized in the literature. The following letter found inside the baptism records of the Church of Christ, Fordsburg, bears testimony to the complexity of white working class identity during this period:

January 2nd, 1907.

My Dear Brother,
A Happy New Year! This afternoon I was calling on Mr. Theodore Johnson at Langlaagte, when the people opposite summoned me across the road and asked me to baptize their baby who is very sick. They are poor Dutch folk Wesleyan Methodists but were very anxious for my ministrations even when they learned that I was an Anglican!

Thus, Phillipus Cornelius, born 13 September 1906, son of Cornelius Jacobus and Magdalena Coetzee, was baptized by the Rev. George Hart and registered as a new member of the Anglican Church.

Notes

[1] Kubicek, R. V., *Economic Imperialism in Theory and Practice: The Case of South African Gold Mining Finance, 1886-1914* (Durham 1979), p. 44. Hereafter *Economic Imperialism*.
[2] Kubicek, R. V., *Economic Imperialism*, p. 54.
[3] Sir Otto Beit (1853-1930), financier and benefactor brother of Alfred Beit, the mining magnate. Came to South Africa in 1890 and joined H. Eckstein & Company. He settled in London in 1898 and became partner in a stockbroking firm.
[4] Sir Lionel Phillips (1855-1936). Born in London. He was closely involved with South African mining from 1875 when he came to Griqualand West as a diamond sorter. He moved to the Witwatersrand in 1889 as a representative of the Wernher and Beit firm. Soon he became a senior partner and President of the Chamber of Mines between 1892 and 1895. His involvement in the Jameson Raid forced him to leave the country. He returned to

Johannesburg in 1906 and was deeply involved in local politics while defending the interests of the mining industry.

5 Sir George Farrar (1859-1915). Mining magnate and politician. Chairman of the Anglo French Exploration Company and of East Rand Proprietary Mines Limited. He was a leading member of the opposition to Kruger in the Reform Committee at the time of the Jameson Raid. In 1904 he became a leader of the Transvaal Progressive Association that supported Responsible Government for the Transvaal. He was elected to the Transvaal Legislative Assembly in 1907. Was a Transvaal delegate to the National Convention 1908-9, and, after the unification of South Africa, a member of the House of Assembly.

6 Cecil John Rhodes (1853-1902). Mining magnate and politician. Arrived in Kimberley in 1870 where became successful in his diamond mining ventures. In 1880 founded De Beers' Diamond Mining Company. Founded Consolidated Gold Fields of South Africa in 1887 and launched the British South African Company in Matabeleland (Rhodesia) in 1889. He started his political career in 1881 as a member of the Cape House of Assembly. He became a Prime Minister of the Cape in 1890 position from which he resigned after the Jameson Raid.

7 On the political and ideological imperatives of the gold mining industry during the 1890s see Bozzoli, B., *The Political Nature of a Ruling Class: Capital and Ideology in South Africa, 1890-1933* (London 1981), pp. 25-62. Hereafter *The Political Nature*.

8 On the causes of the South African War see Marks, S. and Trapido, S., 'Lord Milner and the South African State', *History Workshop Journal*, 8, 1979, pp. 50-80. Hereafter 'Lord Milner'; Phimister, I., 'Unscrambling the Scramble: Africa's Partition Reconsidered', Seminar Paper, African Studies Institute, 1992.

9 Sir Alfred Milner to Major Hanbury Williams 27/12/1900. Headlam, C. (ed.), *The Milner Papers* (Cape Town 1966), volume 2. Hereafter *The Milner Papers*.

10 It is necessary to remember here that while the 1896 Census focused on an area within a three-mile radius of Market Square, the 1904 Census was taken after the boundaries of the city had been extended to a six-mile radius of Market Square and in that sense the definition of Johannesburg differs from one census to the next.

11 The high number of married women in Johannesburg in 1896 probably reflects false returns from prostitutes who were living with pimps. While the returns of the 1896 Census under 'occupations' showed the existence of 114 self-confessed prostitutes, van Onselen has indicated that the actual number of whores in the city was around 1,000. Whether these women chose to pass as married, or to disguise their actual trade under other occupations such as barmaid, is not easy to establish. See van Onselen, C., *Studies in the Social and Economic History of the Witwatersrand, 1886-1914* (Johannesburg 1982), 'Prostitutes and Proletarians, 1886-1914', volume 1, *New Babylon*, p. 104. Hereafter 'Prostitutes and Proletarians'.

12 The returns of the 1896 Census showed under birthplaces a significant number of foreigners in Johannesburg. Amongst them there were: Russians (male: 2,587; females: 394); Germans (males: 1,368; females: 557); Hollanders (males: 526; females 215); Swiss (males: 80; females 31); Swedes and Norwegians (males: 202; females: 59); French (males: 194; females: 150); Italians (males: 173; females: 23); Americans (males: 378; females 93) and Australians (males: 463; females: 201).

13 On the political opposition to the Kruger government and the grievances of the *Uitlanders* see Gordon, C., *The Growth of Boer Opposition to Kruger, 1890-1895* (London 1970); and Cammack, D., *The Rand at War: The Witwatersrand and the Anglo-Boer War* (London 1991). Hereafter *The Rand at War*.

14 These percentages, taken from a sample of 53 mining companies, seem rather low when

compared with the 66.79 per cent of married men who lived with their families in Johannesburg according to the 1896 Census. The discrepancy in the figures can be attributed to the fact that the mining companies fell outside the area within which the 1896 Census was taken. This moreover suggests that the families settled in Johannesburg were largely non-mining families. *Industrial Commission of Enquiry 1897*, Evidence of C. S. Goldman, pp. 118-19. Goldman was a member of the Executive Council of the Chamber of Mines and also a member of the Native Labour Association, the organization put into place by the Chamber of Mines in the 1890s to recruit black workers within the Portuguese colonies.

15. Katz, E., *The White Death: Silicosis on the Witwatersrand Gold Mines, 1886-1910* (Johannesburg 1994), pp. 1-10. Hereafter *The White Death*.
16. *Report of the Small Holdings Commission, 1913* (U. G. 51-13), para. 16.
17. *Industrial Commission of Enquiry 1897*, Evidence of R. Barrow, p. 174.
18. *Industrial Commission of Enquiry 1897*, Evidence of R. Barrow, p. 172.
19. Cammack, D., *The Rand at War*, pp. 69-70, p. 77, and p. 202.
20. The returns of the 1896 Census showed that mining was the single largest skilled occupation amongst the city's population (3,194).
21. *The Star*, 11 October 1890; *The Star*, 13 October 1890.
22. Van Onselen, C., *Studies in the Social and Economic History of the Witwatersrand, 1886-1914*, Johannesburg 1982, volume 2, *New Nineveh*, 'The Main Reef Road into the Working Class: Proletarianisation, Unemployment and Class Consciousness amongst Johannesburg's Afrikaner Poor, 1886-1914', p. 125-6. Hereafter 'The Main Reef Road'.
23. See *Standard and Diggers' News (SDN)*, 28 September 1895 'They don't want work'; 26 May 1896, 'Hard times on the Rand'; 22 February 1899, 'Indiscriminate Alms Giving'. *The Star*, 30 August 1897, 'The Problem of the "Arme" Burgher'.
24. Van Onselen, C., 'Prostitutes and Proletarians', pp. 106-8.
25. The Act provided for the registration and medical examination of prostitutes as a way of preventing the spread of venereal diseases. On the application of the Contagious Diseases Acts in the Cape see van Heyningen, E., 'The Social Evil in the Cape Colony, 1868-1902: Prostitution and the Contagious Diseases Acts', *Journal of Southern African Studies*, 10, 2, 1984, pp. 170-97.
26. (U.W.) (CPSA), AB748/Ba. Minutes of St. Mary Parochial Council.
27. The database has been organized using the program Dbase III. Each record was given a number after which follow the surname of the father, and the names of both parents. Each record reflects the information available in the baptismal records of the Anglican Church. It comprises: date of birth and name of the child, address of the family, trade of the father and name of the godparents. The database has been named Data Base J1. The information will be quoted as follows: Data Base J1., number of the record, and name of the family followed by the names of both parents. The 2,290 families that constitute the database represent 35 per cent of the families settled in Johannesburg at the time of the 1896 Census.
28. University of the Witwatersrand (U.W.), Church of the Province of South Africa (CPSA), AB. 2013 Diocese of Johannesburg: JB.3.2 Belgravia; JJ.2.4.1 Jeppe; JJ.3.1.4.1-4 Johannesburg. The baptismal registers from Fordsburg do not form part of the collection yet, and therefore are not classified. They taken were directly from the Church of Christ in Fordsburg.
29. The identification of British and Afrikaner families has been based on language, distinguishing British surnames i.e. Smith, from Afrikaner surnames, i.e. Smit. When in doubt about the origin of a particular name it has been checked against Malherbe, D. F. du

Toit, *Stamregister Van Die Zuid-Afrikaanse Volk* (Stellenbosch 1966).
30 Of the 144 families whose main breadwinner was a miner it has been possible to reconstruct 26.60 per cent of them.
31 Data Base J1. Record 2119 Bayley, Lennox and Isabelle.
32 Data Base J1. Record 698 Heugh, Samuel and Rosa.
33 Data Base J1. Record 1151 Isaacs, Charles and Jane.
34 Van Onselen, C., 'The Main Reef Road', pp. 113-25.
35 The families of brickmakers that have been reconstructed represent 27.50 per cent of the families headed by a brickmaker who had their children baptized in the Anglican Church.
36 Data Base J1. Record 604 Muller, William and Maria.
37 Data Base J1. Record 1018 Bates, Henry and Maria.
38 Data Base J1. Record 1541 Coleman, George and Ellen.
39 Amongst working class families headed by bricklayers and builders whose children had been baptized in the Anglican Church it has been possible to reconstruct 32.09 per cent of the families. Amongst the families headed by painters and plasterers it has been possible to reconstruct 28.26 per cent of the families.
40 Data Base J1. Record 511 Rose, Benjamin and Minnie.
41 Van Onselen, C., 'The Main Reef Road'. pp. 114-15.
42 The company started in the late 1880s when A. H. Nellmapius, a wealthy and prominent Transvaal farmer, approached President Kruger to obtain a concession to develop a line of horse-drawn trams in the city. The economic potential of the venture attracted mining capital and Johannesburg City & Suburban Transport Company was floated in 1889. The tram service started operating in 1891. By 1896 City & Suburban Transport operated a fleet of about 35 trams and employed 200 drivers. See van Onselen, C., 'Johannesburg's Jehus, 1890-1914', volume 1, *New Babylon*, pp. 165-7. Hereafter 'Johannesburg's Jehus'.
43 Data Base J1. Record 472 Murphy, Edward and Jane.
44 Data Base J1. Record 27 Culvert, William and Anna.
45 Between 1904 and 1906 the number of licensed cabbies fell from 905 to 606. Van Onselen, C., 'Johannesburg's Jehus', p. 185.
46 Data Base J1. Record 1197 Morkel, John and Catherine.
47 In 1899 about 900 young Afrikaners managed to find a job as Zarps. Van Onselen, C., 'The Main Reef Road', p. 113.
48 Amongst the families headed by policemen it has been possible to reconstruct 23.63 per cent of the cases. Data Base J1. Record 224, Shultz, Bernard and Catherine.
49 Data Base J1. Record 1129 Abrahams, Harry and Rebecca.
50 On the complexities of the incorporation of Afrikaner workers into the mines see Katz, E., 'Miners by Default: Afrikaners and the Gold Mining Industry before Union', *The South African Journal of Economic History*, 6, 1, 1991, pp. 61-80 and 'The Underground Route to Mining: Afrikaners and the Witwatersrand Gold Mining Industry from 1902 to the 1907 Miners' Strike', Paper presented to the Symposium on Work, Class and Culture, History Workshop and Sociology of Work Unit, University of the Witwatersrand, 28-30 June 1993.
51 Data Base J1. Record 668 Lopson, Andrew and Elizabeth.
52 Medick, H., and Sabean D. (eds.), *Interest and Emotion: Essays on the Study of Family and Kinship* (Cambridge 1984), pp. 3-4.
53 *Ibid.*
54 (U.W) (CPSA), AB748/Ba. Minutes St. Mary Cathedral Parochial Council, 14 April, 1895.
55 Keegan, T., *Rural Transformations in Industrializing South Africa: The Southern Highveld*

to 1914 (Johannesburg 1986), pp. 22-3. Hereafter *Rural Transformations*.
56 Keegan, T., *Rural Transformations*, p. 25.
57 Van Onselen, C., *'The Main Reef Road'*, pp. 125-33.
58 Grundlingh, A., 'Collaborators in Boer Society', in, Warwick, P. (ed.), *The South African War: The Anglo-Boer War 1899-1902* (London 1980), pp. 258-78. The same can be said of British workers' loyalty to the imperial cause. While British-linked trade unions like the Amalgamated Society of Engineers and the Amalgamated Society of Carpenters and Joiners were loyal to Britain, South African societies such as those catering for printers and engine drivers favoured neutrality. There were also British trade union leaders who like J.T. Bain, the organizer of the Amalgamated Society of Engineers, joined the republican forces. See Tickten, 'The Origins of the South African Labour Party', Ph.D. thesis, University of Cape Town, 1973, pp. 92-3.
59 Hofmeyr, I., 'Building a Nation from Words: Afrikaans Language, Literature and Ethnicity, 1902-1924', in Marks, S. and Trapido, S. (eds.), *The Politics of Race, Class and Nationalism in Twentieth Century South Africa* (London 1987), pp. 95-123, p. 100.
60 The following paragraphs are based on Fourie, J., *Afrikaners in die Goudstad. Deel 1 1886-1924* (Pretoria 1978), pp. 139-57. Hereafter *Afrikaners in die Goudstad*.
61 In 1895, one of the dominies of the Reformed Church in Johannesburg maintained that the spiritual life of the Afrikaners living in the city was in serious decline: "Ook gevoelt men zich op de groote Goudstad niet verantwoordelyk aan elkander, zooals op kleinere dorpen. Velen meenen vaak dat zy onbekend zyn & gaan dan allicht op een dwaalweg voort. De wisswlende aard der gemeente te midden eener delversbevolking maakt velen ook onverschilling dan elders het geval zou zyn. Eene gejaagde besigheid verdringt den huisgodsdienst, vooral 't morgens. Schrikkelyke verschynselen doen zich voor op' n genied der openbare zedelykheid." Quoted in Fourie, J., *Afrikaners in die Goudstad*, p. 147.
62 Fourie, J., *Afrikaners in die Goudstad*, p. 150.
63 On the political importance of these divisions within the Afrikaner population see, Denoon, D., *A Grand Illusion: The Failure of Imperial Policy in the Transvaal Colony during the Period of Reconstruction, 1900-05* (London 1973), pp. 16-19. Hereafter *A Grand Illusion*.
64 According to Hexham, between 1902 and 1909: "Church Councils did all they could to discourage contact with the English. Baptisms and marriages in the English Church were subject to censure and everything possible was done to maintain a consciousness of the distinctive Afrikaner identity of Church members", Hexham, I., *The Irony of Apartheid: The Struggle for National Independence of Afrikaner Calvinism Against British Imperialism* (New York 1981), p. 72.
65 Bozzoli, B., *The Political Nature*, pp. 50-1.
66 On this specific aspect of Milner's policies see Marks, S. and Trapido, S., 'Lord Milner', pp. 61-3.
67 Curtis, L., *With Milner in South Africa* (Oxford 1951), p. 206.
68 Denoon, D., *A Grand Illusion*, p. 9.
69 Streak, M., *Lord Milner's Immigration Policy for the Transvaal 1897-1905*, Rand Afrikaans University Publication, Series B1 (January 1969). The process of keeping emigration within the Empire started in the late 1890s with the creation of the Royal Colonial Institute, founded with the aim of supervizing and directing British emigration within the Empire. Milner himself was quite enthusiastic about this policy, and back in Britain he was very active in encouraging sponsored emigration as an important factor in promoting imperial unity. Newbury, C., 'The March of Everyman: Mobility and the Imperial Census of 1901', *The Journal of Imperial and Commonwealth History*, XII, 2,

1984, pp. 80-101, pp. 80-1.
[70] Stedman-Jones, G., *Outcast London: A Study in the Relationship between Classes in the Victorian Society* (Oxford 1971), pp. 308-12.
[71] The political aspect of the encouragement of immigration cannot be stressed enough. Milner's concern at the end of the war was that if the demographic imbalance were not redressed, a future federal assembly would not be able to secure British hegemony in the Transvaal. Sir Alfred Milner to Major Hanbury Williams, 27/12/00, Headlam, C. (ed.), *The Milner Papers* (Cape Town 1966), volume 2, p. 242. Hereafter *The Milner Papers*.
[72] On this specific issue see Swaisland, C., *Servants and Gentlewomen to the Golden Land: The Emigration of Single Women from Britain to South Africa, 1820-1939* (Oxford 1993).
[73] Sir Alfred Milner to Major Hanbury Williams, 27/12/00, *The Milner Papers*, volume 2, p. 243.
[74] Williams Papers, MSS Afr. s.131. Circular dated 3 June 1902, cited by Denoon, D., *A Grand Illusion*, p. 159.
[75] Sir Alfred Milner to Mr. Spenser Wilkinson, 27/04/03, *The Milner Papers*, volume 2, p. 449.
[76] British Women's Emigration Association, *Annual Report*, 1900, quoted in van Helten, J. J. and Williams, K. '"The Crying Need of South Africa": The Emigration of Single British Women to the Transvaal, 1901-1910', *Journal of Southern African Studies*, 10, 1, 1983, pp. 17-38, p. 22. See also Stoler, A. L., 'Rethinking Colonial Categories: European Communities and the Boundaries of Rule', *Comparative Studies in Society and History*, 1989, pp. 134-60.
[77] Basil Williams had met Lionel Curtis at Brasenose College in Oxford. He had been in South Africa as a soldier and had returned to work with Milner. In 1901, when Curtis was appointed Johannesburg Town Clerk, Basil Williams was his assistant. By 1903 he had left Johannesburg and was organising a new educational system in the Transvaal.
[78] Transvaal Archives Depot (TAD), Colonial Secretary (CS) 104/670/02. Memorandum by the Colonial Secretary.
[79] (TAD) (CS) 117/8613/02. Telegram from the Governor of the Transvaal to the Secretary of State, 28 July 1902. Minutes of a meeting held at the office of the Colonial Secretary, 25 August 1902.
[80] (TAD) (CS) 457/3174/04. Transvaal Immigration Office. Letter from the Private Secretary to the Governor of the Transvaal, 11 May 1904.
[81] *Report of the Working of the Immigration Act, 1902 for the Year 1903* (G. 63-1904).
[82] The remaining 9.59 per cent travelled on deck. (G. 63-1904), p. 4.
[83] (G. 63-1904), p. 7.
[84] Males predominated over females by 63.58 per cent.
[85] Kubicek, R. V., *Economic Imperialism*, pp. 48-9.
[86] Katz, E., *A Trade Union Aristocracy: A History of White Workers in the Transvaal and the General Strike of 1913* (Johannesburg 1976), pp. 109-53. Ticktin, D., 'The Origins of the South African Labour Party', pp. 114-52.
[87] The proportion of females fell to 22.69 per cent as did the number of minors - from 13 per cent in 1903 and 18 per cent in 1904 to 14 per cent in 1905. *Report of the Officer in Charge of Immigration and Labour for the Year 1905* (G. 4-1906).
[88] This bureaucratic reshuffle needs to be read in the context of the ongoing economic depression and the measures taken to overcome labour shortages through encouraging immigration. As C. W. Cousins, the officer in charge of Immigration and Labour, put it in his first report: "From every point of view there seems to have been ample justification for

the formation of this Branch, and for the administration in close association therein of matters so intimately related to one another. The anticipation of labour problems and relief measures would react upon one another. The conditions of the labour market would materially affect the immigration and vice versa." (G. 4- 1906), p. 2.

89 Van Onselen, C., 'The Witches of Suburbia: Domestic Service on the Witwatersrand, 1890-1914', volume 2, *New Nineveh*, pp. 9-13.

90 "It is true that some immigrants take up work in tea-rooms, hotels, etc. but this is not due to a scarcity of suitable situations as domestic servants, but to the fact that some women prefer work as waitresses in tea rooms because as such they have more freedom and are able to lead a more independent life than in domestic service." Letter from Courtnay Shaw, Acting Secretary of the Transvaal Immigration Office, to the Governor of the Transvaal (TAD) (CS) 457/3175/1904.

91 For an account of prostitution on the Witwatersrand see van Onselen, C., 'Prostitutes and Proletarians', pp. 103-62.

92 (G. 4-1906), p. 8.

93 (G. 4-1906), p. 7.

94 *Report on Immigration and Labour for the Year ending 31st December 1906* (G. 21-1907), p. 3.

95 This figure was made up of 5,809 men and 764 children. Surprisingly enough, there was a real increase in the female population, as 427 more women entered than left. (G. 21-1907), p. 5.

96 (TAD), Mayor of Johannesburg (MJB) 5/1. *Report of the Medical Officer of Health for the Period from 31st July, 1904 to 30th June 1906*, p. 75.

97 De Villiers, R., 'Afrikaner Nationalism' in Wilson, M. and Thompson, L. (eds.), *Oxford History of South Africa*, volume II (Oxford 1971), pp. 365-423; Giliomee, H. and Adam, H., *The Rise and Crisis of Afrikaner Power* (Cape Town 1979); Moodie, Dunbar T., *The Rise of the Afrikanerdom: Power, Apartheid and the Afrikaner Civil Religion* (Berkeley 1980); Thompson, L., 'Great Britain and the Afrikaner Republics, 1870-1899' in Wilson, M. and Thompson, L. (eds.), *Oxford History of South Africa* (Oxford 1971), pp. 289-324. A more complete discussion of the different interpretations of Afrikaner history will be developed in the conclusion of this book.

Chapter 3

The Political Economy of White Working Class Housing in Johannesburg, 1890-1906

Introduction

The discovery of gold on the Witwatersrand was followed by the proclamation of public diggings in 1886. At this time, given the uncertainty around the life span of the goldfields, plans for the organization of the area did not go beyond the allocation of claims under the Gold Law of the South African Republic. But soon enough the influx of population made it necessary to replace the *ad hoc* Diggers' Committee with a more permanent form of administration. Thus in 1887 two important events took place simultaneously: the executive in Pretoria appointed a *Gesondheids Comite* (Sanitary Committee) as an organ of self-government; and the area that was to constitute Johannesburg was officially surveyed and stands marked out.

Ten years later in 1897, when Johannesburg was granted municipal status, it had a population of 102,000 inhabitants and extended over five square miles. By 1904 the population had increased to 158,000 and the city covered 82 square miles. This leap had not taken place without conflict and setbacks. Not only did three different administrations control Johannesburg between 1886 and 1899 but municipal government was interrupted by the outbreak of the South African War of 1899-1902. When the first post-war town council was installed, in 1901, the local government was in dire financial straits, its relations with the central government ill defined, and basic urban infrastructure was almost non-existent.

The slow pace in the development of administrative capacity and urban infrastructure in Johannesburg during the 1890s became all the more evident as the city's population expanded. From its earliest days Johannesburg's goldfields and the dream of urban prosperity had attracted both foreign workers and local Afrikaner families who were fleeing worsening conditions in the countryside. By the late 1890s insanitary areas, slum conditions and a lack of appropriate accommodation were some of the problems that a by this time sizeable white working class had to face in the city.

When, in March 1901, British troops commanded by Lord Roberts entered Johannesburg a new stage in the administration of the city started. Major W. A. J. O'Meara became Acting Mayor of Johannesburg and Milner, in his capacity as British Governor of the Transvaal, appointed the members of a new town council.[1] The council based its policies on the Victorian statutes of municipal government. The 18 newly appointed councillors were soon to find that, whatever the basis for their policies, the interests at play in Johannesburg were not easy to reconcile. And even if, as Lionel Curtis said, "just at present one gets things done with a stroke of the pen that in England would entail an act of Parliament and a exhaustive parliamentary enquiry",[2] the councillors had much political convincing to do before they could implement their ideas for Johannesburg's urban development.

Three issues dominated political discussion in Johannesburg during the reconstruction period: rates and taxes, ownership of town lands and the scarcity of housing in the city. Deciding on a system of rates and taxes was part and parcel of the need to define the powers of the local government and to provide the municipality with an adequate financial base. But the assessment rate was far from being a neutral financial problem. It was deeply intertwined with the broader land issue and in this sense touched on the interests of the mining houses which had large holdings of underdeveloped land south of the city centre. The restrictions that the reef's geology imposed upon the mining operations partially explained the mining industry's interest in land. However, soon enough land itself became the most important area of investment outside the gold mines and the mining houses became, through their estate companies, the largest owners of land in and around Johannesburg. Any change in the assessment rate or any policy to discourage speculative holding of land was contrary to their broader interests. These were reflected in the establishment of leasehold townships as opposed to freehold ones. The price and availability of working class accommodation in Johannesburg was directly affected by the concentration of land in the hands of the mining houses and their estate companies. In turn, this impinged on white workers' budgets and acted as a deterrent to their permanent settlement in the city. Against this backdrop, between 1901 and 1906, the Johannesburg Town Council had to reconcile the political objectives of the reconstruction administration with the economic interests of the mine magnates and the needs of the white labour force.

The British immigrants who arrived and settled in Johannesburg with their families, those labouring men who came alone and established their families later, and recently proletarianized Afrikaner families clustered closely together in the freehold suburbs east and west of the city where accommodation was more readily available. Proximity to the mining industry and to the economic activity of the town centre made Braamfontein, Belgravia, Ferreirastown,

Fordsburg, Jeppestown, Marshallstown and Vrededorp the obvious choices of the working class.

The geography of class in Johannesburg was the product of economic and social forces and also, especially after 1901, the result of particular characteristics of the reconstruction period town planning. Socio-economic forces, class interests and (not always successful) political design combined in different ways to shape working class neighbourhoods and their functional relation to the city as a whole. The mining industry's interest in land ownership in Johannesburg had two fundamental effects upon the colonial state's ability to implement its policies. On the one hand, it restricted, to some extent, the availability of working class accommodation. On the other hand, it acted as an obstacle to certain aspects of town planning proposed by the administration.

From a political and ideological perspective negotiation and lobbying as well as protest around these issues took place in a colonial context which meant that urban planning in Johannesburg, and more specifically, the peculiarities of white working class settlement, were, despite their Victorian roots, constricted in new and powerful ways by the racial logic which operated in the colony.

The Origins of the White Working Class Housing Problem: Land and the Property Market in Greater Johannesburg, 1886-1906

At the time of the discovery of the Witwatersrand goldfields in 1886 the distribution of mining claims in the South African Republic was governed by the Gold Law of 1883. This law, however, had been devised to deal mainly with alluvial diggings such as those in Pilgrims' Rest. According to this legislation the diggers were allowed to peg out a certain area of ground, a 'claim', in which, against the payment of a monthly licence, they could dig and wash the alluvial deposits. It soon became evident to the diggers that it was not always either convenient or comfortable to pitch their tents on the claims. Thus, they established their camps on neighbouring ground, on a 'stand' that was not suitable for mining. The owner of such land, whether the government or a private person, asked for a monthly rent payment for the ground. Not only diggers were attracted to the mining areas; traders also made their way to the goldfields and paid a monthly licence for using stands for their purposes.

When goldfields were located over large areas the distribution of stands did not offer major problems. Very little planning was necessary to facilitate circulation between the stands and claims within the area through paths and roads. Geographically constrained areas, such as the Barbeton goldfields, entailed more careful planning of the camp. The experience with the alluvial diggings was extremely useful when gold was discovered in the Witwatersrand

and in 1886 the proclamation of the public diggings and the survey of the area set aside for stands were done almost simultaneously.[3]

The piece of ground known as Randjeslaagte farm, which comprised about 600 acres located between what are today Commissioner Street, along West Street and Diagonal Street northward to a point at the corner of Louis Botha Avenue and East Avenue, was selected for residential stands. The centrality of the area combined with the fact that it was state-owned and therefore a potential source of revenue for the government made the Randjeslaagte farm ideal for stands. In 1886 E. de Villiers surveyed the area and marked out 986 stands of 50 x 50 feet which were auctioned as a 99 years lease for which there was a 10s monthly licence.[4]

The development of the goldfields lured many private investors who bought large tracts of land, marked out stands west and east of the central town and sold them on leasehold. The Gold Law of 1883 made provision for a stand tax (2s 6d) that the government could levy for administrative expenses where the concentration of stands was dense enough to form a *dorp* (small village). In 1891 the government levied a quarter of the licence fees payable for stands proclaimed on private land as a defrayment of the administrative costs.[5]

Under the Gold Law of 1883 stand licences started off as a form of rent paid to the government for the use of a stand, and, although it was assumed that the use of the ground would continue as long as payments were made, the system was not one of a freehold tenure. However, in less than ten years the widespread development of townships on government and private land on the Witwatersrand transformed the right of the diggers to pitch a tent into a *de facto* form of tenure akin to freehold rights and changed the stand licence from a payment for the use of land into a tax owed to the government. This process had great importance when township companies started buying land in and around Johannesburg. On the one hand, it defined the relationship between township companies and the local authorities. On the other hand, it influenced the nature of tenure on both government and privately owned land. The relatively small amount paid in taxes encouraged accumulation of land for presumably speculative purposes, which, in turn, created an artificial scarcity of land, putting up the prices both of land and rented accommodation and reducing the availability of land for building purposes in the city and its suburbs.

The gold laws of 1883 and 1898[6] dealt with two different types of rights: mineral rights (claims) and land rights (stands). They established that both land and mineral rights came into existence with the proclamation of a particular area as a public digging, that is to say, from the moment in which the state declared its right over such land and its mineral resources. This fact had long term consequences for the characteristics of tenure in private townships within mining towns.

The gold law in its two versions established the relations between the state, private owners of land and those who were working mining claims on both state and private land. The laws distinguished between mineral rights and surface rights in a proclaimed area. The 1898 Gold Law guaranteed the exclusive power of the state to distribute mineral rights (i.e. claims) to private persons when the deposits were on government land and to dispose of the mineral rights when the deposits were on privately owned land, and established that only the government could proclaim public diggings.[7]

Those powers did not, however, extend to surface rights (i.e. stands) in the case of privately owned land. When the government decided to proclaim a public digging on private land, the owner had the right to reserve a *mynpacht* for himself and to single out those plots that were part of the homestead and that therefore could not be thrown open to mining.[8] At the same time the owner of the land was entitled to share with the government all licence money from claims and stands on his property. The government had the right to all licence money from claims and stands on state land and to half of the money from the same licences on private land.

Mineral rights on public or private land did not give full title to the use of the surface. Accordingly, Gold Law No. 15 of 1898 established that the remaining portion (what was left once *mynpacht* and homestead had been marked out) of proclaimed mineralized ground could be occupied by the government free of charge and be used for constructing roads, erecting public buildings, and for surveying stands.[9] This condition of this law was to be at the centre of a controversy between the mining companies and the local authorities after the South African War.

The Gold Law of 1898 referred only to proclaimed land. Nevertheless, when township companies bought farm land and created townships in non-proclaimed areas, they established the tenure of the stands within the terms of the Gold Law. Thus, instead of selling them freehold, they sold their stands leasehold, i.e. they sold the use of the land, not the land itself. This system of tenure, which seemed particularly suitable in the context of the uncertain economic future of the goldfields in the late 1880s, actually entrenched the speculative nature of land ownership and the property market.

By the late 1890s three township companies, closely linked to mining interests, controlled most of the land and the property transactions in Johannesburg. The Witwatersrand Township Estate and Financial Corporation was created in 1896 as a supplement to the mining interests of the Abe Bailey group.[10] Through a process of absorption of other estate companies, by the end of the South African War it had managed to acquire 742 acres of land, divided into 5,397 stands spread between the townships of Bellevue East, Fordsburg, Jeppestown, Jeppestown South, North Doornfontein and Wolhuter.

Johannesburg Consolidated Investment Company was formed by Barny Barnato in 1889. It took over the assets of four estate companies that controlled the tract of land immediately north-east of Johannesburg central. But Barnato was not alone in this operation. A. Eckstein, from the Corner House group, was also part of the new company.[11] In total it owned 2,380 acres divided into 5,238 stands that constituted the townships of Berea, Yeoville, Houghton, and Old Doornfontein. Finally, Braamfontein Estate Company had been formed by Eckstein himself in 1892 and it owned the townships of Braamfontein and Parktown.

The dominance of the land market by real estate companies, reinforced through the constant growth of the population and the increasing demand for housing that took place both before and after the South African War,[12] was made possible by a tax system that was highly beneficial to landowners.

Proclamation was the legal procedure by which a township was recognized as such. During the 1890s the fact that proclamation was not enforced by law allowed for an important loophole in terms of taxation.[13] Small residential freeholds in a non-proclaimed town were not different, according to the law, from a subdivision of a farm and therefore paid a farm tax that was substantially lower than the town tax. This system encouraged the accumulation of land by estate companies. Where the ground was not proclaimed they had to pay a farm tax that was negligible and where the ground was proclaimed, the bare land was taxed only at 10s annually regardless of its value.[14]

The fact that during the 1890s most of the land surrounding the Johannesburg town centre was the property of township companies shaped the most characteristic feature of the political economy of housing in Johannesburg.[15] In the years immediately after the South African War the high prices of land and rent resulting from the powerful position of these companies in the land market became stumbling blocks to the permanent settlement of people in Johannesburg.

During the reconstruction period, the project of the extension of Johannesburg's boundaries in 1901, the Rating Bill of 1903 and the Vrededorp Stands Ordinance of 1906 represented three different ways in which the colonial administrators and the municipality dealt with the land issue. While the first two approaches were designed to curtail indirectly the speculative nature of land ownership, the third represented the new authorities' attempt to unify tenure in the city and do away with special rights over town lands.

The need to extend the city's boundaries was related to the process of urbanization that had taken place in Johannesburg from 1886. Lionel Curtis, who had acquired vast experience in municipal government issues in Britain, was appointed Town Clerk in 1901 and took upon himself the motivation for, and implementation of, this project. Curtis argued that sooner or later the prevalent pattern of urbanization in the city would reproduce the separation between affluent and poor neighbourhoods common to London. In Johannesburg the line of the reef had already isolated the well-to-do areas in the north of the city from the mines and their satellite working class neighbourhoods in the south. To begin to change this pattern it was necessary to incorporate the mines and the northern suburbs into the municipal area, extending the jurisdiction of the nominated town council from a three-mile radius of Market Square to a six-mile radius. The extension of the jurisdiction of the town council would imply not only the establishment of a unified administration, but also that rates would be levied on properties belonging to the mines. As soon as the project became known the Chamber of Mines reacted to what it considered a most unfair situation.[16]

Mine property, the chamber explained, could never be seen as an important residential area. Generally unhealthy conditions, derived from the permanent noise and dust, made it unsuitable for habitation purposes for anybody other than mining employees. In addition, the further development of deep level mines necessarily implied that more ground would be taken up for mining purposes and then this ground would, according to the Gold Law of 1898, be immediately excluded from taxation.

Interestingly, in its attempt to avoid inclusion in the municipal area and thus the payment of rates and taxes, the Chamber of Mines seemed to change its politics. While under the government of the South African Republic the mining industry militated energetically for both the political rights of the *Uitlanders* and the need to have British workers settled on the Witwatersrand; in 1901, under a British administration, the Chamber of Mines opposed the inclusion of its workers on the municipal voters roll, an inevitable consequence of the extension of the municipal area, because the nominal rents the workers paid did not qualify them as occupiers. Ironically, the mining companies had to be reminded that the mine workers were "one of the most purely British sections of the population" and in that sense one of the most loyal to the government.[17] It was James Percy Fitzpatrick, who replaced Lionel Phillips as Eckstein's man in Johannesburg, who had the task of convincing his colleagues in the Chamber of Mines as to the benefits of the extension of Johannesburg's boundaries. By the end of 1901, thanks to his mediation, the chamber lifted its opposition to the project and in 1903 the boundaries of Johannesburg were extended to embrace the mines south of the reef line.[18]

In 1901 a report from the town valuator, Richard Currie, showed that by then the concentration of land ownership in the hands of estate companies in Johannesburg had acquired alarming proportions and was pushing up land prices.[19] Curtis himself pointed out the "enormous growth of land values in the centre of Johannesburg" and viewed the development of an electric tram system as a possible solution to the housing problem in the city. The extension of easy and inexpensive transportation, as conceived by Curtis in 1901, could, among other things, lower the price of land in the centre of Johannesburg through competition with more economical new areas further out, freeing workers from the need to live close to their workplace. Nevertheless, it took until 1904 for the town council and City and Suburban Transport, the company operating horse-drawn trams in the city, to reach an agreement and the new electric tram only started operating in 1906.[20]

Whatever the problems that the high prices of land and rented accommodation posed to the settlement of British workers on the Rand, neither the central administration nor the nominated town council were ready to take more drastic measures against the mines' control over the land market in order to make land and housing available in town.[21] In his reply to the Chamber of Mines's comments on the project to extend Johannesburg's boundaries Curtis made it perfectly clear that the reconstruction administration had no intention of undermining the industry's interests because they constituted "the treasure house of the government whose first interest must be to protect their wealth".[22]

Convinced that land and housing markets would sort themselves out once supply caught up with demand, the town council only adopted measures of temporary relief for Johannesburg's homeless such as the pitching of tents on vacant government ground for returning refugees. But by 1903 the supply of houses was well behind the demand for accommodation and rentals for working class houses in Johannesburg were unduly high. In this context Lord Milner appointed a commission of enquiry into the shortage of working class accommodation. In the meantime and with an eye to more immediate solutions, the Finance Committee of the nominated town council prepared a Rating Bill that could have changed somewhat the political economy of housing.

The introduction to the bill proposed taxing every ownership interest in land belonging to the municipality, excluding mineral rights. In other words, the bill proposed an assessment rate on the freehold owner; on the township company as first lessee; and on the stand-owner as second-lessee. With respect to the mines, those portions of the surface used for residential purposes or purposes other than mining were to be valued at the amount the land would fetch on the open market.

Had the bill been passed it would have discouraged the speculative nature of land investment by taxing the capital value of land instead of its rental value. According to the council, this would have had two advantages. On the one hand, it would have encouraged builders to construct houses. On the other hand it would have stopped landowners withholding their land from occupation by keeping it out of the market. The council's argument was that:

> Buildings as such don't make any demands on the Council, but that it is to the population of this community that all municipal services are rendered and neither to buildings nor land. The congregation of this population on the limited area of the Municipality is the cause which has enhanced the value of land beyond that of similar land say 100 miles distant, and it appears to us to be only reasonable that such enhanced values should contribute towards the needs of the population which had created them.[23]

But the Rating Bill was not passed. The administration chose to keep the assessment rate as it was in Britain: based on the annual rental value of land and buildings and not on its capital value.[24] The battle around the site value rate had only started. Its outcome depended largely on the political composition of the municipal council but also on how widespread was information about land assessment rates, and, last but not least, on the pressure that workers' demands could put on local and central government. In 1903, despite the fact that the municipal council was sprinkled with men with a mind for reform, such as Richard Feetham, who had replaced Curtis as Town Clerk in that year, the majority of its members belonged to the propertied class, like Julius Jeppe, the largest shareholder of Ford and Jeppe Estate Company.[25] Members like Jeppe were clearly against a reform that would undermine their interests. It was only ten years later when the Labour Party had a majority both in municipal and provincial government that the assessment rate could be changed in Johannesburg.

The town council's third way of dealing with land and property issues was the Vrededorp Stands Ordinance of 1906 which vested the freehold of the government township of Vrededorp in the municipality of Johannesburg. Under the Republican government destitute *burghers* (citizens of the South African Republic) had been given land rights to stands in Vrededorp. Tenure of these stands was for the life of the original holder and his widow and was only transferable to a lessee belonging to the same social group i.e. poor *burghers*.[26] The reconstruction administration changed this last clause, opening the transference of land rights to any person who wished to buy property in Vrededorp. By 1905, of the 785 stands that constituted the township of Vrededorp, 450 were still under the grant of the Republican government, 321 stands had been transferred to persons other than poor ex-*burghers* under the new administration, and 14 were reserved for schools.[27]

In vesting the freehold of Vrededorp in the municipality, the government was simultaneously giving the town council new financial resources and transforming a "temporary and charitable grant" into a normal lease.[28] According to the municipal government "the charitable" grant given by the republican government had taken the Vrededorp stands off the market and created a group of people that stood apart from the rest of the population because of its access to state charity. In this sense the Vrededorp Stands Ordinance had two functions. On the one hand, through the uniformity of tenure, it returned the stands to the market. On the other hand, it "levelled up" the rights that individuals had to acquire property in this area. The original holders were given four years after the enactment of the Ordinance to buy the new lease in instalments. The prices were £40 or £50 depending on the position of the stand, plus a monthly licence.

In addition to the original beneficiaries of the Republican concession other private investors bought some of the stands that had been freed by the ordinance. The reconstruction administration did not recognize any particular rights to transferees who had acquired their stands after 1901 because, in the town council's opinion, these people had "purchased them as other people would purchase rights for their own interest and of their own motion" and therefore there was no reason "why the community should take upon its own shoulders the burden of making the speculation a success".[29]

During the hearings of the Vrededorp Stands Commission, in 1905, the town council's representatives, councillors Leonard, Buckle and Murray, proposed to treat outside standholders and transferees as having the same rights. The main argument of the elected Johannesburg Town Council was that on the one hand the reconstruction administration had allowed this transference of land rights to take place and on the other that most of the transferees were poor people employed on the railways or in the mines.[30]

Annexure 4 of the report, which listed the persons holding more than one stand, supported the case of the town council. Forty people held 135 stands that had been transferred after 1903. Amongst them only two persons, Solomon Caro, who held 25 stands, and Simon Frenkel, who held 15 stands, had visibly accumulated property in the area.[31] The annexure showed that although a certain element of speculation existed in the transactions that took place in Vrededorp, the vast majority of the population owned only one stand and was either poor Afrikaners or Jewish people.[32]

Put in the context of measures taken by the town council on the land issue, the Vrededorp Ordinance indicates that in the aftermath of the South African War the reconstruction administration's intervention was not so much directed at curbing the already high concentration of land in the hands of a few township companies as at homogenizing land tenure in the city.

Johannesburg's Urbanization and the "Geography of Class", 1890-1906

The emergence of a settled population in late nineteenth century Johannesburg, no matter how unstable, left the government of the South African Republic with the problem of providing the city with an administrative structure and services. In 1890 the executive in Pretoria first conferred self-government upon the new town in the form of a sanitary board, which was an elected body representing the owners and occupiers of fixed property in Johannesburg. This body was responsible for the sanitary condition of the city, as well as for the provision of essential services like water, electricity and transport.

In spite of being an organ of self-government, the Johannesburg Sanitary Board (1890-7) was heavily dependent on the executive in Pretoria, not least because the executive could modify the decisions of board. The true lack of independence of the local government was especially apparent when it came to finances. While the Johannesburg Sanitary Board had its own sources of revenue through fees, fines and taxes and also had borrowing powers, revenues and expenditure were controlled and subject to the approval of the central government.[33] This, plus the fact that Johannesburg's citizens seemed to have been in arrears quite often, made the independence of the sanitary board a political fiction.

The mounting political tension between the Pretoria executive and the sanitary board was also related to these problems. The underlying issues, however, had to do with the threat that de facto British dominance in Johannesburg posed to the Kruger government. The city's white population was largely made up of *Uitlanders* who had controlled the local government from its early days. The Republican government's distrust of British intentions was expressed in political restrictions on the franchise of the *Uitlander* population. The Jameson Raid of 1895, which was a reflection of many of these tensions, brought this situation to a critical point.

While the growing importance of Johannesburg was sanctioned in 1897 with the concession of municipal status to the city, Kruger was careful to put in place the necessary mechanisms to control Johannesburg's independence and to guarantee the loyalty of the municipal council. Half of the new council's members had to be *burghers* elected by *burghers* and the central government reserved for itself the right to appoint the mayor.[34] Given the predominance of *Uitlanders* in the voters roll, this decision turned the council into a less representative body than the sanitary board had been.

In December 1899 the outbreak of the South African War brought the municipal government, as well as most of Johannesburg's economic activity, to a standstill. It was only after Lord Roberts's occupation of the city in March 1900 that local government was re-established. The new authorities took the state machinery out of the hands of what was seen as an inefficient administration and planned to transform it into a modern political structure capable of nurturing economic development based more firmly on the financial resources of the mining industry.[35]

In February 1901, after acquainting himself with the state of affairs in

Johannesburg, Lionel Curtis sent a memorandum to the Colonial Secretary, George Fiddes, laying out the basis for the reconstruction of Johannesburg. Among the suggestions, a municipal government developed along the lines of British municipalities seemed appropriate not only as an administrative structure but also because "a municipal system approximated to that in England would at once be a school of self-government and mark when the time was ripe to confer its fuller privileges on the inhabitants of the Colony at large".[36]

But the administrative situation in Johannesburg was "so removed from the highest types of Municipal government" that Curtis advised the appointment to the municipal administration of at least one person with experience of these matters in large modern cities like Birmingham and Glasgow. Lord Milner took this recommendation seriously and appointed Curtis himself as Town Clerk, due to his experience in the Mansion House Committee on the Dwellings of the Poor in London.[37]

Raising Johannesburg's administrative infrastructure to the standards of British municipalities was not an easy task. Important steps in this direction were the definition of powers vested in the town council, the extension of the city's boundaries and the Rating Bill. Every political decision taken by the nominated council was directed towards transforming Johannesburg into a settled community. In Lionel Curtis's own words:

> What is vital for this community is that Johannesburg should become a place where people will desire to remain rather than a mine of wealth whence men look to rapidly accumulate fortunes for export elsewhere. Everything calculated to make Johannesburg desirable as an habitation will tend to the attainment of the end in view, and it is idle to deny that pure, efficient and cheap local government is a strong inducement for a population to remain, instead of passing like annuals, which have to be resown artificially and never take permanent root. The British administration cannot afford to neglect any measure likely to contribute to this end.[38]

Economic and political developments in the city had a decisive impact on the configuration of working class neighbourhoods in Johannesburg and therefore on the processes of urbanization and settlement of the population to which Curtis was referring.

The character of Johannesburg's neighbourhoods was influenced by the ways in which type and price of accommodation, proximity to the workplace and provision of services combined in the different areas of the city. Johannesburg central, which comprised the area limited by the railway line in the north, Commissioner Street in the south, the Gas Works in the west and End Street in the east, had the greatest concentration of buildings and population in the city (Table 3.1). The mixture of residential and commercial buildings – domestic residences interspersed with shops, banks and offices – created a space where classes, races and nationalities could mix, colonial bourgeoisie with the popular classes, Boer with Briton, and whites with blacks.[39]

Table 3.1 Number and types of buildings, 1890

Neighbourhood	Buildings	Shops	Hotel-Bars	Population
Central Johannesburg	2,118	486	146	8,337
Braamfontein	182	15	2	124
Fordsburg	384	47	8	1,384
Jeppestown	168	11	4	708
Marshallstown	699	119	52	2,432
Ferreirastown	460	39	34	2,263

Source: Johannesburg Census 1896.

Marshallstown was part of the Turffontein private farm, south of Johannesburg proper. It was a semi-government township[40] belonging to the Marshalls Township Syndicate Ltd. It was obtained on leasehold by H. B. Marshall from F. J. Bezuidenhout, the greatest landowner in the area, in 1886. The township comprised 977 stands spread over 67 morgen.[41]

Ferreirastown, on the western side of the city, was bought by P. I. Ferreira and J. P. Meyer from F. J. Bezuidenhout in 1886 on a 99 years lease. In 1887 the lease for the entire area was acquired by the government at a rent of £167 a year. The area of the township was 19 morgen divided into 289 stands of 50 x 50 and 50 x 100 feet.[42] By the end of the first decade of the 1900s, Ferreirastown, which had started off as a residential area for the middle classes, was drastically changed. Local and foreign poor whites and not a few non-Europeans, all of whom eked out a living through mostly illicit occupations, moved into the small and overcrowded houses now characteristic of the area.[43]

In the west end of the city Fordsburg was the other typically working class area. This semi-government township was bought initially by Ford and Jeppe

Estate Company in 1888 and it passed on to the Witwatersrand Township Estate and Finance Corporation when the former sold their assets in 1896. By 1890 poor whites were predominant among a multiracial population of 1,384 inhabitants. Lack of restrictions on the use of plots for business purposes made it easier for poor shopkeepers to live in rooms behind their shops.[44]

Vrededorp's origins as a government concession for the settlement of poor *burghers* decided the social character of this neighbourhood situated north-west of Fordsburg. Vrededorp was an eminently Afrikaner neighbourhood that between 1895 and 1906 sheltered mostly transport riders and cab drivers.[45]

Brickfields-Burghersdorp, on the southern limits of Braamfontein, originated in 1887.[46] The geographical features of the area combined with its social composition to make Brickfields Johannesburg's first slum area.

Finally, on the eastern side of the city, there was Jeppestown, a more upmarket working class neighbourhood, which was acquired in 1886 on freehold from the owner, F. J. Bezuidenhout, by Ford and Jeppe Estate Company. In 1896 the Witwatersrand Township Estate and Finance Corporation bought Ford and Jeppe's assets. The township had an area of 168 morgen (including Belgravia) divided into 2,709 stands. By 1890 it had a comparatively small population, 708 inhabitants.

The returns on occupation in the 1896 Census, although imprecise, give an idea of the socio-economic characteristics of each ward. The different categories referred to the economic sector in which a person was employed and do not necessarily reflect the class composition of each ward. As expected, the three largest economic sectors in Johannesburg were industrial, commercial and domestic.

The mining industry was the single largest employer of white workers. At the same time the needs of the industry in terms of machinery, buildings, transport, and food and clothing for the workers created the economic space for other industries that employed some of Johannesburg's white population. The distribution of these sources of employment had an important part in the configuration of the working class neighbourhoods. Brewing, flour milling and baking, carriage and wagon building, harness making, and brick and tile making were the most important local industries which spread throughout the city's six wards and Brickfields. Each of these industries generated related economic activities. By 1896 the brewing industry had to satisfy the customers of 28 liquor stores and 128 bars, most of which were located in the central areas of the inner city, and which employed 438 barmen and 43 barmaids.

The flour milling business was shared by 21 millers who provided for 35 bakeries in which 341 bakers were employed. The addresses of the majority of these businesses indicate that the inner city streets, especially Commissioner and Market Streets, had the largest concentration of these shops. The transport and construction industries were the ones that employed the largest workforce in town. Until the establishment of the electric tram service in 1906, the need for transport in and around the city kept 96 wagon and carriage builders busy. They built vehicles for private citizens as well as for the 83 cab owners registered in the 1896 Census. These vehicles were driven by almost 2,000 drivers while animals and equipment were cared for by 16 farriers, 165 grooms and 43 harness makers. While the wagon and carriage builders and harness makers had their business located in downtown Johannesburg, farriers worked in Fordsburg and Vrededorp, close by to the stables.

Table 3.2 Population by wards 1896[a]

Wards	Europeans	Malays[b]	Indians	Natives
Ward I	5,409	---	206	603
Ward II	7,380	483	857	1,472
Ward III	7,836	188	192	2,582
Ward IV	7,235	9	575	2,096
Ward V	3,374	2	197	1,043
Ward VI	4,634	---	71	839
Brickfields	3,586	448	2,438	658

Source: Johannesburg Census 1896.

a) By 1896 Ward I comprised: Booysen's Township, Fordsburg, Coolie Location, Braamfontein, Auckland Park. Ward II was constituted by Height's Township, Ferreira Township, Johannesburg, part of Fordsburg, Marshallstown, Braamfontein. Ward III comprised part of Marshallstown and Johannesburg. Ward IV was made up of different portions of the same neighbourhood. Ward V included mining companies' outskirts, Prospect Township and part of Johannesburg. Ward VI comprised the mining companies' outskirts and Jeppestown.
b) Muslim coloured population.

The same is true of cab owners and cab drivers, who tended to live in the west of the city from where they had easier access to Market Square to buy fodder for their animals. In 1896 the construction industry created jobs for 1,648 brickmakers, 431 bricklayers, 185 builders and 89 building contractors, 261 plasterers and some of the 2,203 carpenters who lived in Johannesburg.[47]

Generally the state of the building trade is a good indication of urban prosperity and Johannesburg was no exception to this rule. If the recovery of the mining industry after the 1890-1 crisis brought about renewed confidence on the Rand market which benefited most trades, this was particularly obvious in the building industry. The years between 1892 and 1896 saw a boom in construction activity in Johannesburg, and 1895-6 marked the peak of a period of prosperity.

Table 3.3 Occupations by wards 1896

Occupation	Ward I	Ward II	Ward III	Ward IV	Ward V	Ward VI	Brickfields
Professional	169	403	542	197	453	136	241
Domestic	981	1,034	1,180	626	1,315	908	294
Commercial	502	1,141	1,863	656	1,489	488	326
Agricultural	31	262	91	12	34	21	13
Industrial	1,211	2,232	1,940	822	1,814	1,034	700
Dependants	1,858	571	170	780	526	585	498
Indefinite	1	182	617	2	186	2	3
Unspecified	656	457	433	279	418	460	1,511

Source: Johannesburg Census 1896.

During these years the Johannesburg Sanitary Board approved almost 2,000 plans.[48] Yet most of the construction activity of this period was restricted to the erection of commercial buildings and business premises. The five years of prosperity were followed by the 1897-8 depression that continued during the war years, accentuating the already existing scarcity of especially working class housing in Johannesburg. The chronic shortage of accommodation became particularly acute after the South African War. While in the context of the 1896-7 economic slump the working class complained about the high rents they had to pay,[49] after 1901 rents were not only higher but the actual lack of working class accommodation became a threat to the immigration policy proposed by the reconstruction administration.

The outbreak of the South African War, in 1899, paralyzed construction activity and caused deep disruption in the housing market. In October of that year Kruger proclaimed that, as long as martial law was in force, property owners had no right to demand rents from tenants. In the case of business property the lessees had to pay half. One of the preoccupations of the *Rust en Orde Kommissie* governing Johannesburg between 1899 and May 1900 was the provision of accommodation for the destitute, mostly wives of *burghers* in the field and refugees from the Orange Free State. They were temporarily put up in houses in Braamfontein, Burghersdorp, Doornfontein, Fordsburg and Jeppestown that had been abandoned by the population who had fled to the coast. But there were several instances where destitute refugees themselves simply took over abandoned property.[50] When the British took over the administration of Johannesburg on 31 May 1900, damage to property, unlawful occupation of houses, and a general lack of accommodation for the white population had made the housing problem a critical issue.[51]

During the military occupation the population who had taken refuge from the war in the Cape Colony and elsewhere started coming back. The largest part of the 42,000 white refugees who had fled Johannesburg returned between May 1901 and May 1902. This influx of population into the city made evident the extent of the squatter problem.[52] In August 1901, the treasurer of the Johannesburg municipality wrote to the Secretary to the Governor that, in spite of the establishment of a *burgher* camp, there were still a number of white people inhabiting houses illegally. They were too poor to pay sanitary fees and in many cases they were receiving relief from the administration. Proprietors were prevented by the authorities from evicting their squatter tenants and the town council had to bear the cost of this situation.[53]

To make matters worse, repairs to war-damaged houses were held in check by both the shortage of building material and a dramatic rise in their cost. Although the repatriation stores, organised after 1901, provided some of the necessary materials, the administration decided on a loan scheme. Distressed *burghers* could get an interest-free loan for two years in order to help rebuild their houses.[54] This was not nearly enough to solve the problem. A year later, in 1903, the Director of Public Works of the municipality had to write to the Colonial Secretary asking permission to pitch tents for returning refugees on vacant government land north of Braamfontein.[55] It was then proposed that increased facilities to import building materials, such as the lowering of import taxes, should be established.[56] It was with this idea in mind that the town council addressed a letter to the major township companies asking whether they were considering the erection of white workmen's cottages on their vacant land, and whether they had land available to sell or lease to the municipality which could form the basis of a possible municipal housing scheme.[57]

The lack of accommodation in Johannesburg also represented a problem for the organization of the new administration. According to Sir Alfred Milner, even administration officials had difficulties in finding suitable accommodation for their families.[58] The rents, between £15 and £30 per month, were abnormally high and a civil servant earning £600 a year could not afford to keep his family.[59]

In this context it was proposed that the government pay for the accommodation of its white employees, especially those in the railways, postal and telegraph Departments, as a way of alleviating the crisis.

It is not easy to establish the exact dimension of the housing crisis in Johannesburg after the war. The number of plans approved by local authorities between 1890 and 1902 corresponds with the figures cited in the *Report of the Johannesburg Housing Commission* in 1903. There were by then 17,900 buildings within the municipal area, excluding the so-called Kaffir and Coolie locations in the north-west of the city. The commission made an extremely crude calculation to establish the population density per building. It divided the number of existing buildings by the number of inhabitants in the city without distinguishing between population density in the inner city and its suburbs. With a white population of approximately 91,000 the density was five persons per building.[60] Even subtracting from the total number of buildings those that were exclusively commercial, the density does not change substantially (5.6). Considering that the "average" building had two bedrooms, a dining-room, kitchen and a bathroom, a family with three children would have been moderately comfortable. Compared with cities like London where working class families had to put children in the same bed,[61] overcrowding in Johannesburg had not yet reached dramatic proportions. Nevertheless, by 1903 the accommodation of the working classes had become enough of a problem for the reconstruction administration to appoint a commission of enquiry into it. While the figures do not really support the complaints and concerns about a serious shortage of white working class accommodation in Johannesburg, there are other ways of analyzing a problem the existence of which was confirmed not only by the testimony of most witnesses before the commission of enquiry but also by some of the letters that concerned citizens sent to the editor of *The Star* during 1902.[62]

The scarcity of housing has to be understood in the context of a colonial society where racial hierarchy constituted the basis for political and social domination. The housing problem in Johannesburg was economically, socially and politically constituted. At the economic level the shortage of housing was defined in terms of the affordability of the available houses for white breadwinners. From this point of view there were three main components to the housing problem. First, there were not enough houses available to suit the needs of working class families, i.e. houses with four rooms at a rental of £7 to £10 per month.[63] Secondly, when these houses did exist, rents were unaffordable. Thirdly, suitable accommodation in terms both of price and size usually existed only beyond walking distance from the inner city, making transportation an issue and an additional cost. Lack of appropriate transport and the need to eat in town instead of at home, when the cost of food was already high, made these houses unaffordable in terms of a working class family budget of £25 per month.[64] The control that estate companies had over the land market and workers' need to live close to their workplace accentuated the economic component of the crisis. High land prices made it difficult for a working class family to rent, and even more difficult to buy, property.

Socially, scarcity of housing had its roots in the contradictions between the aspiration to and the need for a certain type of accommodation on the one hand, and the fact that this type of accommodation was unaffordable in the desirable neighbourhoods like Marshallstown, Jeppestown or Johannesburg central on the other hand. Suitable houses were available for rent but only on the borders of the demarcated insanitary area. Although this was appropriate accommodation at the right price, the unhealthy conditions and the multiracial component of the area made it thoroughly undesirable for the British workers who had to live in "those localities affected by the poorer classes" and live in a manner that "is repugnant to those who have been used to associate with their equals".[65]

Finally, the housing problem was politically constituted in as much as the lack of appropriate working class accommodation posed a serious hurdle to the process of settlement of British immigrants:

> To have a contented British population you must have a British family. There are thousands of mining fellows here engaged to girls at Home who would gladly get their sweetheart out and settle down, who would be the wives and mothers and thus help in the most material way to achieve Lord Milner's object and make a British South Africa an accomplished fact. So long as the cost of living is so high we cannot get the right class of people to come out.[66]

At the same time, the existence of, mainly Afrikaner, destitute families who had enjoyed state support during the Republican government, put the new administrators in the position of having to make political decisions on state intervention in the market, which, they thought, might create a "privileged" class of Afrikaners. The appointment of a commission of enquiry to investigate this matter - and the ensuing discussions - showed how much the scarcity of working class accommodation in Johannesburg was seen as a political problem that affected the nature of state power and its relationship with potentially conflicting interests in the colony. With rents that varied between £10 and £23 monthly, white working class families were often compelled to take in lodgers in order to afford the rent.[67] Yet there were families facing a worse fate than having to put up with lodgers. It was reported to the commission that there were families living in bachelor flats such as those in Gordon Chambers, a block of flats located at the heart of the working class neighbourhood of Marshallstown, with no facilities for cooking.[68]

The main implications of this situation were spelled out by Rev. S. J. Hamilton, the Presbyterian minister of Fordsburg, who had wide experience in working class neighbourhoods:

> Men are finding that it is impossible for them to keep their families and the result is that they are sending them home, in large numbers. Therefore the old evil is being intensified, that is, men instead of making their home here are looking upon this place as one in which to make money as speedily as they can and then get out of it. Now this is encouraging the gambling spirit. Our object should be to encourage family life. As it is Johannesburg is threatened with remaining a mining camp instead of being a settled community.[69]

If the evidence heard by the Johannesburg Housing Commission did not completely belie John Buchan's comment that "the annoyances of the Johannesburg proletariat are, as compared with those in Europe, like crumpled rose-leaves to thorns",[70] it at least contradicted some of the contempt shown by the Private Secretary to the High Commissioner in South Africa in his writings about the Johannesburg workers' grievances a year earlier.

In less than two decades the urbanization of Johannesburg had produced most of the evils associated with the great European cities: the working class was separated from the well-to-do by the lack of transport,[71] the high cost of living and the scarcity of affordable accommodation, while slums such as those in the Brickfields-Burghersdorp area were identified in the mind of the ruling class with London's rookeries.[72] Milner's plans to make the Transvaal predominantly British through the immigration of the "right kind" of working men were being undermined by successive economic crises and, not less important, by the working conditions in the Witwatersrand gold mines. The death rate from silicosis amongst underground white workers, 16 per cent between October 1899 and January 1901, prevented many workers from returning to the mines after the war and acted as a further deterrent to workers' immigration to the Rand.[73] The white workers' difficulties in setting up home in Johannesburg due to the shortage of housing and high rents seemed to be accentuating what the mine owners had called in 1897 the "unstable character" of Johannesburg's white working class and to be conspiring in a serious way against the grand political design of the reconstruction administration: to transform the Transvaal into a strong British colony. In this context, the administration's responses to the problem become a crucial element in understanding the social and political dynamics of the period 1901-6.

Social Engineering and the "Geography of Class" in Johannesburg, 1901-1906

The importance attached to efficient municipal government by the reconstruction administrators can hardly be exaggerated. Municipal government in Johannesburg implied more than sound finances: it was necessary to address the problems of urban development in a fast growing city. The British administration of the Transvaal was especially sensitive to the extent to which social problems could undermine the political and ideological control exercised by the mining capitalists. The appointment of the Johannesburg Insanitary Commission of Enquiry, 1902-3, and of the Johannesburg Housing Commission, 1903, and the creation, in the same year, of the Transvaal Immigration Department in order to facilitate and encourage the immigration of single British women to the Transvaal, were of crucial significance. These measures were devised to stabilize skilled workers, facilitate social control and secure British hegemony.[74] Much has been written about the energies devoted to "social engineering" during this period.[75] And while it is undeniable that the Milner administration used the exceptional power derived from not being accountable to an electorate to shape the Transvaal's society and administrative structures, there has not been similar emphasis in the literature on the areas in which state intervention was not so keen or effective.

The ways in which the reconstruction administration dealt with the working class housing issue suggests that both political and ideological reasons prevented Milner's administration from intervening in a more decisive manner to solve the housing crisis.

During the reconstruction period state agency in addressing urban problems was felt in sanitary legislation, in street clearance projects, i.e. the eradication of slums, through the opening of arterial roads, and in the development of a system of public transport in the city.[76] Against the backdrop of widespread Social Darwinism both in Britain and Europe, the idea of sanitation had remarkable strength in inspiring town planning in most Western cities.[77] The ideas behind the public health policies and town planning implemented in South Africa were also broadly in line with these views. The belief in the environmental determination of crime - so pervasive in Britain between the mid-1800s and the early 1900s - also influenced the resolutions of the Johannesburg Town Council in these fields. Street clearance meant improving the sanitation of slum areas and breaking their isolation from the rest of the city as a way of fighting "moral decadence" as well as unhealthy conditions in the poverty-stricken areas of the city such as Brickfields.

The domain of public health was an area in which colonial state intervention between 1901 and 1906 was especially decisive. The appointment in 1901 of

Charles Porter as Johannesburg's Medical Officer of Health heralded a whole new approach to urban social problems. Porter had had wide experience as a Medical Officer of Health in Britain. He was a keen supporter of urban reform along the lines of the English Housing of the Working Classes Act of 1889, and was very much aware of the importance and potential influence of the Medical Officer of Health in identifying and solving urban problems.

A Public Health Committee, comprising a handful of sanitary inspectors, was created under Porter's chairmanship in 1901. The committee depended on the municipal council administratively and financially. It was responsible for most aspects of Johannesburg's citizens' health: the quality of their food and water, the disposal of waste, the sanitary conditions of dwellings and shops, and the control and prevention of infectious diseases. Public health by-laws were passed establishing the powers of sanitary inspectors, police and any authorized servant of the council to act in this regard.[78]

The annual reports of the Medical Officer of Health between 1902 and 1906 show the importance of medical involvement in the quantification, control and education of Johannesburg's population. Statistics on births and deaths, as well as causes of mortality by racial group in each ward, were carefully gathered. Disease, births and deaths were correlated with the general sanitary conditions in each district and explained in the context of its inhabitants' class background.[79] In this sense, ideas in Johannesburg were not that different from the British or European approach to the matter. Crime, as well as disease and immorality, were seen as largely determined by the social environment. And because insanitary and crowded conditions in the poor neighbourhoods of the city were seen as social problems it was seen as the state's responsibility to deal with them.[80]

In this ideological context the action of the Medical Officer of Health and the enforcement of sanitary legislation during the reconstruction period became powerful tools to intervene in urban problems.[81] The fight against overcrowded, unhealthy dwellings and neighbourhoods was part of the larger battle to make Johannesburg a settled community. The opening up of isolated areas to both public view and the authorities' control through new thoroughfares was paralleled by the opening up of the household's private space to the gaze of the sanitary inspector who had the power to enter any house to determine its suitability for human habitation. The activity of the Public Health Committee between 1901 and 1906 was all the more impressive when compared to the work done by the pre-war town council and even more so when compared to the lack of resolve of its predecessor, the sanitary board. Despite this resolve the Public Health Committee had to contend with both the bureaucracy's reluctance[82] to enforce measures such as vaccination after 1901, and the workers' resistance and indifference when faced with non-compulsory health measures.[83]

The second area of state intervention in urban problems was street clearance. Although slum conditions had been prevalent in areas like Brickfields from the very inception of the city, the continuous influx of population, the hardships of the war and cyclical economic crises had worsened the already unsatisfactory state of affairs. In this context the eradication of Johannesburg's slums was a social as well as a political necessity that the first post-war town council took very seriously.

The trend to use apparently non-racial regulations to deal with overcrowding or slum removals as part of an emerging racial framework appeared in Johannesburg immediately after the South African War and became more evident during the hearing of the Insanitary Area Commission of Enquiry between 1902 and 1903.[84] The town council's plea to demolish dilapidated and insanitary houses, and to separate so-called Natives, Coolies and Malays from the white population was a consequence of what M. Swanson in another context has called "sanitation syndrome".[85]

Brickfields-Burghersdorp, Johannesburg's largest slum, included the Malay and Coolie Locations and a section of the neighbourhood of Fordsburg. This area was separated from the inner city by the railway line south of Braamfontein. Soon after Kruger allowed the poor *burghers* to use the clay deposits to make bricks in 1887, Brickfields became a permanent feature of the social geography of Johannesburg. By 1896 the returns of the first census of the city showed a multiracial population of 7,000. From 1897 onwards this area was known as Burghersdorp and was populated by the poorest of the former *bywoners* arriving in the city. When, in 1901, an epidemic of bubonic plague broke out in the coastal cities, this area became the focus of municipal authorities' attempts to prevent returning refugees from bringing the disease to the city.

Despite these immediate concerns it took a year before the Johannesburg Insanitary Area Commission was appointed to deal with an improvement scheme suggested by the municipality. What emerged during the hearings was that both commissioners and witnesses related the area's lack of economic value to its geographical features and social conditions. For all of them the lack of proper streets, drainage and sewage systems, and the "ignorance and natural proclivities" of its 'poor whites'[86] and 'coloured'[87] inhabitants combined to cause the deplorable state of the district.[88] This was aggravated by the difficulties in policing an area of narrow streets and passages that constituted a refuge for the criminal classes.[89] All of this, plus its comparative isolation from the city, militated against the value of Brickfields as a business site.[90]

Against this background, the nominated town council proposed the expropriation of several stands to make the area sanitary and to open a thoroughfare linking the eastern and western parts of the city as a step towards the establishment of a tramway service. But expropriation had to be offset by a rehousing scheme. The town council proposed to build 180 three-roomed houses, 150 two-roomed and 150 one-roomed houses as an alternative for the potentially displaced 1,811 whites currently living in the slum. These houses, built on government ground, would be rented at £3, £2 5s, and £1 10s per month respectively, which made this accommodation, as the council acknowledged, unaffordable for those actually living in the slum area. This, however, was not seen to be important because, as the council put it, "the evicted occupants usually go to some place but little better, and the buildings provided for them are taken by a more prosperous class of people".[91]

Unsurprisingly, due to Curtis's participation in the project, the proposal was conceived along the lines of the English Housing of the Working Classes Act of 1889 and it posed similar difficulties. It dismissed the fact that most evicted families could not afford the new accommodation and it worked on the assumption that moving people out of dilapidated homes would not exacerbate the crisis. In Johannesburg, as years before in London, this approach showed how shortsighted administrators could be. The rehousing scheme was not designed to satisfy the needs of those who would be evicted and, had it been implemented, instead of solving the problem it would have accentuated it.

Despite the fact that the rehousing scheme was not implemented, the town council went ahead with the expropriation, incurring enormous costs related to the compensation of owners of stands in the area. Probably because this was the first attempt by the municipality to clear an insanitary area and because the powers of the local authority were not yet properly defined, the town council ended up giving owners of unhealthy and dilapidated property too high a price for their stands.[92] The cost of expropriation became a serious deterrent to more decisive state intervention in the housing problem and in the years to come what had happened with the insanitary area was used as an example of why the town council should not use expropriation as a strategy to deal with these problems.[93]

The fiasco of the Insanitary Areas Scheme explains only partially why during the reconstruction period no town council in Johannesburg embarked on a permanent housing scheme. Over and above implementation issues there were ideological and political concerns. Among them was the notion that a government housing scheme based on renting out property below its commercial value would create a "privileged class" in terms of its access to state aid. In 1903, during the hearings of the Johannesburg Housing Commission, the nominated council made it clear that such an idea "is not one that should be even contemplated, and the alternative is to let the houses at their fair market value".[94] It is interesting that, despite indications to the contrary, the town council suggested that fair prices ruled the housing market in Johannesburg.

The municipal authorities' optimism about the state of the housing market and the wisdom of leaving housing issues to "private enterprise" was seemingly confirmed by the approval in August 1903 of plans for the building of more than 300 houses by private builders and the decision of Rand Mines to build workers' cottages for 274 families on mine property.[95]

The town council's analysis of the housing shortage was consistent with this optimism. Contrary to cities like London, where the scarcity of housing was caused by the unavailability of land, the council argued, in Johannesburg the crisis was caused precisely by a temporary shortage of houses which in turn had pushed up rental prices. The solution to the problem was to attract capital to the building trades. This, together with the development of cheap public transport, would eventually open up new areas for building and ease the pressure on residential accommodation in the city centre. The reconstruction administrators' non-confrontational approach towards the mining industry and their estate companies made them lose sight of the fact that, in spite of the availability of land outside the "walking city", this land was withheld from the market. High rents for working class accommodation in Johannesburg were certainly due to shortage of housing, but this was caused not so much by the high cost of the materials as by the speculation and locking up of land by companies controlled, directly or indirectly, by the mining industry itself.

Given the close relationship between the mining industry and the reconstruction administration, it is hardly surprising that the Johannesburg nominated town council had done almost nothing to prevent speculation in land.[96] It is not surprising either that, faced with a residential accommodation crisis for white workers, the council had chosen to wait until market forces sorted prices out. Local or central state intervention in the land and property market was not seen as the solution to the problem either in Johannesburg or in Britain. Yet, when it came to the problem of working class housing, British municipal councils, probably due to working class representation in these bodies, were readier to take up municipal housing schemes, or to encourage the private sector to develop model tenements. In terms of insanitary and slum property the English Housing of the Working Classes and Town Planning Act of 1905 gave the municipalities powers either to force owners of such properties to make them sanitary, or to take it upon themselves to make such properties sanitary. Even had Johannesburg's nominated and elected town councils chosen to intervene more directly in these matters, there was actually no legislation to sanction it. Moreover, the socio-economic condition of the white working class in Johannesburg between 1901 and 1906 did not seem nearly as dramatic as in England. The nominated Johannesburg Town Council saw no apparent reason to develop a permanent housing scheme with rents below their market values. These were regarded as emergency measures and as such quite unnecessary according to the council's perception of the shortage of white working class housing in 1903.[97]

The council's *laissez faire* approach was aided indirectly by the lack of working class agitation on the housing problem: despite individual working class evidence given before the Johannesburg Housing Commission and the expression of workers' concern in letters to the press, there was no formal direct political pressure coming from the labour movement on this issue. The fact that no trade union representation was made to the Johannesburg Housing Commission during 1903 can be partly attributed to the fact that the importation of Chinese indentured labour captured all the attention of the labour movement that year. Nevertheless, the relative passivity of labour before seemingly important issues had other causes.

What has been called the apathy of the trade union movement during this period can be explained through the actual position of white workers in the labour process as well as through the internal difficulties and dissension within the trade unions.[98] In the racially organized colonial society the fact that white workers still had the monopoly of the skilled trades and job security conspired against rank and file active participation in their respective unions.[99] Trade union leaders were more concerned about non-white competition in skilled and semi-skilled occupations than were the rank and file. The lack of response from workers was also reflected in the political sphere. In 1904, when the Witwatersrand Trades and Labour Council, the workers' umbrella organization founded in 1900, decided to contest the municipal election, all its candidates but one were defeated.[100] The same happened in 1905 and 1906. If these defeats can be attributed to labour representatives' inability to offer a unified political front, they can also be explained through workers' reluctance to go to the polls.[101]

Whether working class political listlessness derived from workers' apparently safe position in skilled and semi-skilled jobs or from leaders' incapacity to engage with the problems that really mattered to the man on the street, what is certain is that the labour movement did not constitute a formidable political opposition to the reconstruction administration. This did not mean, as the appointment of the Johannesburg Housing Commission proves, however, that working class problems were easily dismissed or taken lightly by Milner and his team of administrators. The stabilization of British workers on the Rand was a fundamental part of the reconstruction administration's policies and therefore, as Curtis put it in 1901, "the British administration cannot afford to neglect any measure likely to contribute to this end".[102]

Conclusion

The reconstruction administration's overall goal of transforming the Transvaal into part of a strong British colony did not only depend on the success of Milner's immigration policy. It was also based on the creation of an efficient colonial state capable of mediating the relationships between the different social sectors and economic interests at play in the colony. The nature of the political power of the Milner administration underlined the central state's capacity to intervene in all aspects of the organization of the colony. The fact that between 1902 and 1905 there were more commissions of enquiry appointed than in any other period in South African history bears testimony to the interventionist nature of the reconstruction administration. Part of this intervention was indirectly designed to define the scope of the political, economic and social rights of the population whether they were mine owners, landowners or workers.

The analysis of the political economy of white working class housing provides an insight into the contradictions between the general political aims of the state, the different forms of its intervention in society, and the social and economic processes that took place in Johannesburg during the period 1890-1906.

The reconstruction administrators' approach towards white working class housing relied on their belief in the fairness of the market left to itself. Even if between 1902 and 1903, during the hearings of the Johannesburg Insanitary Commission, and the discussion of the Rating Bill, in 1903, the nominated town council had considered a more interventionist approach, both the rehousing scheme and the change of the rate system were eventually abandoned. Between 1901 and 1906 no directly articulated pressure was coming from the white working class to force the state to undertake a permanent housing scheme. The idea of building model dwellings involving private investors was dismissed by the town council as an unnecessary and unwanted feature of urban life in the colony. This view was partially based on the fact that the British workers who actually settled in Johannesburg expected to be better off there than at "home". For both the administrators and the workers themselves being better off meant living in houses not in flats, enjoying the privacy of family life without sharing common spaces with neighbours, and having enough room to engage the services of a 'kitchen boy' to help out with menial tasks.

The *Report of the Johannesburg Housing Commission* of 1903 showed that neither the local administration nor the colonial government were prepared to intervene in the housing problem beyond some relief measures. This was due, in part, to the reconstruction administration's non-confrontational approach to the mining houses and therefore to their land interests. But it was also related to broader political issues.

The Gold Law of 1898 had hastened the speculative nature of land ownership in Johannesburg and opened the way to the high concentration of urban land in the hands of a few estate companies linked to the mining houses, and the reconstruction administration did very little to change this situation. When, during the discussion of the project to extend Johannesburg's boundaries, the nominated town council challenged the Chamber of Mines' approach, it was the political issue, the incorporation of British mineworkers as voters, more than the actual land issue that was at stake.

Milner and his team of administrators took on an unusual amount of planning and political intervention to guarantee the political and ideological shaping of the British Empire in the South African colony. In this regard one of the greatest challenges they faced was the amalgamation of British workers and recently urbanized Boer population, whether petty bourgeoisie or unemployed, into a politically defined single identity expressed in terms of loyalty to the Empire. Two main strategies were designed to achieve this. On the one hand, there was the immigration policy that was to create a British demographic majority. Not less important was the role that the political system itself was called to play in nurturing a sense of loyalty to Britain. In this context Curtis's apparently inane idea that a municipal system was a school of self-government and a stage in the concession of further privileges to the inhabitants of the colony acquires its full political and ideological force.

When the nominated town council took over Johannesburg's administration in 1901 some of the most distinctive aspects of the "geography of class" of the city were already in place. The working class lived in the centre of the city and in the neighbourhoods east and west of it from where they had easy access to their workplaces. Lack of proper urban infrastructure and accelerated processes of urbanization combined with the cyclical movements of the economy to produce slum areas where very poor Afrikaners and a few British newcomers eked out a living.

Johannesburg's local government addressed the social problems generated by urban growth through the development of infrastructure; the creation of a system of rates and taxes; the attempt to unify land tenure in the city; and the implementation of legislation to promote public health. The liberal credo with its faith in the market forces was far stronger in the colony than in Britain and prevented a more decisive intervention in Johannesburg's social problems. Resistance to the creation of a class "privileged" by its access to public credit and, more explicitly, resistance to the favouring of the, largely Afrikaner, lower strata of the working class, was the justification for the absence of state agency in the housing problem. State intervention in social problems was not seen as furthering the homogenization of the working class. Citizenship, and by implication loyalty to the Empire, was the reconstruction administration's recipe for the homogenization of the colony. And this was not created through privileged access to state charity, but, as Curtis put it, through inclusion in the political system and the benefits of a sound administration. Consistent with this conception, social engineering during the reconstruction period operated almost exclusively at the ideological and political level. As a consequence, the resulting geography of class of Johannesburg was often more a product of lack of state intervention in the land and housing market than of an actively pursued social engineering design.

Eventually successive economic crises, unemployment, the emergence of the poor white problem in the city and greater militancy of the labour movement combined with changes in the form of the state to transform both local and central government's approach to urban problems and to generate a more active, if different, form of social engineering.

Notes

[1] The nominated town council was replaced after 1903 with an elected council that conceived its work pretty much on the same lines as its predecessor.
[2] Curtis, L., *With Milner in South Africa* (Oxford 1951), p. 217. Hereafter *With Milner*.
[3] *Third Report of the Financial Relations Commission*, 1906, pp. 13-14. Hereafter *Report of the Financial Relations*.
[4] *Report of the Financial Relations*, p. 14.
[5] *Report of the Financial Relations*, p. 15.
[6] The first law in which the state of the South African Republic asserted its right with respect to precious minerals was Law No. 1 of 1871. From 1871 until 1898 there were no less than 18 laws passed dealing with precious minerals. Law No. 15 of 1898 was commonly known as the Gold Law and it was the law in operation when the British administration took over the South African Republic in the aftermath of the South African War. In 1901 Sir Alfred Milner appointed a commission of enquiry into the working of the 1898 Gold Law which produced its report in 1902. See *Report of the Gold Law Commission, 1901-1902*, 1902. Hereafter *Report of the Gold Law*.
[7] *Report of the Gold Law*, 1902, p. xxx.
[8] "The owner of a farm on which minerals have been discovered is entitled to obtain from the Government a "mynpatch" equal to one tenth of the area proclaimed, and to hold this under the form of a mineral lease, usually called a "mynpatch brief". The Government is entitled as a consideration for this lease, to exact from him either the sum of 10/- per morgen per annum, or 24 per cent of the gross income made by him working the "mynpatch"." *Gold Law No. 15 1898*, Article 25.
[9] *Report of the Gold Law*, p. xxiv.
[10] Abe Bailey had been in Johannesburg from 1887. As a stockbroker he acquired sufficient shares in the mining industry to allow him by 1895 to sit on the boards of nine mining companies. He formed South African Gold Mines in 1897. One of his more

decisive backers was Julius Jeppe. At the time of the formation of Witwatersrand Township Estate and Financial Corporation Bailey acquired the assets and expertise of the Jeppe family in the real estate business. See Kubicek, R.V., *Economic Imperialism in Theory and Practice: The Case of South African Gold Mining Finance, 1886-1914* (Durham 1979), pp. 158-9. Hereafter *Economic Imperialism*.

[11] On Johannesburg Consolidated Investment Company see Kubicek, R.V., *Economic Imperialism*, pp. 120-4.

[12] See *Report of the Transvaal Leasehold Townships Commission, 1912* (U. G. 34-12), Appendix D. Hereafter *Leasehold Townships Commission*.

[13] "But proclamation was at the time (1890s) not a law but a custom and the practice of formal proclamation was gradually broken down in the neighbourhoods of towns like Johannesburg and Pretoria. The township owners as a rule confined themselves to selling leases of stands marked out on the diagram. The freehold of the township as a whole did not pass and remained undivided and registered as one portion of a farm and subject to one farm tax only." *Report of the Financial Relations*, para. 34.

[14] *Report of the Financial Relations*, paras. 35-36.

[15] Some of the features of social life in Johannesburg greatly benefited the interest of landlords and property owners in the city centre during the 1890s. As van Onselen has argued, by 1896 a significant portion of central Johannesburg was devoted exclusively to prostitution. Brothel keepers were prepared to pay high cash rentals for houses. One consequence of this development was that rents in central Johannesburg were so high that lower-middle and working class families were pushed away from the city centre. Van Onselen, C., 'Prostitutes and Proletarians, 1886-1914', volume 1, *New Babylon*, pp. 114-15.

[16] "And it may be taken for granted that dealing with such delicate and difficult questions as the valuing and rating of mining property, the town, if it possesses the power, will shift the leonine portion of taxation from its own shoulders onto those of the mines." Reply of the Transvaal Chamber of Mines to the project of extension of Johannesburg's boundaries. Cited in Curtis, L., *With Milner*, p. 277.

[17] Curtis, L., *With Milner*, p. 289.

[18] On the mines' final acquiescence in the project see Maud, J.P.R., *City Government: The Johannesburg Experiment* (Oxford 1938), p. 74. Hereafter *City Government*.

[19] "The policy pursued hitherto by the big land corporations of Johannesburg through being able to hold in freehold tracts of land free from taxation in any shape or form, has forced the inhabitants to purchase at exorbitant prices small pieces of ground in stands of 50 x 50 feet and of 50 x 100 feet for residential purposes with the exception of Parktown." Town Valuator Report. Cited in Curtis, L., *With Milner*, p. 298.

[20] For a more detailed account of the development of a system of public transport in Johannesburg see, van Onselen, C., 'Johannesburg's Jehus, 1890-1914' in *Studies in the Social and Economic History of the Witwatersrand, 1886-1914*, volume 1, *New Babylon* (Johannesburg 1983), pp. 163-203.

[21] The power exercised by the mining industry in the city affairs is best reflected in the Johannesburg Municipality Amendment Ordinance No. 41 of 1902 which established that any by-law affecting a mining company had to be first submitted to the Chamber of Mines for its consideration. See Maud, J.P.R., *City Government*, pp. 61-2.

[22] Curtis, L., *With Milner*, p. 294.

[23] Transvaal Archives Depot (TAD), Mayor of Johannesburg (MJB) 1/1/2, 1903. Rating Bill.

[24] Lever, M.R., 'Johannesburg's Adoption of Site Value Rating', Honours Dissertation, University of the Witwatersrand, 1993, p. 59.

25 Jeppe was also involved in the gold industry as chief backer of the mining venture of the Abe Bailey group. See Kubicek, R., *Economic Imperialism*, pp. 158-9.
26 *Report of the Vrededorp Stands Commission, 1905*, Report of H.O. Buckle and C. Murray, paras. 1-3. Hereafter *Vrededorp Stands Commission*.
27 *Vrededorp Stands Commission*, Evidence of A.M. Niven, member of the Johannesburg Town Council, para. 87.
28 (TAD), Governor of the Transvaal (GOV) 961/17/109/06. Vrededorp Stands Ordinance.
29 *Vrededorp Stands Commission*, Report of H.O. Buckle and C. Murray, para. 14.
30 *Vrededorp Stands Commission, 1905*, Evidence of Councillor Leonard, para. 17. This evidence is confirmed by some of the letters addressed during 1906 to Lord Selborne by the Vrededorp Standowners' Committee, and by individuals. (TAD) (GOV) 961/17/109/06.
31 No information about these persons has been found in the *Vrededorp Stands Commission*.
32 *Vrededorp Stands Commission*, Annexure 4, p. 29.
33 (TAD), Colonial Secretary (CS) 3/270-370, 1901. Memorandum from Lionel Curtis to the Colonial Secretary; Maud, J., *Johannesburg and the Art of Self-Government* (Johannesburg 1937), p. 10. Hereafter *Johannesburg and Self-Government*.
34 Maud, J., *Johannesburg and Self-Government*, pp. 15-16.
35 Bozzoli, B., *The Political Nature of a Ruling Class: Capital and Ideology in South Africa, 1890-1933* (London 1981), pp. 49-50. At the municipal level this implied close co-operation between the central and local authorities. According to Maud this co-operation was especially obvious in the relations between the first nominated town council and the central administration of the Transvaal colony between 1900 and 1903. Maud, J.P.R., *City Government*, p. 62.
36 (TAD) (CS) 12 3/270-370, 1901. Memorandum from Lionel Curtis to the Colonial Secretary.
37 Curtis was replaced in 1903 by Richard Feetham who arrived in Johannesburg in 1902. Curtis himself was moved to Pretoria as Assistant Colonial Secretary charged with reforming legislation regulating municipal government in the Transvaal.
38 Curtis, L., *With Milner*, p. 258.
39 Macmillan, A., *The Golden City* (London n.d.), p. 118; pp. 157-8.
40 Semi-government townships were those private leasehold townships laid out under the provisions of the Gold Law but for which the state received only a share of the stand licences.
41 *Leasehold Townships Commission*, pp. 78-80.
42 *Leasehold Townships Commission*, p. 70.
43 Scully, W., *The Ridge of the White Waters* (London 1912), pp. 207-9; 210-12; 213-14.
44 *Leasehold Townships Commission*, pp. 45-6.
45 *Report of the Vrededorp Stands Commission*, Report of H.O. Buckle and C. Murray, paras. 1-2.
46 For a detailed account of the development of the brickmaking industry in this area see van Onselen, C., 'The Main Reef Road into the Working Class: Proletarianisation, Unemployment and Class Consciousness amongst Johannesburg's Afrikaner Poor', *Studies in the Social and Economic History of the Witwatersrand, 1886-1914*, volume 2, *New Nineveh* (Johannesburg 1982), pp. 116-21.
47 The last two paragraphs are based on the *1896 Census* of Johannesburg and on the *Longland's Johannesburg and District Directory 1896*.
48 Van Onselen, C, *New Nineveh*, p. 117.
49 See *Industrial Commission of Enquiry 1897*, especially, R. Barrow's evidence, pp. 172-4.
50 Cammack, D., *The Rand at War, 1899-1902: The Witwatersrand & the Anglo Boer War* (London 1990), p. 76, pp. 169-71.

51 The Special Criminal Court established in Johannesburg immediately after the British occupation passed judgement on numerous cases of breaking into abandoned houses in the city.
52 The history of South Africa from 1948 onwards has loaded certain terms with such a specific meaning that their usage, apparently out of context, needs to be explained. Here 'squatter problem' is the term used in the sources to refer to white illegal occupiers of public ground and/or private houses in Johannesburg immediately after the South African War. As will be seen in the next chapter the term continued to be used at least until the 1910s.
53 (TAD) (CS) 31/4161. Letter from the Johannesburg Town Council Treasurer to the Secretary to the Transvaal Governor, 19 August 1901.
54 (TAD) (CS) 168/14366/02. Letter from the Refugee Department to the Colonial Secretary, 1902.
55 (TAD) (CS) 117/8608. Letter from the Director of Public Works to the Colonial Secretary, 6 August 1902.
56 (TAD) (MJB) 1/1/6. *Minutes of the Johannesburg Town Council*, 5 August 1902.
57 (TAD) (MJB) 4/2/35. Letter from the Johannesburg Town Clerk to Johannesburg Consolidated Investment Company and Witwatersrand Township Estate and Financial Corporation, 12 August 1902.
58 An investigation by the General Purpose Committee established that there were only 100 houses in Johannesburg in condition to be let. (TAD) (MJB) 4/1/6, 08/08/02; (MJB) 4/2/35, 08/08/02.
59 (TAD) (GOV) 119/446. Letter from Sir Alfred Milner to Joseph Chamberlain, 22 September 1902.
60 *Report of the Johannesburg Housing Commission, 1903*, p. 8. Hereafter *Johannesburg Housing*.
61 White, J., *Rothschild Buildings: Life in an East End Tenement Block 1887-1920* (London 1980), pp. 49-54.
62 See the letters published under the heading 'Regulation of Rents' in *The Star* editions of 9 April 1902; 11 April 1902; 15 April 1902; 17 April 1902, 18 April 1902, and 25 April 1902. See also the leading article 'The Housing Problem' in *The Star*, 18 April 1902.
63 "The asserted scarcity of housing accommodation was based upon facts especially affecting a certain kind of dwelling namely those containing two, three and four rooms, kitchen, pantry and bath. During the past two and a half month I had received applications for at least 110 unfurnished houses of which hardly 10 % were larger than those mentioned whilst the number of houses brought to me for letting purposes stood in no proportion whatsoever to those required." *Johannesburg Housing*, Evidence of P. Japhet, estate agent, p. 2. The evidence to this commission of enquiry was not published. The manuscript is housed in the State Archives, Pretoria. The state of the document prevents the automatic indication of the precise paragraph of a quote.
64 "I know that considerable number of people hold stands in Richmond and Melville with the purpose of building as soon as there is a prospect of locomotion but at present they could not get out and in. The class of people who are really interested in this matter want to go home for their midday meal and the result is they crowd in the Braamfontein district." *Johannesburg Housing*, Evidence of Rev. S.J. Hamilton, para. 557-9.
65 *Johannesburg Housing*, Evidence of P. Japhet, para. 1.
66 *Johannesburg Housing*, Evidence of Rev. S.J. Hamilton, Second Day of Sitting, 31 July 1903.
67 "Another instance is a three-roomed iron house, rooms very small, neither pantry or bathroom, rent for 8 pounds a month. The two bedrooms are let and the family sit, sleep and

live in the dining-room." *Johannesburg Housing*, Evidence of Rev. S.J. Hamilton, 31 July 1903.
68 *Johannesburg Housing*, 1903, Evidence of P. Japhet, para. 5.
69 *Johannesburg Housing*, 1903, Evidence of Rev. S.J. Hamilton, 31 July 1903.
70 Buchan, J., *The African Colony: Studies in the Reconstruction* (London 1902), p. 321.
71 For the same problems in the case of the London working class see Stedman-Jones, G., *Outcast London: A Study in the Relationship between Classes in Victorian England* (Oxford 1971), pp. 217-18. Hereafter *Outcast London*.
72 "I beg to inform you that I visited the location known as the Brickfields and Indian Location yesterday in company with the Health Officer. These places are not laid in any kind of order, and it is quite impossible to make any kind of arrangement for keeping a watch on the low class of people living in the place, or for an effective guard over the property of people living in the town. The place is full of narrow passages, in some places not two feet wide, running irregularly at all angles and communicating numerous sheds and outhouses, which themselves are thoroughfares for those who wish to use them as such. It would be impossible to maintain any watch on such places and a criminal once getting into the place would almost certainly escape and be practically free from successful pursuit." Letter from the Commissioner of Police of Johannesburg, E. Showers, to the Town Clerk, February 1902. *Johannesburg Insanitary Area Commission of Enquiry, 1902-1903*, p. 10.
73 Katz, E., *The White Death: Silicosis on the Witwatersrand Golf Mines, 1886-1910*, (Johannesburg 1995) pp. 93-121.
74 Van Onselen, C., 'The World the Mine Owners Made: Social Themes in the Economic Transformation of the Witwatersrand, 1886-1914', volume 1, *New Babylon*, p. 28. Hereafter 'The World the Mine Owners Made'.
75 Marks, S. and Trapido, S., 'Lord Milner and the South African State', *History Workshop Journal*, 8, 1978, pp. 50-80; S. Marks and S. Trapido (eds.), *The Politics of Race, Class and Nationalism in Twentieth Century South Africa* (London 1987), pp. 1-70; van Onselen, C., 'The World the Mine Owners Made', pp. 1-43.
76 The general implications of the creation of a system of public transport in the city have been examined in van Onselen, C., 'Johannesburg's Jehus, 1890-1914', volume 1, *New Babylon*, pp. 163-204.
77 Dubow, S., 'Race, Civilisation and Culture: The Elaboration of the Segregationist Discourse in the Inter-War Years', in S. Marks and S. Trapido (eds.), *The Politics of Race, Class and Nationalism*, pp. 71-94.
78 (TAD) (MJB) 1/1/3. *Minutes of the Johannesburg Town Council*, February 1902.
79 (TAD) (MJB) 5/1. *Report of the Medical Officer of Health for the Period from 31st July 1902 to 30th June 1903; Report of the Medical Officer of Health for the Period from 31st July 1904 to 30th June 1906.*
80 Stedman-Jones, G., *Outcast London*, pp. 191-3.
81 Powerful as it was medical intervention should not be overstated. S. Parnell has demonstrated that a fully-fledged public health policy with its characteristic segregationist overtones was only in place during the post-Union period. See Parnell, S., 'Origins of South African Public Health and Town Planning Legislation', *Journal of Southern African Studies*, 19, 3, 1993, pp. 471-88.
82 (TAD) (MJB) 5/1, *Report of the Medical Officer of Health, 1904-06.*
83 (TAD) (MJB) 1/4/1/, Public Health Committee, Circular on Vaccination, 1901.
84 S. Parnell situates the emergence of the racial framework at the time of the unification of South Africa in 1910. Parnell, S., 'Johannesburg Slums and Racial Segregation in South African Cities, 1910-1937', Ph.D. thesis, University of the Witwatersrand, 1993, pp. 24-5;

pp. 28-9.

[85] Swanson, M., 'The Sanitation Syndrome: Bubonic Plague and Urban Native Policy in the Cape Colony, 1900-1909', *Journal of African History*, XVIII, 3, 1977, pp. 387-410. See also Bickford-Smith, V., *Ethnic Pride and Racial Prejudice in Victorian Cape Town: Group Identity and Social Practice, 1875-1902* (Cambridge 1995); Bickford-Smith, V., 'South African Urban History, Racial Segregation and the Unique Case of Cape Town?', *Journal of Southern African Studies*, 21, 1, 1995, pp. 63-78; Deacon, H., 'Racial Segregation and Medical Discourse in Nineteenth Century Cape Town', *Journal of Southern African Studies*, 22, 2, 1996, pp. 287-308.

[86] 'Poor whites' refers to unskilled workers, largely of Afrikaner descent, who were especially exposed to prolonged periods of unemployment and/or could not find employment due to the racial division of the labour market that characterized all four British southern African colonies.

[87] Coloured people, population of mixed racial origin, i. e. white and black. They came largely from the Cape Colony and spoke Afrikaans.

[88] "Many if not most of its inhabitants are coloured persons or poor whites whose ignorance and natural proclivities would not tend to make their dwellings models of sanitation." *Johannesburg Insanitary Area*, 1903, para. 39.

[89] *Johannesburg Insanitary Area*, p. 8.

[90] *Johannesburg Insanitary Area*, pp. 11-12.

[91] (TAD) (MJB) 1/4/3. *Minutes of the Town Council*, 1903 Housing Scheme. The non-white population would be moved into locations.

[92] The municipality was forced to pay £1,145,046 for land that was only worth £393,000 in 1912. Maud, J.P.R., *City Government*, p. 134.

[93] See *Report of the Transvaal Leasehold Townships Commission, 1912* (U. G. 34-12), para. 86.

[94] (TAD) (MJB) 1/1/4. *Minutes of the Johannesburg Town Council*, August 1903.

[95] (TAD) (MJB) 1/1/4. *Minutes of the Johannesburg Town Council*, August 1903.

[96] The alliance between the mining industry and the reconstruction administration went through different stages. While Milner's support of the Chamber of Mines and the mining industry as such is quite clear, the Chamber itself was divided in its support of Milner's imperial project. The relations between the mining industry and the Transvaal British administration blossomed around the Chinese labour importation crisis in 1903. According to Denoon, 1904 and 1905 marked the highest stage of the cooperation between the Chamber of Mines and the Transvaal colonial administration which was expressed by the Transvaal Government sharing information with the chamber's executive and withholding it from the Imperial Government. Denoon, D., *A Grand Illusion: The Failure of Imperial Policy in the Transvaal Colony during the Period of Reconstruction, 1900-05* (London 1973), p. 184. See also, pp. 160; 182; 190.

[97] "No action should be taken, in our opinion, that may tend to discourage this process unless the strongest reasons could be found for it." (TAD) (MJB) 1/1/4. *Minutes of the Johannesburg Town Council*, August 1903.

[98] Katz, E., *A Trade Union Aristocracy: A History of White Workers in the Transvaal and the General Strike of 1913* (Johannesburg 1976), p 182. Hereafter *A Trade Union Aristocracy*.

[99] Craft unions had been founded in the Transvaal after the discovery of gold on the Witwatersrand in 1886. They were deeply influenced by the traditions brought by British and Australian artisans. Workers' general satisfaction with their working conditions and the perception of the Kruger government as open to addressing workers' grievances contributed to the lethargy of the trade union movement in the Transvaal before the South African War.

Katz, E., *A Trade Union Aristocracy*, p. 24.

[100] The elected candidate was Peter Whiteside, the organiser of the South African Engine Drivers' and Firemen's Association and President of the Witwatersrand Trades and Labour Council between 1902 and 1904.

[101] Katz, E. *A Trade Union Aristocracy*, p. 193. See also Ticktin, D., 'The Origins of the South African Labour Party', Ph.D. thesis, University of Cape Town, 1973, pp. 179-210.

[102] Curtis, L. *With Milner*, p. 258.

Chapter 4

White Working Class Housing and the Emergence of the Urban Problem in Johannesburg, 1907-1922

Introduction

Johannesburg municipal elections on 9 December 1903 were followed by three years of negotiations and political agitation around the granting of self-government to the Transvaal. The Liberal Party victory in the 1905 British elections accelerated the discussions and in 1906 the Transvaal was granted Responsible Government. The following year *Het Volk*, a broadly Afrikaner nationalist formation, created in 1904 by Louis Botha and Jan Smuts, won the first general election.

The change in the form of the state tilted the political and ideological balance in a direction that would have been quite unthinkable for the reconstruction administration. The growing preoccupation with social issues, which characterized politics in the Transvaal after 1907, became national with the unification of South Africa in 1910. This, however, was not the sole result of political change: serious unemployment and increased working class militancy, brought about by successive and ever deeper economic crises, constituted the backdrop against which the notion of 'social problem' emerged in colonial white politics.

The period immediately before the Transvaal 1907 election had been filled with anxiety and foreboding for the mine owners who were particularly concerned about the effect that the repatriation of Chinese indentured labourers, announced by *Het Volk*, would have on the industry.[1] At the same time a fall in the price of gold in 1906 combined with prevailing political uncertainty to create a full-scale economic depression that lasted until 1908.

Unemployment and indigency affected most areas of the Transvaal during these years but became especially obvious in Johannesburg where the local government not only had to deal with its own unemployed people but also with a growing influx of poor unskilled Afrikaners from the Transvaal countryside. Inevitably immigration accentuated the still unsolved structural problems of the city. Unemployment, the high cost of living and the continuous immigration of 'poor whites' to Johannesburg were, well into the 1910s, the constitutive parts of a social problem with serious political consequences, which were not ameliorated by successive profitability crises in the mining industry before and after World War I (1912-13; 1919-22).

Between 1907 and 1922 the political scene was dominated by three political parties: the South African Party, led by Botha and Smuts, the Labour Party, founded in 1910, and the National Party, founded by J. H. B. Hertzog in 1914, who were competing against each other to win the white working class vote. As for the working class itself, by 1914 Milner would have found it difficult to recognize in the mining workforce the "most British element of the population" since the incorporation into the mines of hundreds of Afrikaner workers since 1907 had somewhat diluted the original British character of the industry.

Johannesburg itself was also changed. Economic expansion and demographic growth became a mixed blessing when production booms gave way to economic slumps and their social consequences. Of course, unemployment and urban degradation were far from being social problems exclusive to Johannesburg. However, that before and after the First World War the governments of Great Britain, continental Europe and Latin America were also contending with the 'social question', should not detract from the fact that in the colonies unemployment, indigency, and urban degradation were seen through the lens of a racial hierarchy. It was this racial hierarchy that allowed both the political parties and the state to turn unemployment and urban degradation into a political issue affecting the governability of the colony.

This chapter analyzes Johannesburg's urban problem between 1907 and 1922 to show that economic and social developments during this period changed the ruling class's perception of the city and the approach of the government and political parties to the housing of the white working class.

The Land Issue in Johannesburg: Taxation, Slum Property and Shortage of White Working Class Accommodation, 1907-1922

During the period 1907-1922 four legal instruments dealt with the issue of land tenure in Johannesburg. Under the *Het Volk* government the Townships Amendment Act of 1908 provided a legal instrument to establish the municipalities' powers over townships and the definition of land tenure in the cities. After the unification of South Africa, three commissions of enquiry appointed by the central government dealt with these problems from different perspectives: the Transvaal Leasehold Commission (1912); the Small Holdings Commission (1913); and the Local Government Commission (1915).

The Townships Amendment Act of 1908 presented two main innovations in the way it dealt with township land. First, it gave the municipal councils control over townships. Secondly, it converted all leasehold titles in government townships into freehold and prohibited the sale of stands on leasehold after the act was passed. These changes meant not only that now municipalities had much greater power to deal with their land but also that land tenure was the same in all government townships.[2] The conversion of leasehold into freehold provided Johannesburg's local government with the opportunity to have the city re-surveyed. Three areas were targeted particularly this survey: Brickfields-Burghersdorp, the area known as Prospect Township on the farm Doornfontein south-east of Johannesburg, and Vrededorp.[3]

In that which was Brickfields after the nominated Johannesburg Town Council had expropriated most of the stands constituting the demarcated insanitary area in 1903, not much had been done in terms of the planned new township. In the context of the Townships Amendment Act of 1908, Newtown, as the area was re-designated, was to be developed in line with the original 1903 project. In addition to the usual licence money standholders had to now pay monthly instalments for their freehold titles.[4]

Two years after the application of the Township Act there was an unexpected depreciation in the price of leasehold stands which made necessary a revision of the law. In 1910 Governor-General Lord Selborne appointed the Transvaal Leasehold Commission with this purpose. The commission, under the chairmanship of M. R. Greenlees, a Johannesburg lawyer, was composed of H. Pim, an accountant by profession and a member of the council since 1903, H. Graumann, the Mayor of Johannesburg, and F. A. W. Lucas, the Labour Party member of the town council, as its secretary. The commissioners examined two related issues: the circumstances of the creation of private leasehold and semi-government townships, and the terms of the conversion from leasehold to freehold.[5]

According to the commissioners the unforeseen drop in the price of leasehold stands that followed the implementation of the Township Amendment Act was caused by the fact that township owners holding vacant stands that could not be sold on leasehold, and the freehold value of which would not increase, began to offer their stands at freehold prices below the market rates. The owners of stands already sold on leasehold, however, did not have the same problem. Leaseholders were asked to pay values that had been fixed at prices prior to the conversion to freehold. This difference generated deep dissatisfaction amongst those whom the law disfavoured and created a very unequal situation in the property market, though it was short-lived.[6]

The Leasehold Commission found that the system of private leasehold townships was a form of land speculation that at the same time inhibited the work of building societies as short leases encouraged the erection of flimsy structures instead of permanent buildings.[7] Moreover, the fact that the nominal owner was actually a tenant, vulnerable to forfeiture and confiscation if, for whatever reason, he or she was not able to fulfil the lease, was also seen as a deterrent to the erection of solid buildings.[8]

While the commission briefly considered expropriation as a way of dealing with leasehold tenure of urban land, the experience of the previous Johannesburg Town Council in 1903 with the demarcated insanitary area caused the councillors to look into other alternatives.[9] The solution proposed, and advocated by Lucas in particular, was to introduce taxation based on the value of the land.[10] In justifying the commissioners' view the *Report of the Transvaal Leasehold Townships Commission* argued that since it was urban development and human occupation which gave value to land, property site value was, according to the report, "the value resulting from the presence, activity and expenditure of the community".[11]

Coincidentally, as the commission came to a conclusion that implied the changing of Johannesburg's rating system the city council itself passed a resolution that favoured the principle of rating land values only. However, this resolution was re-enacted by the Transvaal Provincial Council as the Local Authorities Rating Ordinance No. 6 of 1912 which kept the rating system as it was, based on land together with improvements. This event, which partly curtailed Johannesburg City Council's independence, was a consequence of the political differences between the city council and the provincial council which derived from the political composition of each of these bodies.[12] Party politics, of course, not only decided the outcome of the Johannesburg Town Council resolutions but also dominated the town council itself. While before 1907 the town council's composition and action were based on the concept of the best man government, after that date, and especially after the 1911 Labour victory in municipal elections, the town council was dominated by party politics.[13]

While political parties and township companies were busy disagreeing on the taxation system the high demand for land and housing both in and around Johannesburg did not abate. It was in this context that the central government thought the establishment of smallholdings[14] in or near the mining districts would be a way of alleviating the pressure for land in the cities, particularly Johannesburg, and of providing a healthy occupation, especially for miners affected by silicosis. With this idea in mind a commission of enquiry into smallholdings in the Transvaal was appointed by Governor-General Gladstone on July 1912. The Small Holdings Commission, which counted F.W. Lucas among its members, heard evidence from 66 witnesses of whom 28 were workers.

The report of the commission emphasized the unsettled nature of the working population of the Rand. Despite the fact that the number of married miners with families in South Africa had increased from 20.13 per cent in 1902 to 42.32 percent in 1912, the existence of 1,963 (8.37 per cent) married workers with families overseas and 11,550 (49.31 per cent) single workers employed in the mines was seen as a sign of the workers' reluctance to make the Rand their permanent home.[15] Interestingly, this perception of the working class was reinforced by the workers themselves, especially married and settled workers, who were constantly moving from mine to mine along the reef in search of higher wages, improved conditions of employment or better housing.[16] The problem of accommodation on the mines brought the commissioners' attention to the broader, and seemingly more permanent, issue of the scarcity of housing on the Rand. The evidence pointed once again at the cost of accommodation representing more than a quarter of a workman's wage and at accommodation itself being both unsuitable and expensive.[17]

Under these circumstances the establishment of smallholdings seemed a plausible solution to working class accommodation. An investigation into the availability of land for this purpose brought the commissioners face to face with some of the complications arising from the proclamation of this land under the Gold Law of 1898. The commission concluded that even were the legal obstacles to utilising existing lands within a ten mile-radius to the south and north of the Main Reef to be removed there would still be economic reasons why landowners would not sell their properties. Land taxation was so negligible that it did not encourage the utilization of the land but rather its retention for speculative purposes.[18] Under these circumstances the commission suggested that the best way to make land available was to tax the capital value of the land. The South African Labour Party organized its 1911 municipal electoral campaign along this line, mirroring developments in labour parties in Britain, Australia and Canada.[19]

The opposition of the Township Owners' Association to the development of smallholdings, and to any change in the method of taxation, was voiced by Julius Jeppe, president of the association. Disagreement from the propertied class and the mining industry with the commission's recommendations made the provincial government appoint yet another commission of enquiry to deal with the problem of municipal taxation. The terms of reference of the Local Government Commission, appointed on 13 November 1912, were to enquire into the advisability of altering municipal taxation and the results of rating land values in the rest of the world. Moreover, the commission had to report on whether elected or nominated councils were a preferable system of local government. The commission was chaired by H. J. Hofmeyr, a member of the local government since 1894, and had six other members, Julius Jeppe,

T. Kleinberg, J. H. Findlay, R. Feetham, J. S. Preddy, and G. B. Steer, a Johannesburg municipal councillor and Labour Party supporter.

By the time that the Local Government Commission presented its report in 1915 the political climate in the Union had changed. Two major strikes, one by miners in 1913 and one by railway workers in 1914, which had occasioned widespread worker protest and the call to general strikes, were heavily repressed by government troops. Workers' dissatisfaction with the collapse of the strikes and with the South African Party's policies in general was expressed in the March 1914 elections when the Labour Party for the first time won a majority of seats in the Transvaal Provincial Council. The municipal elections showed similar results and the Johannesburg Town Council was dominated by Labour. This gave a clear opportunity for the Labour Party to change Johannesburg's rating system.

Industrial and political unrest did not dissipate the differences amongst the members of the Local Government Commission. On the contrary, the commission produced three reports. The majority report signed by Hofmeyr, Jeppe, Kleinberg and Findlay clearly rejected any change in the system of municipal taxation.[20] It argued that the fall in the real value of stands in Johannesburg after 1902 proved that the previous rating system had not furthered the landlords' interests. Moreover it was suggested that a municipal tax exclusively based on the value of the land would eventually cause a drop in those values, shaking confidence in the market. The majority report insisted that given the small number of ratepayers amongst the municipal registered voters (15 per cent in the case of Johannesburg) the government should be warned against the danger of:

> Making rate on land values the sole means of municipal taxation and thus putting a small minority of property owners at the mercy of a large majority of voters whose pockets would be unaffected by the rates which they might decide to impose.[21]

This comment probably reflects the unspoken fear of the development of a strong Labour Party capable of galvanizing white workers' political discontent. The Chamber of Mines had seen a similar connection between political citizenship and economic power in 1901 when the extension of Johannesburg's municipal boundaries was to include the mining companies, making them liable for municipal rates and taxes.

Contrary to other commissions of enquiry, the *Majority Report of the Local Government Commission* saw overcrowding not as an effect of the taxation system but as a consequence of people's inability to pay rents. The report maintained that given the high cost of building, letting houses was unprofitable, and that even using cheap land, the cost of labour was so great that a family inhabiting a couple of rooms in a slum property could not pay enough rent for the landlord to invest in providing better accommodation.[22]

While the majority report clearly represented the opinion of the Township Owners' Association, the two minority reports, albeit with certain differences, accepted that site valuation was a sound political measure not only to stop land speculation but also to combat overcrowding and insanitary conditions. The first minority report, signed by Feetham and Preddy, proposed to increase site value taxes without entirely excepting improvements as a way of avoiding too high an increase on land taxes, and of keeping adequate levels of revenue in most municipalities.

The Labour Party had the necessary votes both in the Johannesburg Town Council and in the Transvaal Provincial Legislature to change the municipal tax system. Nevertheless, the central government withheld assent. It took the Labour Party three attempts to get the 1916 Rating Bill passed, and the bill which was eventually accepted incorporated the suggestions of Feetham and Preddy's minority report. For a transitional period, 1917-1919, the system of taxation was still mixed. And it was only after 1919 that the Johannesburg Town Council imposed its rates on site values only.

The Labour Party saw rate reform as an essential component of a much broader social reform which also encompassed the battle against slum property. This latter part of the reform had to take place in the area of public health and town planning, and in this Labour was not alone.

The Urban Problem in Johannesburg: Public Health and Town Planning, 1907-1918

Between 1896 and 1911 the white population of the city grew from 39,454 to 121,857 and by 1914 Johannesburg's total population was around a quarter of a million. Population growth and immigration increased the demand for housing and exacerbated the social problems derived from accelerated capitalist development. In the 15 years that separated the granting of self-government to the Transvaal from the mining strike of 1922, the proponents of urban reform as well as the different governments were fundamentally concerned with slum property, insanitary conditions in white working class neighbourhoods, miscegenation and increasing criminality among white people. After the proclamation of the Union of South Africa in 1910 public health and town planning became the tools of a new wave of social engineering that was especially targeted at averting the mixing between black and white population in whichever form it took place.[23]

The economic depression that started in 1906 produced an unusually high number of unemployed people and had an obvious impact on white workers' capacity to pay their rents.[24] The *Report of the Transvaal Indigency Commission*, appointed in 1906, pointed out that since it was almost impossible to stop the immigration of poor whites into towns, preventing the development of "squalid, unhealthy and demoralising poor white settlements" was an essential element in fighting "the perpetuation of indigency and crime".[25]

The Indigency Commission heard evidence from people who had vast experience in working class neighbourhoods, both in Johannesburg and abroad. Such was the case of the Anglican Sister Evelyn[26] and D.B Gilchrist, the District Surgeon in Fordsburg. Both their testimonies pointed to high rents as one of the causes of indigency in Johannesburg. In Fordsburg, for example, a house with three bedrooms and kitchen and little or no yard cost £9 per month. Houses costing £14 and £15 in Fordsburg were prohibitively expensive for men earning the average wage of a skilled worker, £20. Faced with these prices poor white people showed a strong spirit of resourcefulness. While some families took in lodgers to help pay the rent,[27] others, more desperate, resorted to more radical solutions. In November 1907, 800 unemployed men and their families took over Milner Park in Braamfontein and established a squatter camp. It is not clear how the municipal authorities dealt with these people who were living in tents and had nowhere to go. Yet by the end of the month there were only 60 families left. A similar event, although of smaller proportion, occurred in Vrededorp. Episodes like these exacerbated the view that poor whites were not only a public health hazard but also a threat to public order.[28]

The perception of slums as both unhealthy and unruly was accentuated by the prevalent racist view of society. This seemed to be confirmed by urban development itself because in 1906, as in 1902, the more unhealthy and economically depressed areas of Johannesburg were multiracial in composition. A series of small buildings at the bottom of Fountain St and Pine Avenue in Fordsburg were often cited during the hearings of the Indigency Commission as an example of the unhealthy combination of races in the city: "In the back you have Hottentots and in the front the lowest class of whites who are living on liquor selling and prostitution."[29]

Between 1908 and 1919, when the Union government's first Public Health Act was passed, it became clear that the slum problem in Johannesburg had important implications at three different, although complementary, levels. First, the multiracial character of these areas raised the question of what to do with the non-European population, especially the "natives", who had settled in the city. Secondly, the presence of poor whites in these areas meant that any slum clearance would have to be followed by a process of resettlement that guaranteed that no new slums would develop. Lastly, the very existence of slums contradicted the modern notions of town planning and the settlement of a respectable working class.

The urban reform initiatives of the 1910s, particularly in terms of racial segregation, were conceived as a means of containing white indigency in the city and in this sense the 'poor white problem' is central to any explanation of the rise of segregation in South Africa.[30] However, the relation between the establishment of African locations around the city and the 'poor white problem' was not always clearly stated in government circles. Moreover, there was not an official policy indicating where and how the African population should be housed. This, in part, reflected the contradictory interests at play amongst land and property owners in and around Johannesburg. The mining companies that in terms of the Gold Law of 1898 controlled surface rights of the areas where mining operations took place and the different ratepayers' associations were all opposed to rehousing schemes. While the mining companies were jealous of their privileges in terms of municipal taxes, the ratepayers' associations were more often than not comprised of the owners of the properties that African workers were renting.[31]

Attempts by the Johannesburg Town Council in 1912 to have African people removed to a location in Klipspruit Farm, 20 west of the city, failed due to the cost of transporting them in and out of the city. Employers of black African labour were then issued with permits to establish compounds for the housing of their workforce on their premises. In debating the comparative merits of locations and barracks for the housing of "natives" in the city, the Estates and Parks Committee of the town council pointed out that:

> It cannot be forgotten that those open locations in close proximity to large white populations are very difficult to police and control. They are the haunts of loafers and criminals, both white and black, who are a great source of trouble to the Police Authorities.[32]

Only a year later, in 1913, this time in the context of the reports of the Commission of Enquiry into Assaults on Women and of the Select Committee on European Employment and Labour Conditions, the government focused again on the issue of African workers living in the city. The official preoccupation with the numbers of the African population in Johannesburg should not come as a surprise. As Table 4.1 indicates, between 1904 and 1911 the African population in the city had increased from 59,605 to 101,971, reflecting the accelerated process of African proletarianization.

During their investigations into alleged sexual assaults on white women by black men the members of the Commission of Enquiry into Assaults on Women examined the socio-economic characteristics of the city. The commission found a direct relation between the existence of multiracial slum areas within Johannesburg and growing criminality. The report indicated that the layout as well as the social composition of the slums were objectionable:

> Narrow passages, or so called yards, exist into which open the doors of single rooms which are often let at 20s a month or more; and in these dwell whites, Chinese, Indians, natives and others on terms of equality, whilst latrines provided are for the common use of all.[33]

Table 4.1 Population of Johannesburg, 1904-1921

Year	European	African	Coloured	Asiatic	Total
1904	83,363	59,605	7,326	5,348	155,642
1911	119,953	101,971	15,180	----	237,104
1921	150,286	115,120	11,351	6,214	282,971

Source: Maud, J. P. R., *City Government*, p. 384.

But what the commissioners found most disturbing was that social interaction between black and white people seemed to have led to consensual sexual intercourse among them. This was seen as an indication of the level of degeneration to which the poorer sector of the white working class had sunk. The enormous preoccupation that miscegenation was for the colonial order and the particularly deleterious effect that poor white behaviour had in this regard, was clearly spelled out in the report of the commission:

> It is asserted that whilst these whites are sinking in the scale the natives are rising and that the poor white children are becoming the dregs of the population.[34]

In order to prevent any further development of these evils, the commission suggested the relocation of the "native" population in racially segregated areas of the city.[35]

A year after the appointment of the Commission of Enquiry into Assaults on Women, another government-initiated investigation was launched. This time the topic was unemployment. The Select Committee on European Employment and Labour Conditions was appointed by the House of Assembly and in the course of its work it explored some of the same problems that the commission of enquiry had been dealing with. The committee concluded that the living conditions found in the cities - insalubrious neighbourhoods, racial mixing and general moral degradation - were responsible for much of the poor white problem. Members of charitable organizations, the police and various churches who gave evidence before this committee often referred to Ferreirastown, Fordsburg, Marshallstown and Vrededorp as poor white areas where all forms of vice and miscegenation took place.[36]

Miscegenation, its effects and possible solutions became a pervasive social issue during the 1910s. Reports from various government bodies whether at the local or at the national level echoed the conclusions of the Commission of Enquiry into Assaults on Women. 'Unattached natives', 'menace to the poor white population' 'illicit liquor traffic' became tropos in a discourse constantly preoccupied with the dangers that a subversion of the social order might cause for the government of the colony. Thus, talking about the need to relocate the 'native' population, a report by the Parks and Estate Committee of 1916 noted that:

> We feel that the Council should at once take in hand the housing of those natives who are at present living in insanitary back-yards - a menace to the poor white population and a danger to themselves. Should the Government, in face of the Report of the Black Peril Commission and the Reports of the Police Department, fail to assist the Council in this matter, we feel that they would be not serving the best interests of the community.[37]

The allocation of land to house black workers, which was a specific concern of the Parks and Estates Committee of the town council, also fell under the Medical Officer of Health. Health in the Union of South Africa, as in much of the Western world was a complex concept that opened the door for state intervention in the private ambit of the family and of the individual. Social control of the working class, and separation of the dangerous classes from the working class, were parallel movements that took the guise of sanitation and urban renewal in most Western cities on both shores of the Atlantic.

In South Africa the wide area of influence of the Medical Officer of Health made this office pivotal in addressing the urban problem. In this sense, the activities of the Medical Officer of Health are essential in understanding the importance that public health and town planning were acquiring during this period. The task had fallen on Charles Porter, who was appointed Medical Officer of Health of Johannesburg by Lord Milner in 1901. Porter was a tireless publicist of the British principles of town planning. As Medical Officer of Health of Johannesburg between 1901 and 1914, and as a member of the

Public Health Council of the Union after 1918, he lobbied for the implementation of local legislation along the lines of the Housing of the Working Classes Act and of the Town Planning Act passed in Britain in 1890 and 1909.

In the day-to-day handling of sanitary problems in Johannesburg Porter seemingly had two main objectives. On the one hand, to inculcate hygienic habits in the white working class. On the other hand his office had to deal with insanitary properties both to avoid infectious diseases and to get rid of dilapidated buildings and dwellings considered unfit for human habitation.

The fulfilment of the educational part of the work of the medical officer of health was based on the activity of health visitors who had as their responsibility systematic house-to-house inspections to detect and remedy sanitary defects. Since health visitors' inspections, whether to help in the face of disease or to instruct inexperienced mothers in the art of child rearing,[38] were not made compulsory by law these officials were expected to win the confidence of the families they visited, a task that was not always easy.[39] Control of the sanitary condition of Johannesburg's dwellings, the second most important objective of the Health Department, required the deployment of sanitary inspectors who visited the properties, reported on the conditions they observed, located the owner of a particular stand and took him or her to court if public health by-laws had been broken.

Lack of accommodation and high rents in Johannesburg created the space for boarding houses that, legal or illegal, were cheaper than renting a house. On 21 March 1908, the Medical Officer of Health reported to the police the existence of an illegal boarding house on 12 Lilian Road in Fordsburg that accommodated mainly Italian and Montenegrin immigrants. Sanitary inspectors found two more illegal boarding houses in Fordsburg. One, also on Lilian Road, had space for 20 boarders, and had nine full boarders, all foreigners, at the time of the inspection. Boarders were paying £6 a month. The second one was on High Road; it accommodated 15 boarders, seven women and eight men, the majority of whom had Italian names, who were also paying £6 a month for board and lodging.[40] Louise Morgan, owner of the property on stand 3093, De Korte Street in Braamfontein was subpoenaed to appear in court in August 1911 due to the state of the building and yard on her property. Mrs. Morgan rented out the rooms in her property and, according to the sanitary inspector, there was stercus and wastewater on the ground.[41]

In 1912, after the outbreak of smallpox earlier that year, slum property became the focus of public attention. In August the *Transvaal Leader* ran two articles on the matter. The first one praised the action of the Medical Officer of Health during the emergency and at the same time criticized the town council's inability to put into practice measures that could have prevented the epidemic.⁴²

Analyzing the smallpox cases, the journalist established that most cases started amongst the black and coloured population, which, the writer argued, indicated the need to regulate the conditions under which they were to be allowed into municipal areas. The other serious problem the municipality should deal with, the article continued, were the rookeries which "are at present an eyesore to the town and a breeding-place for all kinds of infectious diseases". The newspaper urged the municipal government to make the further existence of rookeries impossible through town planning and the passing of legislation that would give local governments the capacity to deal with land and property matters.⁴³ A second article, 'The Scandal of Slums', went further in relating slum property to disease, arguing that disease originated in the dirt of the slums and flourished through the ignorance of its inhabitants.⁴⁴

The article criticized the owners of slum property who, the author maintained, were responsible for endangering the health of the whole community:

> Asiatic and half caste slums have sprung up amidst the white population all over South Africa mainly because of the selfish greed of a few property owners who regard their pockets as more important than public safety.⁴⁵

In a memorandum sent by Porter to the Johannesburg Town Clerk in February 1912 he indicated that slum conditions were prevalent in City and Suburban, Ferreirastown, Fordsburg, Marshallstown and Old Doornfontein and proposed three measures to deal with slum property. First, he advocated granting powers to the local authorities to condemn dwelling-houses unfit for human habitation. Secondly, he proposed the establishment of locations for "natives", "coloureds" and "Asiatic"; and thirdly, he suggested that the municipalities should be given the power to compel "coloured" people and "Asiatic" to live in such locations.⁴⁶

The following year in a memorandum sent to the Johannesburg Public Prosecutor listing several landlords from Ferreirastown who had infringed health by-laws, the Public Health Department described the houses in the neighbourhood as constituting one vast slum.⁴⁷ The population of Ferreirastown in the early 1910s was mainly made up of the unemployed, poor working white people and "coloureds" whose lack of hygiene made the medical officer compare their houses with a *kraal*:

> Yards and closets which are cleaned up under the personal direction of the Sanitary Inspector in the forenoon, may be found strewn with refuse or filthied with excrement in the afternoon, and it is a matter of great difficulty to maintain even a semblance of decency in these places; for in

practice, the condition of a previously cleaned yard, after twenty-four hours habitation is not incomparable to that of a clean kraal into which a number of animals have been driven and kept for a similar period.[48]

Between 1910 and 1914, as the perception of Johannesburg's slums as places of multiracial mixing was gaining currency in the public discourse, racial segregation became an essential part of the sanitation movement at the same time that the multiracial character of the slums brought the issue of rehousing schemes for whites back into the political discussion. Porter's keen interest in these matters, his frequent correspondence with British town planners and his readings kept him updated on the developments in this field. In 1914 Porter attended the Town Planning Summer School in England from where he returned an even greater supporter of the garden cities movement, which proposed the establishment of working class houses outside towns as a way of eradicating slums. But the implementation of these ideas needed supporting legislation conferring upon the local authorities powers to deal with slums. As he started lobbying for this war broke out in Europe and Porter himself took leave from his position as Medical Officer of Health to assume war duties as the Union's Sanitation Officer. It was only after the war that issues of public health and housing were taken up again, this time at a national level.

Public Health and White Working Class Housing, 1918-1922

The more powerful action taken by the state after 1918 in dealing with urban problems has to be read against the industrial unrest that took place on the Witwatersrand before World War I and the inflationary tendencies that followed it. The industrial and political unrest of 1913 and 1914 went hand in hand with economic crisis. The 1913 miners' strike had been precipitated by the measures taken by the Chamber of Mines to offset a profitability crisis.[49] The 1914 strike of railwaymen was triggered by the government threat to lay off railway and harbour employees. Unemployment was unusually serious during these years. While skilled workers found it difficult to make ends meet given the high cost of foodstuff and rent, unskilled workers' inability to pay rents gave rise to an increase in slum properties.

Partially in response to the 1913 strike a commission of enquiry was appointed in September of that year to investigate the cost of living, wages and conditions of white labour throughout the Union. The *Report of the Economic Commission* was finalized the following year. The commission linked the high cost of living for the working classes with the prices of transport and recreation. The commission's analysis indicated that rent corresponded to about a half of a working class family's expenditure.[50] A comparison with the cost of housing in England showed that:

> The predominant cost of working-class housing in England is about 5s 6d per room per month including the kitchen which is there used as a living room. The cost in Johannesburg, including the cost of the same local services and including the kitchen, which is seldom so suitable for a living room as in England, is about 24s per month.[51]

Lack of working class accommodation in Johannesburg was blamed on the fact that house property was not a good investment due to the depreciation of dwellings through wear and tear and workers' inability to pay rents. But this was not only due to high rents. The commission found that the low wages paid to unskilled workers was a major cause of slum creation. The government had acknowledged this situation by including in the terms of reference of the commission an investigation into the feasibility of establishing a minimum wage. Examining this matter, the commission argued that:

> Put it in the coldest and most prosaic terms, it is purely a question of securing for white people wages enough to live upon in order that the efficiency of white labour may not be undermined, slums may not be created and a standard of existence beneath what is recognised commonly decent for the white population may not be fostered.[52]

Poor whites became an important variable to take into account when recommending the establishment of a minimum wage:

> At present a considerable number of men are earning at unskilled or partially skilled work a wage that would be below any minimum standard legally imposed and the effect of such imposition, under South African conditions, would be to throw this work into the hands of black or coloured workers.[53]

The outbreak of World War I temporarily displaced these preoccupations. The large numbers of white workers who left South Africa to join the South African troops on the front improved the bargaining powers of those workers who remained. Wages increased in most trades during the war years while better conditions of employment, which followed from increased war-time production, helped to keep down industrial unrest. Nevertheless, the cost of living and especially rents increased between 1914 and 1918. By the end of the war deteriorating urban conditions and a shortage of working class accommodation in most cities of the Union were once again the object of official investigation.

In 1918, as the men who had been part of the Defence Force were demobilized, unemployment was looming large in the official mind. Amidst this a public health conference was held in Bloemfontein between 16 and 18 September, only weeks before the outbreak of an influenza epidemic that left a death toll of 150,000 nationwide.[54] The main goal of the conference, which gathered representatives from all South African municipalities, medical officers of health and organizations directly or indirectly involved in public health matters, was to discuss the provision of a bill on public health. The issues examined during the conference were political and ideological as well as technical. The fact that a public health portfolio was going to be created opened the discussion about in which ministry it should be located and whether or not a member of the medical profession should be appointed to the post. Moreover, the relations between local and central authorities at both the political and the financial levels were once again thoroughly examined.

The opening address by Thomas Watt, chairman and Minister of the Interior, placed the conference firmly within the context of recent political events:

> The war had made people realise as never before the importance of national health - the value of a numerous, fit and healthy population, not only from the point of view of national defence in the present crisis in our history, but in the years of industrial and economic struggle which lie ahead. The time has come for a forward movement - a health offensive - in this country and action in the matter could not longer be delayed.[55]

The health offensive proposed by Watt had several prongs especially because social conditions played an important role in spreading the diseases the medical profession was intent on combating: tuberculosis and venereal diseases. In this sense, it was agreed that town planning was an essential component of any legislation on public health. Dr. Mitchell, the Union Medical Officer of Health, stated that:

> As regards town planning, many of the greatest difficulties with which Health Authorities had to contend arose from the fact that this aspect of health administration had, up to quite recently, been almost entirely neglected; towns had been allowed to grow up anyhow and the results had been disastrous from the health point of view - surely town planning in the Union was a public health matter. The root of the tuberculosis problem was housing conditions.[56]

The Public Health Act was finally passed in June 1919. Most of its chapters referred to infectious diseases, epidemics, venereal diseases and health control at the Union's ports and inland borders. Chapter VIII, Sanitation and Housing, which a few years later was called by Porter 'South Africa's town planning charter',[57] gave the Medical Officer of Health of every local authority the power to inspect and make recommendations with respect to overcrowded and insanitary buildings and dwellings. The eagerness with which Union municipal officials requested powers to control slums and to prevent the development of disease was especially evident amongst Johannesburg Town Council's officials. The interest in urban reform in the city was reinforced by a new electoral victory of the South African Labour Party in the 1919 municipal elections. The record number of seats obtained by the Labour Party in the national election of the same year put them in a powerful position to pass legislation to deal with the issue of the lack of white working class housing.

The Public Health Act was followed almost immediately by the 'Bill making provision for the improvement of unhealthy areas in urban localities and for matters incidental thereto'. This bill expanded section 132 of the act, granting local authorities power to expropriate of insanitary land and buildings. It also made local authorities responsible for housing those persons displaced by the application of the act.[58]

Despite the obvious connection between housing and public health, there was no public health legislation that could redress the actual shortage of housing *per se*. Aware of this, Thomas Watt, now Minister of Public Works, appointed a Housing Committee in August 1919. This committee was tasked with establishing whether it was advisable for the government to assist financially local authorities to provide housing accommodation to persons of limited resources and with what amendments should be made to the Unhealthy Areas Bill.

The committee presented its report in December 1919, having heard evidence in Cape Town, Kimberley, Port Elizabeth, East London, Pietermaritzburg, Durban, Bloemfontein, Pretoria and Johannesburg. The witnesses before the committee were mostly representatives of municipal councils, medical officers of health, town engineers and valuators, members of building societies and office bearers of professional associations representing builders and architects. No trade union representation was made to the committee.

Persons of limited resources were defined in the report as those individuals earning salaries or wages of up to £50 a month and not possessing other financial means. Nevertheless, it was the lack of housing amongst the poorest section of the white population that posed the biggest challenge to any attempt by the state to redress the shortage of working class accommodation.

The committee's investigation showed that the major urban areas were experiencing were a shortage of housing which affected clerks, artisans, unskilled workers and poor whites as well as the African, so-called coloured and Asiatic population. The shortage was put down to the inflationary tendencies that followed World War I and their effect on already existing conditions. According to the committee's report there were three immediate problems that exacerbated the housing crisis. First, the scarcity and high cost of imported timber. Secondly, the marked increase in the price of bricks and tiles after 1913; and thirdly, and most importantly, the shortage of skilled labour in the building trades.[59]

The committee found that the houses being erected in Johannesburg, mostly in the new northern and eastern suburbs,[60] were just sufficient to meet the normal increase of the population. The committee also observed that most of these houses were built to be occupied by the owners and would not help to remedy the housing problem. The situation was such that private enterprise alone could not help in overcoming the shortage of housing, particularly when the scarcity was principally of small working class homes. Thus to offset the current conditions of working class housing in Johannesburg it was necessary for the state to build 1,600 houses:

> In all the circumstances we consider private enterprise alone cannot be relied upon to meet the shortage of houses of moderate size. As regards houses for the poorest classes of white people, coloured, native and Asiatics, there can be no doubts that, as private enterprise has not in the past met the need, it would be futile to rely on its doing so in the future. In these circumstances means must be devised for making good the shortage of housing within a reasonably short space of time, and it is only the authorities, local or central, which can be expected to take action.[61]

The fact that the housing crisis affected all sections of the white working class and the non-European population opened the debate about who was to take responsibility for a housing scheme. According to the report it was a widespread feeling amongst local authorities that, while they were prepared to accept responsibility for the housing of the working white population, they were reluctant to tackle the problem of both poor white and non-European housing. In this regard the Housing Committee maintained that:

> So far as the local authorities are concerned, we think that they must be held responsible for their (poor whites) housing as for other services rendered in the town. It would be quite wrong to say that the local authorities are responsible for the well-to-do citizens but not for the poor citizen. We therefore consider that as between the local authorities and the state the local authorities must be responsible for the provision of adequate

housing for white and coloured persons, natives and Asiatics in the urban areas.[62]

This approach constituted a quantum leap from the position held during the reconstruction period, which had relied on market forces left to themselves to solve the 1903 housing crisis in Johannesburg. Yet the report stated that its recommendations were due to the abnormal situation experienced in the country. Under normal circumstances the Housing Committee would have objected to municipal housing on the same grounds as had the Johannesburg Town Council 16 years before: municipal housing could not successfully compete with private enterprise; municipal intervention in the housing market would be a deterrent to private enterprise; local authorities would always pay higher prices for land; and, last but not least, the political argument against subsidized housing on the grounds that it would create an unduly privileged sector in the population was voiced again.[63]

But in 1919 the situation was extremely serious because the war had accentuated a problem that had been worsening for years:

> But judged by their own standards of living the hardships which these classes (poorer whites) are enduring through shortage of houses and through the consequent overcrowding in dwelling houses, shanties and hovels, which would not, in other circumstances, be occupied at all, are in a great number of cases extreme.[64]

The shortfall in new housing stock and the inability to keep up with demographic growth and with the deterioration of old buildings was a problem common to all cities in the Union, but it was probably at its worst in Johannesburg. The report stated that a great number of houses in Johannesburg were occupied by two or even three families and that there were many families who had to occupy one room in the poorest type of dwelling.[65] Once again it was pointed out that the lack of accommodation for both whites and Africans encouraged racial mixing.[66]

Given that this situation was, to a greater or lesser extent, to be found in most South African cities and that:

> There is no question that the health of the people suffers, and suffers seriously, from such a state of affairs - physical and moral deterioration are the result, bringing with them disease and the evils of poverty, drink, immorality and crime. In protecting public health and in combating these evils the State is called upon for the expenditure of large sums of money annually for hospitals, asylums, gaols and the like, whilst at the same time through an abnormally high death rate - an appallingly high death rate

amongst coloured people in the towns - it is losing annually large numbers of citizens and prospective citizens and the loss of these is a loss of wealth to the community.[67]

The committee called upon the state to intervene where local authorities, due to either a lack of effective powers or for other reasons, had failed. But even though the principles of, and political reasons for, state intervention were clear, the implementation of a housing scheme posed difficulties of its own. In terms of the actual form that state intervention should take, the committee proposed the creation of a permanent housing commission under the Minister of Health which would be responsible for the allocation of funds to local authorities and the approval of different housing projects. The immediate objective of such a commission would be the construction of around 21,000 houses nationwide at a cost conservatively estimated at £7,000,000 minimum.[68] The houses were classified in three groups. Class A had three to five rooms suitable for clerks and artisans; class B had two to four rooms suitable for poorer white, so-called coloured and Asiatic people; and class C comprised dwellings for so-called natives and Asiatics.[69]

Four possible sources for financing the construction of houses were indicated by the committee. First, the few individuals who could afford to own their houses. Secondly, building societies which could advance a proportion of the sum required to buy the sites and build the houses. Thirdly, municipalities who either had the money or were in a position to raise a loan from the provincial or central government. Finally, the central government who would have to finance the largest proportion of the costs.

With regard to the government contribution to the housing scheme, the debate centred around whether government assistance should take the form of direct or indirect rent subsidies. Given the contemporary experience in Britain where, after the war, the government took it upon itself to subsidize the construction of houses for the working classes, the debate was certainly pertinent. The support for temporary subsidies was based on the abnormally high prices of building materials after the war and the dislocation that local industries experienced during the same period. On a more general level, it was suggested that housing schemes should not be considered to be a purely financial transaction and that the country should be prepared to make some sacrifices to benefit the white community as a whole.[70]

The committee argued that in South Africa the housing problem was twofold. On the one hand there was an acute shortage of housing as a consequence of the war. On the other hand there was a need for housing reform for the poorer classes. This latter need existed before the war and, according to the committee, any attempt to solve it in the context of the current shortage of material and labour would be unwise. It was stated, moreover, that the amelioration of the conditions of the poorer classes was a problem that subsidized rents could not possibly solve because it did not strike at the causes of their poverty.

According to the Housing Committee there was an ideological limit to what the state should do in regard to the poorer classes:

> Housing reform does not merely mean building better houses, it means also the building up of character. The essential thing in regard to housing the poorer classes, particularly at the present time, is to eliminate as far as possible overcrowding and the unhealthy and immoral conditions which exist. The very fact of doing this should provide opportunities and excite the imagination of the people to desire to earn increased wages to enable them to pay higher and economic rents in order to enjoy the amenities of more comfortable homes.[71]

The limit to what the state should and could do for the poorer classes became particularly obvious when it came to the provision of housing for poor whites. It was not difficult to agree that this section of the working class could not pay economic rents and that the state would have to subsidize rents if poor whites were to be rehoused.

> The poor whites as we have seen are living in the most degrading and undesirable conditions in many of the towns, and having regard to the preponderance of black population and the importance, as all believe, of maintaining the prestige of the white race, this class of people not only cannot be permitted to remain as they are, but should be compelled to re-instate themselves in what must be their proper standing in the social scale. So far from assisting in the achievement of this most desirable object, we are firmly convinced that state or municipal charity in the shape of uneconomic rents in towns would act as a perpetual drag in the other direction.[72]

In his evidence before the Housing Committee Charles Porter made three points clear. First, that the construction of working class dwellings would check miscegenation and the social problems that derived from the interaction between blacks and whites in the cities. Secondly, that the removal of the African population to appropriate locations was an essential part of town planning. Thirdly, that subsidized rents for whites earning less than £15 a month, that is to say poor whites, constituted charity and could not be afforded by the municipal governments or the state.[73]

On 19 August 1920, the Housing Act was passed. It made provision for the creation of a housing loan fund by provincial administrators from which money could be advanced to local authorities to build houses. Loans would be made available to societies or individuals after the approval of their building projects. The repayment of loans was organized in instalments spread over 40 years for societies and 20 years for individuals. Loans would be secured by a first mortgage on the land on which the dwelling was to be constructed. There was no indication in the act of any form of state subsidy for those individuals who could not afford houses on their own. In other words, the Housing Act created the instruments to develop low cost housing for the white working class but did not make provision for the housing of poor whites.

Conclusion

Between 1907 and 1922 Johannesburg's municipal authorities took a more active role in addressing urban problems in the city. This was due both to the social threat that poor whites were perceived to pose to the racially organized society as a whole and to the political parties' need to win the white working class vote. As during the reconstruction period, municipal action was focused on three main issues: land ownership and taxation; public health; and town planning. Nevertheless, the powerful position of the Labour Party in the City Council and the militant outlook of the working class guaranteed a more radical approach to these issues than that which had been taken between 1902 and 1906.

The attempts to change the system of rates and taxes and to unify land tenure in Johannesburg indicated a drive for reform not seen in the previous period. The fact that the Labour Party's 1916 Rating Bill faced so many objections before being enacted showed the lack of sympathy the Union Government had for the Labour Party's increasingly powerful position in the local and provincial government. But it also speaks of the resilience of mining companies' and township corporations' interests.

In the terrain of public health and town planning, local authorities were even more successful. Although urban reform can by no means be attributed to the action of one individual, it is true that Charles Porter's actions as Medical Officer of Health of Johannesburg left an impression on local and national legislation. Leaving aside the smaller aspects of the reform, important as they were, the greatest achievements in urban reform, from the point of view of town planning, were the Public Health Act and the Unhealthy Areas Act. Both pieces of legislation established the socio-political importance of public health and town planning at the same time as conferring on local authorities the much needed powers to deal with slum properties, amongst other problems.

Public health legislation and town planning regulations were early mechanisms of racial segregation with two main functions: on the one hand, to alleviate the poor white problem and to foster a respectable white working class and, on the other hand, to secure the racial division of urban spaces at a time when regulations on African urban settlement were still incomplete and ineffective.[74] However, the state's reluctance to subsidize poor white housing as was expressed during the debates that preceded the passing of the Housing Act asks for a more nuanced interpretation of the nature and scope of local and central state intervention in the poor white problem.

The fact that the Housing Committee openly objected to subsidizing low income houses for poor whites indicates that the political preoccupation with this section of the population had not yet reached such a climax as to prompt direct state intervention. Moreover, the top income of those persons considered as of limited means by the Housing Committee, £50 per month, was well above the monthly earnings of even skilled workers.

Taking into account the different stages of the debate about state intervention in regard to poor whites' housing it seems appropriate to make a distinction between the objects of two different aspects of public health and town planning legislation between 1907 and 1922. While the eradication of slums and the drive to make working class neighbourhoods sanitary can be seen as a social strategy aimed at stopping miscegenation and controlling poor whites, the housing policy was clearly directed at the upper end of the white working class, and at the establishment of dwellings for the African population. These differences must be explained in terms of the ruling class's changing conceptualization of the poor white problem between 1907 and 1922, an issue which will be examined in Chapter 6.

Notes

[1] On the relations between *Het Volk* and the mining industry see Jeeves, A., 'Het Volk and the Gold Mines: The Debate on Labour Policy, 1905-1910', Seminar Paper, African Studies Institute, University of the Witwatersrand, 1980.

[2] The owner of a township had to satisfy the Townships Board, the official body that granted permission to lay out a township, that he was equipping the township with properly laid out streets, a water supply and was reserving stands for public purposes. Transvaal Archives Depot (TAD), Governor of the Transvaal (GOV) 1157/PS53/36/08, Township Amendment Act 1908.

[3] (TAD) (GOV) 1157/PS53/36/08, *A Bill to Amend the Townships Act 1907*, Part II. art. 34.

[4] (TAD) (GOV) 1157/PS53/36/08, *A Bill to Amend the Townships Act 1907*, Part II. arts. 31-34.

[5] *Report of the Transvaal Leasehold Townships Commission, 1912* (U.G. 34-12), para. 1. Hereafter *Leasehold Commission*.

[6] "Nothing but dissatisfaction can be expected from a leaseholder who having paid a few years ago £1,000 for a plot of ground subject to an annual rental of £12 - for which the

conversion price asked is £180 - finds his landlord selling adjoining equally valuable and similar plots at £580 in freehold", *Leasehold Commission*, para. 47.

[7] *Leasehold Commission*, paras. 20-28.

[8] *Leasehold Commission*, para. 52.

[9] Expropriation would not help in abolishing the system of private leasehold. It was not a financially sound operation because, particularly in the case of expropriation by public bodies, they had to pay more than the full value of the property taken and finally, ascertaining fair expropriation values was a problem of great complexity. *Leasehold Commission*, paras. 83-86.

[10] For an account of Lucas's campaign for the rate of site values see Lever, M.R., 'Johannesburg's Adoption of Site Value Rating', Honours Dissertation, University of the Witwatersrand, 1993, pp. 74-81.

[11] *Leasehold Commission*, para. 71.

[12] On the conflicts between the Johannesburg Town Council and the Transvaal Provincial Council since the unification of South Africa see Maud, J.P.R., *City Government: The Johannesburg Experiment* (Oxford 1938), pp. 89-93. Hereafter *City Government*.

[13] Maud, J.P.R., *City Government*, p. 74.

[14] According to the commission of enquiry a smallholding is a piece of land used for agricultural purposes in the most general sense. A smallholding has a minimum extension of one acre and a maximum extension of 400 acres. *Report of the Small Holdings Commission* (U.G. 51-13) paras. 8-10. Hereafter *Small Holdings Commission*.

[15] *Small Holdings Commission*, para. 93. The figures provided by the commission did not distinguish nationalities amongst single workers, and it was simply assumed that most of them were foreign, which was probably an exaggeration given the rapid incorporation of Afrikaner workers into the industry after 1907.

[16] *Small Holdings Commission*, para. 29.

[17] *Small Holdings Commission*, paras. 34-35.

[18] *Small Holdings Commission*, para. 96.

[19] Lever, M.R., 'Johannesburg's Adoption of Site Value Rating', Honours Dissertation, University of the Witwatersrand, 1993, pp. 1-25.

[20] *Report of the Local Government Commission, 1915* (T.P. 3-15), para. 38. Hereafter *Local Government Commission*.

[21] *Local Government Commission*, para. 72.

[22] *Local Government Commission*, para. 96.

[23] It is worth stressing, once again, that the developments that were taking place in Johannesburg and in most South African cities were in line with tendencies and preoccupations elsewhere in capitalist societies. Not only was the site values rate being discussed in Britain and its dominions, but town planning and public health also constituted a fundamental part of the social and political reforms that were taking place on both sides of the Atlantic. See Ward, D., *Poverty, Ethnicity and the American City, 1840-1925* (Cambridge 1985), and King, A., *Colonial Urban Development: Culture, Social Power and Environment* (London 1976).

[24] In 1907 2,422 unemployed white workers, mostly unskilled, were registered with the Office of the Inspector of White Labour. The office had been created by the *Het Volk* government in the aftermath of the 1907 miners' strike. (TAD) Secretary of Mines (MM) 172/1893/07.

[25] *Report of the Transvaal Indigency Commission, 1906-1908* (T.G. 13-08), para. 119. Hereafter *Report Indigency Commission*.

[26] *Evidence of the Transvaal Indigency Commission, 1906-1908* (T.G. 11-08), paras. 1714-1723 and 1725-1727. Hereafter *Evidence Indigency Commission*.

27 *Evidence Indigency Commission*, paras. 5700-5704.
28 (TAD) Mayor of Johannesburg (MJB) 1/1/12/ 1907. *Minutes of the Johannesburg Town Council*, 21 November 1907.
29 *Evidence Indigency Commission*, para. 5702.
30 Parnell, S., 'Johannesburg Slums and Racial Segregation in South African Cities, 1910-1937', Ph.D. thesis, University of the Witwatersrand, 1993, pp. 18-19.
31 See (TAD) (MJB) 1/1/21, *Minutes of the Johannesburg Town Council*, 14 May 1912.
32 (TAD) (MJB) 1/1/21. *Minutes of the Johannesburg Town Council*, 14 May 1912.
33 *Report of the Commission of Enquiry into Assaults on Women, 1913* (U.G. 39-1913), para. 98. The evidence to this commission of enquiry was not published. It is housed in the South African Archives Bureau (SAB) K.373. Hereafter the report of the commission will be referred to as *Report Assaults on Women* and the evidence will be referred to as Assaults on Women.
34 *Report Assaults on Women*, para. 100.
35 *Report Assaults on Women*, para. 152.
36 *Select Committee on European Employment and Labour Conditions*. (S.C. 9-13), Evidence of Colonel T. G. Truter, Commissioner of the South African Police, para. 1232.
37 (TAD) (MJB) 1/1/30, *Minutes of the Johannesburg Town Council*, 18 July 1916.
38 (TAD) (SGJ) 41/3233/1911. Letter from Mrs. Sisterson to Medical Officer of Health, 14 November 1911.
39 (TAD) (SGJ) 41/3233/1909, Document from the Public Health Office, Manchester, establishing the duties of health visitors; and 41/3233/1911, Letter from Charles Porter to the Town Clerk, Johannesburg, 10 March 1911. Also (TAD) (MJB) 1/1/20/1911. *Minutes of the Johannesburg Town Council*, 5 July 1911.
40 (TAD) (SGJ) 12/430/1/1908. List of unlicensed boarding houses in Fordsburg.
41 (TAD) (SGJ) 66/3698/1911. Court of the Resident Magistrate District of Johannesburg, 23 August 1911.
42 "It will be remembered that just before the recent outbreak occurred the Medical Officer of Health submitted to the Council a list of houses which he declared unfit for human habitation. If energetic measures had been taken to deal with the MOH's recommendation, the disease would have been located much earlier and more easily than it actually was and the danger of its spreading would have been greatly lessened." *Transvaal Leader*, 16 August 1912.
43 The author did not specify what area of the city he was referring to as rookeries, but it is probable he had in mind parts of City and Suburban Township, Ferreirastown, Fordsburg and Marshallstown.
44 *Transvaal Leader*, 23 August 1912.
45 *Transvaal Leader*, 23 August 1912.
46 (TAD) (SGJ) 187/4086/1, 1912, Memorandum by M.O.H. Johannesburg in reference to slum property within the municipal area, pp. 1-4.
47 (TAD) (SGJ) 5/5698, 1913, Memorandum from M.O.H. to Public Prosecutor, pp. 1-2.
48 (TAD) (SGJ) 5/5698, 1913, Memorandum from M.O.H. to Public Prosecutor, p. 2.
49 On the 1913 strike see Simons, H. J. and Simons, R. E., *Class and Colour in South Africa, 1850-1950* (Hardmondsworth 1969), pp. 156-60; Katz, E. *A Trade Union Aristocracy: A History of White Workers in the Transvaal and the General Strike of 1913* (Johannesburg 1976), pp. 321-60; Davies, R., *Capital, State and the White Working Class in South Africa, 1900-1960: An Historical Materialist Analysis of Class Formation and Class Relations* (Brighton 1979), pp. 120-5.
50 *Economic Commission, 1914* (U.G. 12-1914), para. 20. Hereafter *Economic Commission*.
51 *Economic Commission*, para. 17.

[52] *Economic Commission*, para. 70.
[53] *Economic Commission*, para. 72.
[54] On the influence of the 1918 epidemic on public health measures see Phillips, H., 'The Local State and Public Health Reform in South Africa: Bloemfontein and the Consequences of the Spanish 'Flu Epidemic of 1918', *Journal of Southern African Studies*, 13, 2, 1987, pp. 210-23.
[55] (TAD) (TPS) 53/TA 9907, Minutes of the Bloemfontein Public Health Conference, 16-18 September 1918, p. 5.
[56] (TAD) (TPS) 53/TA 9907, Minutes of the Bloemfontein Public Health Conference, p. 11.
[57] (TAD) (SGJ) 187/4086/2, Town Planning Past and Present by C. Porter.
[58] *Bill to Make Provision for the Improvement of Unhealthy Areas in Urban Localities and for Matters Incidental thereto*, 1919, arts. 13-16.
[59] *Report of the Housing Committee* (U. G. 4-1920), paras. 122-130. Hereafter *Housing Committee*.
[60] Although the report did not mention which suburbs it was referring to, they were probably Observatory, Bezuidenhout Valley, Kensington, Malvern and Orange Grove in the east and Parkhurst, Dunkeld, and Melrose in the north.
[61] *Housing Committee*, para. 109.
[62] *Housing Committee*, paras. 112-113.
[63] "The whole of any class requiring housing must be dealt with; otherwise either the remainder of the class suffers an injustice, or the portion dealt with gets an undue advantage. This is perfectly true. It is also true that to supply houses to artisans etc. and to make up the deficiency out of the rates means ultimately that the ratepayers are taxed for the benefit of employers. The possible effect upon municipal politics must not be overlooked, for the tenants of municipal houses, when such form a considerable group, with an effective voice in municipal elections, might bargain their votes for reduction of rent, with very undesirable consequences." *Housing Committee*, para. 114.
[64] *Housing Committee*, para. 115.
[65] *Housing Committee*, para. 64.
[66] *Housing Committee*, para. 71.
[67] *Housing Committee*, para. 117.
[68] *Housing Committee*, para. 143.
[69] *Housing Committee*, para. 105.
[70] *Housing Committee*, paras. 181-184.
[71] *Housing Committee*, para. 192.
[72] *Housing Committee*, para. 202.
[73] (TAD) (SGJ) 110/9608. C. Porter's evidence to the Housing Committee.
[74] Parnell, S., 'Creating Racial Privilege: The Origins of South African Public Health and Town Planning Legislation', *Journal of Southern African Studies*, 19, 3, 1993, pp. 471-88. See also Parnell, S. and Mabin, A., 'Rethinking Urban South Africa', *Journal of Southern African Studies*, 21, 1, 1995, pp. 39-61.

Chapter 5

White Workers' Daily Life in Johannesburg, 1890-1922

Introduction

Johannesburg's origins as a mining town not only conditioned the economic development of the city and its inhabitants but it also shaped the city's daily life in many ways. While the booms and slumps of the mining industry decided the fortunes of both mine magnates and mining employees, some of the tasks performed on the mines unavoidably filled the city with noise and dust. And behind the noise and the dust, and underneath the arrogance of cosmopolitan complacency, which some found characteristic of Johannesburg, there were the lives of its people. From the point of view of a social history of the white working class what really matters is the close-up view that can tell people apart in a crowd. Rescuing the experience of individual labouring men from the "enormous condescension of posterity",[1] however, is not sufficient to understand the lives of the men and women who made Johannesburg their home between 1890 and 1922. It is in the intersection between the experience of the individual and that of the collective that identities are formed and communities take shape. This chapter explores the development of a sense of community amongst white workers in Johannesburg between 1890 and 1922. This sense of community often ran across the ethnic boundaries between English-speakers and Afrikaans-speakers, involved men as well as women and children, and grew in the often multiracial environment of the white working class neighbourhoods.

Community as a sociological or anthropological concept, and even more so as a historical process, raises a series of theoretical and methodological issues. From a theoretical perspective two main questions emerge. On the one hand, if it is accepted that community is not a precondition to the existence of a social group but a process, the immediate question is about the elements involved in such a process and their interactions. On the other hand, if community is a concept that helps to bridge the distance between the theory of a class and its reality, what is the role of material conditions and culture in moulding a community? At the methodological level where should historians search for the constitutive elements of identity, and, how should they piece them together so that the emerging narrative is not a complete imposition of the historian's mind onto forever changing shadows?

The argument of this book is built on the assumption that experience, that is to say, the empirical relations - whether material or emotional - between the individual and the social world, is a substantive component of an individual's understanding of himself or herself, and that similar experiences create the basis for the formation of collective identities which operate at different levels of society. These identities, which will be expressed and talked of discursively, might or might not be galvanized into political or social action. However, political action is not definitive or necessary in the constitution of identities. This assumption owes a great deal to Thompson's analysis of the English working class. For him class was constituted through common experience which in turn was defined by the relations of production in which men were born, and which expressed itself in cultural terms as class consciousness.[2] Nevertheless, the stress here is not on class experience as derived largely from male workers' position in the relations of production. On the contrary, the focus of this book and especially of this chapter is on those aspects of class experience that are not confined to the workplace. Family, domestic life and its physical and social extension, the neighbourhood, seem to have been essential elements in forging white working class identity in Johannesburg.

Material Conditions of Existence in Johannesburg's White Working Class Neighbourhoods, 1890-1922

No traveller who arrived in Johannesburg between 1890 and 1900 could have found the city either beautiful or comfortable. Gas and electricity only became available in 1891 through the Johannesburg Lighting Company. Until well into the first decade of the twentieth century drinking water in many areas was still supplied through wells and the disposal of night soil was as primitive as could be. Most newcomers remarked on both the lack of beauty and newness of a city where everything was "raw and fortuitous, as uncivilized and certainly as ugly as the desert ridge on which Bezuidenhout planted his homestead".[3]

Disfavourable opinions on the city's layout and architecture were accompanied by disparaging comments about its inhabitants. Not only were British travellers convinced of the uncivilized character of the Boer population but they also had serious reservations as to the kind of immigrants that the new city was attracting because, as the British journalist and novelist Violet H. Markham pointed out, "the financial adventurer who has wandered to the Transvaal is not the type of man who would demonstrate the highest side of European civilisation to the Boers".[4]

Speculation, greed, and rapid growth also had other, more immediate, consequences for people's daily existence. Life in Johannesburg was fast moving. People came and went according to their fortunes and even the pulse of city life was marked by a frantic and noisy pace noticed by most travellers. As early as 1887 it was necessary to send the mounted police to patrol the streets and to arrest those exceeding the speed limit of seven miles per hour. Downtown Rissik and Eloff Streets were the cabbies' favoured racecourses. Especially on Saturdays, they would drive four abreast, shouting and whipping their horses while carrying merry and rather tipsy workers from the railway station south of Braamfontein to see the horse races in Turffontein.[5]

As ugly as European travellers found Johannesburg, indubitably it had made enormous progress in its architecture from its days as a diggers camp in the 1880s. By the 1890s timber and corrugated iron buildings had replaced the diggers' tents and as the 1900s unfolded more permanent structures of brick and granite slowly started filling the skyline.[6]

Since the city has its roots in the discovery of gold it is not surprising that its first solid and respectable buildings were those of the mining houses and the financial institutions. And even if, as Violet H. Markham thought, the mining offices and the banking establishments were "huge meretricious buildings as remarkable for their costliness as their lack of artistic merit",[7] the sight of the downtown main arteries stood in strong contrast to the working class suburbs of the city.

While the failure to enforce existing building regulations in Johannesburg might be partly attributable to the inexperience of the Republican government, which was more familiar with the administration of market towns than of rapidly industrializing cities, the state of the working class neighbourhoods of the city was the consequence of a range of social, economic and political problems.

The basic structure of the houses in Fordsburg in the west end of the city was a square of corrugated iron roofing supported by four wooden posts. The spaces between the wooden posts were filled in with green bricks, made of clay and straw, that needed to be protected from summer rain and thunderstorms by corrugated iron sheets. Most of these houses had four rooms. The green bricks kept the interior cool in summer and warm in winter and the papered walls prevented the mine dust from creeping in. Ceilings were originally made of canvas or cotton sheets nailed to the rafters, but these were eventually replaced by wood.

In terms of services, floods and lack of potable water were serious problems in Fordsburg. Part of the neighbourhood fell outside the jurisdiction of both the Water Works Company and the Braamfontein Estate Company, the two suppliers of water in Johannesburg, while in the areas that fell within the water companies' jurisdiction, some people could not afford to pay for the service. During the early 1900s most of Fordsburg's water came from wells located in dirty yards and easily polluted by animals. In 1901 Charles Porter reported that from 28 samples of water taken in the area 16 were polluted.[8]

The incline of the ground in this area did not make things easier. A large part of Fordsburg was susceptible to flooding during the rainy season, between December and March.[9] The District Surgeon, Dr. R. Mackenzie, told the members of the Insanitary Area Improvement Commission (1901-3) that on 2 December 1902, after heavy rain, he could not drive through some of Fordsburg's streets. Park Lane Street and Fountain Road were under water and, as streets were closed, the residents were outside their houses wading about.

When Charles Porter gave evidence before the Insanitary Area Improvement Commission, he indicated that in Fordsburg's lower area there were 110 dwellings of which 86 were passable, 13 insanitary but rectifiable, eight to be condemned and three in ruins. Porter's general opinion was that even the passable buildings were not good enough - too small and dilapidated.[10] The description of the houses and streets in Brickfields-Burghersdorp, north of Fordsburg, was just as bad.[11] Most buildings in Brickfields were either small and ill-ventilated tin shanties or green brick sheds with an earth floor, considered unsuitable for human habitation.

The demarcated insanitary area, however, was not the only part of Johannesburg in which unseemly houses and unhealthy conditions prevailed. Drinking water in Vrededorp and in some areas of Jeppestown, in the east of the city, also came from wells constantly exposed to pollution. Diseases originating from polluted water were fairly common in working class neighbourhoods and in 1902 there was an epidemic of enteric fever in Jeppestown attributed to soil polluted by slops. The report of the Medical Officer of Health pointed out that most of the mine workers' houses on McIntyre Street, where the majority of the enteric fever cases were detected, were crowded together and dirty with both pail and rubbish receptacles being "very offensive" and too close to the kitchens and backrooms.[12]

Typhoid was the other disease endemic in the city and the total mortality rate for whites during the year 1902-3 was 13.8 per cent. Most of the victims were between 15 and 40 years old and the highest number of cases appeared in Brickfields, City and Suburban, Jeppestown and Vrededorp where poor drainage contributed to the development and spread of the infection.[13] Similarly diarrhoea was responsible for more than half the cases of infant mortality (262 per 1000 in 1902). Higher numbers of deaths occurred in the poorer and less sanitary areas such as Brickfields and Vrededorp.[14]

According to the report of the Medical Officer of Health, between 1902 and 1903 pneumonia was the greatest health risk to Johannesburg's white population in general and to the white workers in particular.[15] But amongst occupational diseases silicosis was the lung disease which, still not fully diagnosed by the medical profession, took the most lives amongst the Rand's working population.[16]

Endemic diseases, the enormous health hazards of working in the mining industry, and the lack of appropriate working class accommodation, amongst other problems, conspired against the permanent settlement of British immigrants in Johannesburg. The number of hotels, boarding houses and bars give an image of Johannesburg as a stopover for passengers in transit in the wider industrial world of the Atlantic. Nevertheless, the mushrooming of temporary accommodation cannot be reduced to the presence of a single male population, but has to be read in the context of the complexities of the demography of the white working class in Johannesburg and the general shortage of housing of the early 1900s.

Johannesburg's expansion from the city centre to the neighbourhoods in the east and the west as well as the growth of these areas is reflected in the street directories. In 1897 the *Longland's Directory* recorded 95 buildings in Johannesburg, all of them in the city centre, that is the area between the railway line in the north, Commissioner Street in the south, Sauer Street in the west and End Street in the east. Nearly half of the buildings were on Commissioner Street. They were mostly commercial although some of them had one of the usual three storeys, often the top floor, devoted to residential purposes. By 1903 the directory recorded 166 buildings, reflecting inner Johannesburg's rapid growth. In 1897 the main arteries of Fordsburg did not even figure in the street directory. Six years later, data on Avenue Road, Fordsburg's principal street, was incorporated in its pages. Despite Fordsburg's remarkable growth, in 1903 Avenue Road still offered a very different sight to the traveller when compared with Commissioner Street: small houses and rooms, a few shops - often run by Chinese immigrants - two bakeries, a photographer's studio, a butchery, a watchmaker, and Universal Engineering Works along with Green & Harvey varnish merchants.

A decade later, on the eve of World War I, a newcomer could marvel at the buildings on Commissioner Street and at the shops on Market Street. Steam driven cars and the electric tramway had replaced carts and the horse tram in 1906. West of the city centre the sight was rather different. The residents of Fordsburg were used to unpaved streets, small dilapidated houses, children playing in the mud, overcrowded yards and the unabated noise of the mine's battery stamps. Here there were far more bicycles than cars and city centre's tall and imposing buildings were replaced by small working class houses while the glamour and glitter of shop windows on Market Street gave way to darker grocery shops and laundries along with bars and hotels that were not always reputable.

Briton and Afrikaner, employed and underemployed, lived side by side with the Chinese shopkeepers, the so-called coloured and black families and a very cosmopolitan assortment of Oriental people - mostly Arabs and Syrians - who often caught the attention of the newcomer.[17]

Poor and wealthy alike agreed that Johannesburg was an expensive city. Even in the leaflets published in Britain containing information for immigrants it was stressed that prices in the Transvaal's leading industrial city were higher than at home.[18] Most witnesses before the Industrial Commission of Enquiry (1897) stressed this problem, but it was the testimony of two mining employees, R. Barrow and A. Buchan Fyfe, that perhaps showed most clearly the hardships faced by working class families in Johannesburg before the South African War.

According to A. Buchan Fyfe, the average wage of a carpenter was £1 a day which amounted to £27 at the end of the month. In a mining boarding house for single workers food cost £6 a month and sometimes there was a charge of 10s a month for a room. If the worker was married he also had to provide for his wife and children who did not live on the mine property. The rental of a small house averaged £7 monthly. After deducting the expenses for food and board a carpenter had £6 left to buy clothing, send his children to school, save money for an emergency, buy tobacco, and pay for a little entertainment. Buchan Fyfe remarked that keeping a family on the Rand was almost impossible, particularly when one accepted the fact that most workers were all-round miners earning not £27 but £20 a month. He related his own experience of illness and how it eroded the already tight family budget. In March 1896 he fell sick with typhoid fever and was out of work for 16 weeks. Buchan Fyfe calculated that once the actual costs of the illness and the money lost for being out of work were added, his illness had cost him £200.[19]

Taking a rock driller's monthly wage of £23 16s 8d, R. Barrow compiled the following budget for a worker's family:

Rent	6	10	0
Butcher	2	10	0
Baker	2	0	0
Milk	0	15	0
Groceries	8	0	0
Fuel	1	1	0
Total	£20	6s	0

Other expenses like clothing, schooling, doctor's fees, a 'kitchen boy' and railway fees would amount to a further £10. In other words, the expenses of a rock driller with a family of five (wife and four children) would have been £7 above his wage.[20]

Between 1896 and 1899 several newspaper articles pointed out the economic crisis and the seriousness of unemployment in Johannesburg.[21] *The Star* suggested on 24 July 1897 that one of Johannesburg's mysteries was how a married man with a wife and two children who was earning £20 to £25 managed to make ends meet. Similarly, in 'Hard Times on the Rand', the *Standard and Diggers' News* told its readers of the contrast between affluent and poor neighbourhoods and of the serious spells of unemployment faced in Johannesburg by adventurers and unskilled men.[22]

The outbreak of the South African War worsened the effects of the economic slump and by May 1900, when the British troops commanded by Lord Roberts occupied Johannesburg, scarcity of food, high prices and unemployment had increased the number of indigents amongst the working class. During the days of the military occupation, between May 1900 and April 1901, no butcher was allowed to trade in Johannesburg and all the food supplies were controlled by six government stores that distributed 300 tons of food per week among 35,000 white people. Throughout this period there were never less than 5,000 white persons on the relief list although less than 3,500 actually received assistance.[23]

In this context it was little wonder that when the announcement of the peace was made on Sunday 1 June 1902 the general reaction was one more of incredulity than joy. Bitterly cold weather had kept people at home and, as bars were closed under martial law, the news was received in an uninviting and inhospitable climate both in the houses and in the streets.[24]

As Johannesburg's population slowly returned to its pre-war routine some of the city's structural problems became more apparent. Lack of affordable accommodation was amongst the most serious problems white workers had to face. The organizer of the Amalgamated Society of Engineers, A. Raitt, told the Johannesburg Housing Commission in 1903 that a threefold increase in the price of accommodation since the outset of the war was forcing working class families into slum dwellings while artisan men were obliged to sublet part of their houses, destroying "true home life". Alternatively, married artisans and miners, unable to support their families, were sending them back to England. In the case of shopkeeper the increase in rents was transferred to the prices of domestic goods thus impacting in the general rise of the cost of living.[25]

Shortage of affordable accommodation and the inability to pay the rent of a cottage meant that working class families had to develop new strategies to keep a roof over their heads. One possibility was to incorporate the work of women and children into the family economy. Children were taken out of school to become breadwinners[26] and women sought work in one of the many city laundries. Working parents and elder siblings meant that the younger members of the family were often left unattended, able to wander in the streets "at the open doors of shameless continental women".[27] Other solution to the housing crisis were either to take in lodgers to help pay the rent, or to reduce the size of the family accommodation. Although most workers tried to resist the former option because, as a bricklayer put it to the Housing Commission, "if I get a house I want a home and do not want to be crowded out by a lot of lodgers",[28] taking in lodgers or being a lodger was fairly common during the first decades of the 1900s.[29]

In 1906 the Rand High Court heard a case in which a Mrs. C. Bell petitioned for a judicial separation after 12 years of marriage because her husband, who "never came home sober on Saturdays", had had a fight with the lodger, accusing him of having an affair with Mrs Bell.[30] A similar case, though of more dramatic proportions, happened in Fordsburg in 1908 when Mr. van Jaarsveldt found his wife sleeping with their lodger, a miner by the name of J. J. Fouche. Confronted by her husband, Mrs van Jaarsveldt decided to abandon him and took up with Fouche.[31]

During the hearings of the Transvaal Indigency Commission (1906-8) some witnesses linking the presence of lodgers in working class houses to the weakening of family ties:

> The absence of home life is decidedly injurious for woman and children, as it may tend in certain cases to make the former careless, lazy and improvident. It is also bad for the children, they frequently see and hear things better unseen and unheard.[32]

As it transpired from the commission's work the economic recession affected both skilled and unskilled workers. The Secretary of the Federated Association of Mine Employees, a union subsidized by the Chamber of Mines, indicated that carpenters, bricklayers, wood turners and clerks as well as handymen were amongst the growing indigent Johannesburg population. Married men with two children could not live on the average wage paid on the mines at the time, £17 per month.[33]

For the unskilled worker, particularly those of Afrikaner descent, the days of self-employment as brickmakers or cab drivers were already past. What was left was competition with black migrant labourers who, due to their access to subsistence farming, were paid lower wages and were therefore the preferred workers in unskilled jobs. Although there were some official attempts to offset unemployment through the implementation of relief work by the municipality and the railways, the wages paid, 5s or 6s per day, were clearly not enough to keep a family.

During the 1906-1908 recession the number of families dependent on charity increased considerably. In 1907 the Rand Aid Association, which had been established in 1903 by the Milner administration with the support of the mine owners, gave 410 monetary grants, 19,915 parcels of provisions and 416 parcels of clothing by way of outdoor relief. The association admitted 3,042 men to its home in Fordsburg, and served 45,729 meals to men who were not inmates.[34]

The Transvaal Indigency Commission concluded its investigations by suggesting that a reduction in the cost of living depended to a large extent on skilled white workers further reducing their standard of living. Despite the fact that the results of a comparison between the cost of living in England and Johannesburg showed that neither skilled nor unskilled workers could make ends meet in the Transvaal,[35] a perception of white workers as improvident had been gaining momentum amongst the ruling class and was to become an important element of their understanding of the poor white problem in the mid-1910s. For the moment, however, the 1908-9 investment spurt in the mining industry and the political confidence that followed the unification of South Africa in 1910 did contribute to economic recovery and eased some of the social tensions.

The upturn in the economy did not modify to any significant extent the issue of working class accommodation or the state of the city's slums, which were increasingly viewed as the sites where misery, demoralization and crime merged with miscegenation, thus embodying the worst fears of the colonial middle classes. Predictably, given the pervasiveness of Social Darwinism in the colonial world, this view of social decay was not limited to the local middle class. Visitors from the rest of the Commonwealth saw Johannesburg's slums with the same lens as their local counterparts. The Australian journalist Ambrose Pratt visited Johannesburg in 1910 and ventured outside Johannesburg's main thoroughfares to find "a network of streets and lanes that cries shame upon the Rand. Dirty, mean little houses, broken almost impassable roadways, squalor" extending for miles where poor whites, black and coloured people lived in close proximity. There Pratt heard "the clashing polyglot of a score of diverse foreign tongues" and saw "white children scattered through the murk playing in the gutters, picking up the words and vices of coloured scum".[36]

These visions of squalor and criminality were echoed a year later by Irish-born William C. Scully, a keen and sharp witness of the social conditions in southern Africa since the 1890s, who repeated the tale of small crowded houses, demoralization and poor whites associated with illicit liquor dealing, which was becoming more and more a tropos in both government and broader colonial society expression.[37]

The South African Party government as much as the Labour Party and, since 1914, the National Party created by James B. M. Hertzog, were concerned about the position of poor whites in a racially divided society.

And all the commissions of enquiry and selected committees on these issues appointed between 1912 and 1914 began to explain the situation of the white working class in general, and of its lower rank in particular, against the characteristics of the colonial society.

The Economic Commission, which submitted its report to government in 1914, saw the housing problem as much as the labour issue as consequences of the racial organization of society. Thus the commission suggested that whatever the increase in the cost of living in South Africa there were a series of social pressures specific to the colony which weighed heavily on working class families:

> A white man might be capable of living in comfort on a smaller income, but there is a feeling that in lowering his social position he would lose in prestige where there is a large non-white population. For instance, in some places convention ordains that every white family should have at least one native servant whether the family is of the servant-keeping class, according to English standards or not. In England working class families tend to underhouse themselves, in parts of South Africa they would certainly seem to make the mistake of overhousing themselves.[38]

And referring to the general organization of South African society the report of the commission noted:

> Broadly speaking the economies of South Africa are dominated by the fact that the population consists of two races in industrial partnership with nothing in common in their traditions and standards of living. They form a distinct social strata and there is a gap between them very imperfectly filled by whites who have abandoned white standards of living (known as poor whites).[39]

Despite the neat social stratification suggested in the Economic Commission, social dynamics were far more complex and fluid than this three-tier stratification with poor whites "(imperfectly) filling" the social distance between the white and black populations of South Africa. In a context of social and economic crisis, employed and unemployed workers, both skilled and unskilled, developed their own forms of resistance and strategies of survival. While the employed men organized and went on strike in 1913, 1914, 1917 and 1922, the families of the unemployed resorted to relief work, when available, odd jobs, liquor dealing and prostitution. However, the fine line separating employed and unemployed, skilled from unskilled and white from coloured was easily crossed due both to the action of economic forces and to some of the social interactions that took place in the working class neighbourhoods of Johannesburg.

White Working Class Social Networks in Johannesburg, 1890-1922

One of the fundamental historical issues argued in this book is that the presence of working class families in Johannesburg during this period was more significant than has been previously thought. This, however, does not simply mean that there was a relatively high proportion of married couples in the city, but that the manner in which these families were formed had lasting consequences for the understanding of white working class identity up to the 1922 Rand Revolt. The greater relative importance of both families and relations between families in the life of the white working class in Johannesburg between 1890 and 1922 forces a revision of the characterization of working class culture as predominantly male and organized around drinking, prostitution and gambling.[40] The separation between home life and an overwhelmingly male realm of work, bars and brothels seems less clear cut when read against the importance of family and neighbourhood networks. A shortened distance between family life and the world of work permits a more careful exploration of the role that working class families had in the development of working class culture and therefore in moulding a sense of community and identity amongst the white working class in Johannesburg.

Similarly, this characterization of the white working class directs the historian's attention to more fluid and complex social exchanges than those circumscribed to bars and brothels. This section analyzes some of the social interactions that took place between families, men and women, Afrikaner and Briton, employed and unemployed, children and adults, petty criminals and law abiding citizens, and blacks and whites in the broader context of the working class neighbourhoods.

In a young city like Johannesburg the population of which was made up of immigrants drawn largely from the industrialized world of the northern hemisphere and of newly urbanized Afrikaners coming from the South African countryside, family formation was more than an important stage in the life cycle of men and women. It was also the creation of kinship, a network of relationships and solidarity that had to fill the space left by the lack of actual extended families in the emerging urban centre of the new country. Workers linked by a common "ethnic" background,[41] similar experiences in the workplace, the neighbourhood or their trade, developed emotional ties of solidarity and friendship. These were often expressed in a fictive kinship relationship articulated through the bonds of godparenting.

Relationships that seem to have had their origin in the church itself were continued over the years even when the characteristic high mobility of working class families in Johannesburg had taken a particular family far away from the church where their children or godchildren had been baptized.

Caleb Dunstan was a mason who lived with his wife Martha in Braamfontein. In 1895 they had a baby boy who was baptized in the Anglican Church of Christ on 1 Park Drive in Fordsburg. The chosen godfather was John Donovan, a painter, still unmarried at the time of the baptism. Three years later Caleb and Martha Dunstan moved to a house on 6th Street, Vrededorp, closer to the Church of Christ, where they had three more children, all of whom were baptized in this church. Fifteen years had passed since the baptism of Caleb Dunstan's first child when John Donovan, now married, had his first child.[42] And, although John and his wife Alice lived in Benoni, in 1910 they had their daughter baptized in the Church of Christ in Fordsburg. Looking at this case it is possible to speculate that the friendship between the Dunstans and the Donovans and John Donovan's attachment to the church where his godson had been baptized made him and his wife decide to come all the way from Benoni to baptize their own daughter in Fordsburg.[43]

In other cases sharing a trade combined with the physical closeness of working class neighbourhoods to defy ethnic boundaries.[44] The relationship between an Afrikaner and an English family, the van Niekerks and the Kirbys, shows how personal relationships could sometimes reinforce the ties within a community and thus influence people's decisions. William and Elizabeth Kirby's family[45] lived for at least five years in Fordsburg (1893-8) during which time William was successively employed as a blacksmith, a labourer during the 1896-7 recession, and as a self-employed cab owner in 1898. It was in this year that William asked his neighbour and fellow cab owner, Stefanus van Niekerk,[46] to be godparent to his son, who was baptized in the Church of Christ in Fordsburg. In 1905 Stefanus and Phoebe Van Niekerk wanted to have their daughter, Irene, baptized. They also had it done in the Church of Christ and William Kirby was chosen as godfather.

Sometimes it was the women, rather than the men, who reinforced friendship ties between two families through fictive kinship. This was the case with Margaret Bentley, married to one Edward Bentley,[47] a labourer and resident of Fordsburg. In 1893 Margaret, still single, had been chosen as godmother to the child of Thomas and Sarah Fitzgerald[48] who were also living in Fordsburg. So when Margaret married Edward in 1896, she brought with her, in the person of her godchild, a new relation into her own family. Similarly, it was Maria Truter, the wife of a bricklayer from Brickfields,[49] who was to be the godmother to the baby boy of George Becker,[50] a miner, and his Afrikaner wife, Letitia. The Beckers were living in Fordsburg in 1897 when their son was born. In the same way Ada Johnson[51] became the godmother to the Sharps'[52] baby girl in 1905. Both couples were living in Fordsburg and the fathers were a bricklayer and an engine driver respectively.

In a society where there was no historical community to underwrite important moments in the life cycle people created a cross-cutting sense of community that, no matter how small or inchoate, had a fundamental role in developing ties of solidarity. Men were not the only ones to actively incorporate new relationships into the nuclear family, through their work or their neighbourhood acquaintances; women also had an important role in the creation of family networks. The ways in which some of these relationships were created and cemented suggest that the separation between workers of Afrikaner and of English descent was perhaps not as marked as contemporary politicians and later historiography thought, and gives even more rationale to the participation of working class families in the 1922 Rand Revolt.[53]

The comparatively important presence of Afrikaner families or Afrikaner-English families in the baptismal records of the Anglican Church acquires in this context its full cultural dimension. Noteworthy in this regard is that by 1908 the existence amongst the working class of a population who had English names and spoke Dutch was acknowledged by people who had wide experience of working class neighbourhoods.[54]

If some of the reasons behind the existence of "inter-ethnic" marriages were, at least until 1904, demographic, i.e. the greater proportion of Afrikaner women in the female population of Johannesburg, it seems that personal interactions had a substantial part in the development of a South African white working class and its particular solidarity between 1906 and 1922. While during the 1907 miners' strike the employment of Afrikaners as blacklegs showed the contradictions between class consciousness and the desperate situation of the unemployed in the western suburbs of the city,[55] the 1913 and 1922 miners' strikes showed a more united working class front. If solidarity between British and Afrikaner workers in 1913 and 1922 can be explained through the incorporation of growing numbers of Afrikaner men into the industry, the fact that in both strikes many working class families[56] took to the streets in support of the strikers points to a more complex sense of identity and class consciousness amongst white workers.[57]

Both workplace and neighbourhood were instrumental in the creation of fictive kinship relationships in the form of godparenting. But physical closeness made way also for other forms of social interactions, such as acquaintanceship, that, although less formalized, were just as important in the configuration of a working class identity and sense of community.

At first glance working class family life was not public in Johannesburg in the sense that it was public in London during the late nineteenth century.[58] The absence of tenement blocks allowed for a larger degree of privacy as families did not share sculleries, privies or a common backyard. The everyday noises and conversations of the one family were not necessarily heard by their next door neighbours.

However, people did share backyards, privies and wells, particularly in the poorer neighbourhoods such as Burghersdorp, Ferreirastown and Fordsburg. And when families took in lodgers, or themselves lived as lodgers, a great part of their privacy was taken away. But even when families did not live under the same roof, they still frequented the same public space. They often bought vegetables from the same Chinese shop,[59] got meat from the same butcher, their children went to the same school, they were seen by the same district surgeon, and men drank and played billiard games in the same bars. And all of this took place in a context where economic fluctuations and structural conditions often obliged people to find alternative modes of coping with daily life.

The high cost of living, especially in regard to rental accommodation, along with spells of unemployment, made working class families develop different strategies of survival. But whatever the hardships most working class families experienced, they were exacerbated in the case of the families of unskilled workers whose capacity to compete in the labour market was checked by the presence of a cheaper African workforce.

Until the creation of the office of the Inspector of White Labour in 1907 there was, with the exception of the Rand Aid Association, no state organization for the unemployed to turn to in their search for a job. And even then finding employment was not easy for unskilled workers. Charity, such as that provided by the Rand Aid Association, was not always welcomed by the workers. In this context Johannesburg's streets offered to men and women not only opportunities for society and entertainment but the possibility, though not always necessarily within the law, of eking out a living.

Alcohol and prostitution were two of the most important of these illicit survival strategies. Both had been important features of Johannesburg's social and economic life since the very beginning of its history. Nevertheless, the character and organization of liquor selling and prostitution changed over time in response to the state's ability and determination to curtail and control both occupations.

The production of alcohol was a fundamental means of capital accumulation for the agriculturally based Boer republics during the nineteenth century. At the initial stages of mining production the mine magnates saw no contradiction between their interest in exploiting large numbers of African migrant workers and the selling of alcohol to their workforce. On the contrary, indebtedness to the liquor sellers acted as a guarantee of black migrant labourers, ever-longer periods of work in the mines.[60] This seemingly satisfactory arrangement changed dramatically by the mid-1890s, when the deep level mining requirement of a disciplined workforce made contradictory the interest of Hartherly Distillery, the producer of spirits in the Transvaal, and the mine magnates.

Moreover, the British interests behind the Empire's entry into a colonial war with the Boer republics were focused on gold and not on liquor.[61]

During the military occupation of Johannesburg bars remained closed, the sale of alcohol to the general public was banned, and a special prohibition on selling alcohol to black people was established. However, Johannesburg's population was not going to go endlessly without a drink. The Transvaal Liquor Commission, appointed by the British administration in 1901, came up with some regulations for the retail business. Bars were still closed but men could have a drink with a meal between 12 and 2 pm and 6 and 9 pm.[62] Teetotallers and supporters of state control of the liquor traffic[63] as well as concerned Johannesburg women approached both Lord Milner and Joseph Chamberlain, Secretary of State for the Colonies, to express their opposition to these measures.[64] In the meantime, as mining operations were slowly resumed and the new administrators tried to find a way of dealing with alcohol, black mine workers were back in town and again became a good market for those trying to make some money while the Rand economy had not yet fully recovered from the impact of the South African War.

The introduction of alcohol in the Transvaal during the reconstruction period depended on licensed wholesale dealers who imported spirits from Hamburg and Trieste in casks, decanted them into bottles, and distributed them to retail outlets spread along the line of the Reef.[65] Between 1901 and 1903 many cases of illicit liquor dealing were brought before the local magistrate. In 1902, the new administration had passed an ordinance penalizing the sale of alcohol to black people. Nevertheless, most of the cases brought to court involved small operations uncovered by a police force that seemed more determined than in the past to curb illicit liquor dealing. The Criminal Investigation Department set traps to catch the offenders. Black constables stood in as potential buyers, paying the dealers with marked coins. Using this strategy the police seldom seized more than a couple of bottles of brandy and took to court a few poor whites who were operating from their houses.[66]

In 1906, there was an attempt to crack down on large-scale liquor traffic along the Reef. An amendment to the previous ordinance was passed which prevented anybody from removing more than 12 bottles of liquor at a time from a bottle store without a permit. This measure restricted the importation of large quantities of crude spirit and seriously checked the wholesale liquor merchants. It, nevertheless, did not stop the traffic but merely changed its modality. The new source of illicit liquor dealing was the retail bottle store keeper. Whether directly involved or not, they became an essential link in an economic chain that often started off with a poor white person - man, woman or child - running from liquor store to liquor store in town buying a few bottles to be handed over to the professional dealer.

The idea that there was a link between poverty and illicit liquor dealing emerged quite clearly from the hearings of the Transvaal Indigency Commission (1906-8), which pointed to liquor dealing as the occupation of many poor whites living in Fordsburg and Vrededorp. Witnesses before the commission did not fail to make the Social Darwinist connection between poverty and criminality. As Johannesburg's Acting Commissioner of Police, Lieutenant Colonel Mackey O'Brian, explained, poor Dutch people:

> Are unfit in every way for town life and so they sunk into a very low scale of society and have taken to crime, illicit liquor selling being the easiest way in which a man can get money.[67]

Police statistics showed that during the worst year of the economic recession, 1907, there had been 3,464 prosecutions under the Liquor Law of which black people selling alcohol to black people accounted only for 718 cases.[68] This meant that there were 2,746 cases of poor whites selling alcohol to black workers. This was undoubtedly a large enough figure for the authorities and the general public to start worrying about the current number of poor whites and their potential recruitment into the liquor traffic.[69]

At the beginning of the new decade Robert Shanks, the Inspector of White Labour, indicated that there were 4,376 registered unemployed people in Johannesburg.[70] The total number of black inhabitants of the city in 1911 was 103,668, and the number of black workers employed by the mining industry was 213,880. Over 300,000 potential customers certainly made a sizeable market for the illicit liquor dealers and offered a good opportunity to the unemployed in an occupation that paid more than relief work.

Illicit liquor dealing had been an ever present yet varying problem on the Witwatersrand since the early 1890s, however, it was only in the early 1910s that the ruling class's preoccupation with the social consequences of the illicit selling of alcohol to the black population reached the general public in the form of a moral panic. The "black peril" was construed around the alleged increase of indecent assaults by black men against white women and concentrated the attention of charitable organizations, the police, and different churches.

In 1912 the South African Party government appointed a Commission of Enquiry into the Assaults on Women, the report of which, suggesting that illicit liquor dealing was one of the causes of the increase in indecent assaults, had remarkable influence in both defining the poor white problem and in characterizing the behaviour of black men (and white women) in terms that suited the mores and ideology of white colonial society. Thus, contemporary and successive investigations into social and economic conditions during this period echoed one way or the other the conclusions of what was called the 'Black Peril Commission'.

Jacob de Villiers Roos, Secretary of Justice, in his evidence to the Select Committee on European Employment and Labour Conditions explained that those involved in liquor dealing were "people who are left behind in the race for life and the result is that they follow the least line of resistance".[71]

A description of the extent of the traffic and its actual mechanisms came from the evidence of Major T. E. Mavrogordato, who was in charge of the Criminal Investigations Department, to the Commission into Assaults on Women. According to Mavrogordato:

> All women in Ferreira Town are running about all day buying bottles of liquor. If they get sixpence a bottle and buy a dozen in a day they have made six shillings. You see a woman going about with a perambulator containing a baby buying bottles and hiding them under the baby.[72]

And in the major's experience children were also part of the chain:

> A little girl brings a ticket that is supposed to come from her father, or her uncle or her aunt, and the bottle storekeeper supplies the liquor. Other runners see the children and ask "How much are you getting", and they say three-pence. "I will give you sixpence", says the runner. The child gets the liquor, the man goes round the corner and is sometimes seen disposing of the liquor to the natives. But children soon learn that instead of getting three-pence or sixpence from the runner, it is more profitable to sell the liquor direct to the natives themselves.[73]

Illicit liquor dealing was, however, neither a means of accumulation nor an alternative to proletarianization. Poor whites were the visible and active, though least important, part of a successful enterprise. How successful liquor dealers were can be measured by the lengths to which they went in order to keep their "runners". When poor whites were arrested by the police, the dealers took upon themselves the support of the family of the convict until he was released.[74] It is not difficult to imagine the guarantees that this trade offered, despite its obvious risks, to white working class families living in the slums of Ferreirastown or Fordsburg. Each member of the family bringing in 6s a day obviated the need for erratic and insufficient charity.

The identification of poor whites with Afrikaner folk created the impression that those involved in illicit liquor dealing were of Afrikaner origin. There is, however, enough evidence in the commissions of enquiry appointed between 1906 and 1913 about the presence of unemployed British men and women living in slums and taking part in the traffic.[75] In his wanderings in Johannesburg slums during 1911 Scully had a picturesque encounter which confirms the more arid and sober accounts of the official reports:

> In the same slum I made the acquaintance of an elderly European woman who was apparently living with a coolie. Mislead by her accent, I asked her what part of the Cape Colony she came from. With many lurid oaths she repudiated being a Colonist. She would, she assured me, be____ well ashamed to belong to such a____ country as South Africa. No; she was an Englishwoman and was ____ well proud of the circumstance. What sort of a____ (this, that, the other) was I, she wanted to know to take her for a____ nigger? I subsequently ascertained that this lady had twice "done time". She had served a sentence of six months for illicit liquor dealing and a like period for keeping a brothel for Natives.[76]

For poor white women prostitution was sometimes also an alternative to unemployment. During the 1906-8 economic recession and, more especially, in the 1910s there was a strong association between white prostitutes and illicit liquor selling to black men. But this type of prostitution was only one of the forms that commerce in sex could take. Professional prostitution became a permanent feature of Johannesburg's social life soon after the city was formed as a mining camp. Two waves of prostitutes arrived and worked in Johannesburg between 1886 and 1902. The first wave was made mainly up of southern African women who worked either as full-time or part-time prostitutes from the back of canteens and hotels in the city. Whether they rented rooms in the hotels or worked as barmaids in the canteens, what characterized these women was their independence from pimps.[77] By 1895 the extension of the railway line helped to connect the interior of the country with the international migration arriving from Delagoa Bay. This opened the door to a second wave of ladies who came from Europe and arrived accompanied by pimps. These pimps had broad international experience which allowed them to counteract the state's bid to make the sex commerce illegal with an exceedingly effective system of police bribery.[78]

This was the situation when, in 1902, the new imperial administration assumed its duties in the Transvaal. At a measured pace, perhaps too measured in the opinion of Johannesburg's concerned citizens and Whitehall, the British administration of the Transvaal made provision in the Immorality Ordinance of 1903 for the dismantling of brothels and the prohibition of soliciting in Johannesburg, which was only fully implemented in 1905. By then most brothels had been shut down, soliciting in the streets had been gradually reduced and most prostitutes were working independently from their own homes.[79]

By 1907 when the newly elected *Het Volk* government started its fight against "organized vice", the Rand economy was in the throes of a serious recession. In the context of the economic slump the working class neighbourhoods of Fordsburg and Vrededorp provided a new group of prostitutes. Some local white women, who, responding to the colonial prejudice against manual work, refused to take employment as domestic workers, started selling sexual services to make a living. Some of these women chose to become full-time prostitutes to support themselves and their families. Others were part-time or, in the contemporary expression, amateur prostitutes:

> We do not have open prostitution in Fordsburg. The prostitutes there are women who have sunk so low that they will probably do a day's washing and then go into the drink again and start this kind of thing.[80]

The existence of "amateur" prostitutes in the white working class neighbourhoods made it especially obvious that prostitution was a response to social and economic hardship. And in this sense it constituted a central preoccupation of state and private organizations when analysing the poor white problem.

A full study of prostitution would be necessary to unfold the ways in which these women worked and the services they offered, how much they earned and how they spent their money.[81] Short of this information some of the answers can only be guessed at.

White working class avoidance of work in menial occupations side by side with equally unskilled black labourers was widely stated in the sources throughout the period 1908-22.[82] In the case of working class women this manifested itself as refusal to work as maids for the richer white population. It was also argued that white women preferred the independence of other types of employment to the restraining hours of domestic work:

> One reason is that somehow they think it is degrading to work for another white person in a house. Perhaps that is not the greatest reason. I think the greater reason is that in most cases they have to remain with the family in the evening. If they go to a laundry they can work 12 hours and then they are free for the rest of the day. Their desire for freedom is, I think, a great check to them going into domestic service.[83]

Thus, relatively unskilled laundry work along with serving in a shop became avenues to escape from domestic work. But serving in a shop demanded some level of education and therefore this type of job was closed to most of the very poor and uneducated women.

During 1912 and 1913 most witnesses giving evidence before the Select Committee on European Employment and the Commission of Enquiry into Assaults on Women pinpointed the association between laundry work and prostitution. The fact that most laundry owners were Chinese and that some women workers were prepared to have sex, not always for money but also in exchange for favours, with oriental men contributed to the demonization of both laundry work and working class women:

> And is it true they (white women) are immoral. I mean, do they lend themselves to prostitution largely? - That has been said to be the case, and, I am afraid, it is supported by the fact that they do go for immorality. - I think we had a little evidence on that point here. Is it so that many of them are living with Chinamen and coolies? - Yes, and they work for them. They work in Chinese laundries.[84]

It is difficult to quantify the contribution of women's work in laundries to working class family economies. By 1913, a woman could earn between 15 shillings and £1 per week doing unskilled laundry work. In the best of cases £4 a month was not enough to keep a single person in Johannesburg. To ascertaining which women in a family went to the laundries and which became part-time prostitutes and why, is not easy either. The oft repeated opinion that poor white males lived off the laundry work of their wives and the prostitution of their daughters, aside from being an expression of middle class disapproval, may well have reflected a social reality. The preoccupation with the rescuing of working class girls points in this direction:

> Do you think that the women folk of these people should be rescued? That it would provide a solution to this question if these people could be brought to take positions in domestic service and in that way improve themselves? - I think that is certainly one of the greatest things that could happen. It would be a great step towards their improvement. I think this false pride should be preached against and everything should be done to assist this people to go into housework, although to our shame, it is the usual impression among these people that they can earn their living in other ways, no proper ways.[85]

In whichever way their income was disposed of, it cannot be said that prostitution was exclusively the occupation of young single females. Towards the end of the first decade of the 1900s deserted women with children, whether married or not, also found in the selling of sexual services a way of coping with their circumstances.[86]

In 1913 witnesses before the select committee and the commission of enquiry pinpointed a third way of entering prostitution. Women involved in illicit liquor dealing resorted to it, either as a way of obtaining protection from the police or as a way of making some extra money to take home:

> In many instances women sell it (the alcohol) directly to the natives and we have had evidence that frequently it happens that the woman to avoid being trapped will submit herself to the embraces of the native trap and then he does not go on trapping that woman.[87]

The fact that most customers of the illicit liquor trade were black men made this type of prostitution one of the targets of the 1913 moral panic. In the words of the *Report of the Commission on Assaults on Women*:

> These people (involved in illicit liquor trade) are one of the causes of the natives losing respect for the white race, which is one of the strongest factors calculated to restrain him from even entertaining the idea of the possibility of having any sexual relations with a white woman.[88]

Finally, there were two other types of commercialized sexual activity. There were women who lived off the prostitution practised in their lodgings in hotels, where they apparently had to pay the owners to let them have male visitors. There were yet other women who could not really be called prostitutes but whose sexual liaisons with men were relatively commercialized. These were mainly young women employed as waitresses or barmaids who had a few, more or less stable, clients/friends from whom they not always expected or accepted cash payment. Relations between men and women in these cases were not confined to the secluded space of the women's rooms and implied more than the selling of sexual services to a small and well-known clientele. These women had a social relationship with their male clients which took place in the wider space of neighbourhood bars, the bioscope[89] or even the races. The camaraderie of sorts that these relationships implied could also slide into far more complicated situations when greed or vice intervened.

In 1914, John McCurry, a 50-year-old rigger of Irish descent, was murdered in Saville House, a hotel of ill repute on the corner of Fraser and Commissioner Streets in downtown Johannesburg. The events surrounding his death and the persons directly or indirectly involved in it illustrate some of the complex social interactions that took place in Johannesburg's white working class neighbourhoods. The testimonies given during the inquest provide a description of places and relationships in the city that indicate that as central as bars were for male working class culture in Johannesburg, they were not the exclusive domain of working men.[90]

John McCurry was married with two daughters. He and his family lived at 2 West Avenue, Village Deep. Three days before her husband's death in April Mrs McCurry and her daughters left town for Heidelberg on the far east Rand where McCurry planned to join them. McCurry and his friend and fellow mineworker, William Hadley, took the family to the railway station but contrary to the family plans, McCurry never got to Heidelberg and neither did he answer his wife's letters. He died in Johannesburg on 17 April 1914 of an overdose of morphine administered by mouth.

Mrs McCurry left Johannesburg without knowing that her husband had been retrenched from his position as a rigger at the Village Deep Gold Mine, apparently due to an argument with the foreman. On 15 April McCurry had met John Davidson, an old business acquaintance from J. Davidson and Sons, auctioneers, at his house. Davidson advanced him £35 against the security of the house furniture. The following day McCurry and Hadley packed the family belongings in the Village Deep house and John announced that he had found another job at the Premier Mine. Having moved out of the family house, that night McCurry slept at the Manchester Hotel in Commissioner Street whose owner, Henry Millett, was, like John, a member of the Wemmer Pan Sailing Club. According to Millett, McCurry expected to win a rowing competition on Saturday afternoon.

On 17 April, McCurry got £7 as his last wage payment from the Village Deep Mine. With the £35 advanced by Davidson and his weekly wage in his pocket he cycled in to town. He stopped at the Richmond Hotel and had a drink with the bookkeeper, Leopold Nathan, who lived in the hotel, and the proprietor of the establishment, who in the inquest recollected that they chatted about Ireland, and Johannesburg's old days. At the Richmond Hotel McCurry met, apparently not for the first time, Mabel Crocker. After having a drink with Mabel and the female friend who accompanied her McCurry left the hotel to take Mabel to Belcher Brothers, pawnbrokers, in Sauer Street, where he bought her a pair of earrings. Thus ingratiated with Mabel, he walked with her to the corner of Fraser and Commissioner Streets, to Saville House where Mabel lived. From Saville House McCurry went to the Stock Exchange Bar, just across the road, where he drank with Andrew C. McKinnan, a barman, before both men were joined by Wilfred Smith, a chemist from the Troye Pharmacy, in the Beaconsfield Buildings on Commissioner Street. The drinking spree did not finish at the Stock Exchange. McCurry and McKinnan went to the Ascot Bar, on the corner of Fraser and Commissioner Streets, from where McCurry returned to Saville House, this time to Mabel's room.

The inquest established that in Mabel's room a, by now, fairly drunk McCurry met Annie Gissing; Elizabeth von Plaster; Douglas Cay; Andrew Croll; and was also seen by Dora Boscher; Madge Wilson; Ada Connolly and Ellen de la Rosa. By the time Mabel Crocker left her room at Saville House the consensus was that McCurry was not just drunk, as she said, but drugged. He was found dead next morning lying on Mabel Crocker's bed, his trouser pockets turned inside out and no money on his person.

Each of the characters present in Mabel Crocker's room and their evidence during the inquest give a vignette of working class life in Johannesburg on the eve of World War I. Twenty-year-old Annie Gissing, also known as "Baby", was a waitress at the Empire Cafe, 144 Commissioner Street, and lived in a room at 4 von Wielligh Street. She knew Mabel Crocker fairly well and on Friday, 17 April she went to visit her at Saville House to fetch a skirt and a blouse that Mabel had promised her. Annie Gissing was apparently born in Durban and had been in Johannesburg for 18 months. She was friendly with an unemployed rigger from the Premier Mine named Andrew Croll who shared a room on 45 Marshall Street with a fellow worker from Turf Mine, Jack Tiserary. Apparently the men not only shared the room but from time to time they also shared Annie Gissing.

Elizabeth Von Plaster was a widow living with Fred Smith and her three sons, aged 18, 15 and 10 years respectively, at 1 Simmonds Street. Mrs von Plaster's eldest son, an electrician, was the only employed member of the family. The relationship between Mrs. von Plaster and Mabel was surely friendly enough since the reason why Mrs. Von plaster was there was to collect some money that she had lent to Mabel.

Douglas Cay, the other character present in Mabel's room, was an unemployed cabinet-maker who, like Croll and Tiserary, lived at 45 Marshall Street, and was being helped out by his sister and brother-in-law.

Dora Boscher and her husband were the caretakers of Saville House where Madge Wilson, Ellen de la Rosa and Ada Connolly lived. All four women gave evidence at the inquest and were more or less familiar with all the men gathered in Mabel's room the day of McCurry's death and certainly knew each other fairly well.

When Mabel Crocker left her room at Saville House she went for a night out that took her and Fred Smith to Gambrinus Bar, 47 Commissioner Street, where they were joined by a Fritz Rinke. From there they took a cab to the Stadium, on the corner of Main and End Streets, stopping on the way at Douglas Bar, corner of Fox Street and Von Brandis Street, and then had a few more drinks on their way back. By midnight all of them were drunk and quite oblivious of the fate of John McCurry who was already dead in Saville House. Next morning Dora Boscher called in the police and the murder investigation started.

As a result of the inquest Mabel Crocker was tried for the murder of John McCurry. There is not much information about Mabel Crocker in the inquest. She was married, but her husband had either deserted her or left to live in another city. Most of her friends knew she was a morphine addict and that she went through good and bad financial spells, though she did not have any fixed occupation. It was acknowledged she was a prostitute of sorts.

This case shows that the type of prostitution practised by Mabel Crocker, Annie Gissing and, presumably, by some of the other women living at Saville House, was not restricted to their lodgings and that sexual services were not exchanged exclusively for money. But aside from the relationship between the prostitutes and these men, and between the prostitutes and the hotel keepers, to whom it seems Mabel had paid some money in order to take McCurry up to her room, the events of that week in April offer a glimpse into other aspects of working class social life.

Family relations were based on the camaraderie of the workplace as much as on the physical intimacy that came from living in the same neighbourhood. Sporting activities and business deals further cemented social acquaintance. The conversations of occasional drinking pals had a common reference point in the shared experience of the city's history and, sometimes, the memories of home, Ireland in this case. The women involved in the tragedy also shared different levels of familiarity and solidarity. They lent each other money and clothes, they knew of the unemployment of each other's husbands and lovers, they advised each other on health matters and they sought out each other's company. Working class social life in Johannesburg often developed in overlapping circles in which workplace, trade, neighbourhood, clubs, bars and bioscope intersected to provide a space for communication and fraternal and superficial links between the employed and unemployed, men and women, proletarians and some members of the demi-monde.

Social interaction and familiarity with the city as a physical space was not confined to the adult population of these neighbourhoods. Neither was the danger and the treachery exclusive to the adult world. Working class children moved around town quite freely. For those who went to school, freedom and knowledge of the space was mostly restricted to their neighbourhood. The walk back from school was often marked by stops at the neighbourhood Chinese shop to buy fruit or sweets. For those who could not attend school the degree of freedom was larger as they were catapulted into the adult world of work at an early age. In 1909 the Committee of the Witwatersrand Central School Board established that 850 boys and 850 girls aged 13 left school to join the ranks of the wage earners. It was estimated that about 500 boys annually became "recruits of the unskilled portion of the population".[91] Their experience and knowledge of the city was quite different from that of their peers and this was seen as a serious social problem by the churches, charitable associations and the government. Witnesses before the Indigency Commission (1906-8) underlined the corrosive influence of street life on the children of the working class:

> These children have grown up in a house where there is no order and they go into the streets and sell newspapers and so on. There are more children sinking into degradation in Johannesburg than we know of for that reason. They go to the market and they steal as much as they can get hold of there. They sell newspapers in the streets with all the evils connected with it. These little boys club together.[92]

The most alarming part of it was, according to the Chief Magistrate of the Witwatersrand, that:

> Small native boys in towns are fraternising with European youngsters and looking upon themselves as youthful Dick Turpins doing all sorts of horrible things and in some cases we have instances of these youngsters assaulting white girls of nine and ten years of age, attempting rape and things of that sort.[93]

Children did not need to be part of a criminal gang to know the city, or their neighbourhoods. They knew which houses were empty, who lived where, who owned the shops, and they recognized the faces of people working or living in their neighbourhoods. In 1902 there was a case of rape of a minor that shows some of the dangers that city life afforded children. On 22 January 1902, nine-years-old Sophy Devine was raped by William Waterboer, a coloured man, on her way back from school in Fordsburg. She had often seen her assailant in the neighbourhood. Sophy was enticed into accepting some sweets bought at the local Chinese shop and accompanied Waterboer to have a look at an empty house that, according to her own testimony, aroused curiosity amongst the neighbourhood's children because it was owned by "a woman who speaks funny". At four in the afternoon Sophy Devine was raped just around the corner from her home in Burghersdorp. Scared and no doubt ashamed about what had happened, the child did not confide in her mother until the next day when she was taken to the District Surgeon for a medical examination. The testimony of the family maid, who also knew Waterboer by sight, enabled Sophy's father to catch the man and bring him to the police station in Fordsburg. Waterboer was tried and found guilty of rape.[94]

Aside from serious and hideous crimes such as rape and murder there were other offences that, although minor, tell more about social life in Johannesburg than about its criminality. Some of these misdemeanours took place in the ubiquitous bars that became the stage where tension and greed were openly manifested. Sometimes personal animosity, prejudice or sheer frustration combined with alcohol caused full-blown fights and excited and drunken patrons ended up in a display of manly skills only interrupted by the arrival of the police.[95] Fights and breaking of the public order were, according to police reports, fairly common occurrences in Johannesburg.

Other forms of petty crime also took place in the city's bars. The miners' custom of coming to town on payday to "drink their cheques", or at least part of them, was the pickpockets' and thieves' occasion to do their job. Drunken miners were easy prey for the town crooks. As Major Mavrogordato put it in 1912:

> When you are acquainted with the details of ordinary life in Johannesburg, it comes quite as a matter of course. There are hundreds of white people there who lived by robbing whites. It is quite a common thing on Saturday night for the white miners to come into town. The stiffs, as we call them, are out there to make a living for next week. They enter into the bars, pick up their customers, possibly stand them a drink, drugged them and rob them, and then they have got enough money to carry on to the next Saturday.[96]

There was another type of crime against property that had workers as its target: the theft of bicycles. In 1907 the police registered 1,738 bicycles stolen, valued at £15,824. If we take into account the importance of this means of transport to the working class, it is easy to understand that the loss of bicycles was more serious for workmen than the actual monetary value involved.[97] Mavrogordato's report did not mention whether bicycle theft was a well organized operation, but even allowing for this possibility, court cases suggest that it might have been an individual "criminal" enterprise aided by the negligence of the public, used to leaving their bicycles about at the entrance of bars and shops in town.

Conclusion

The fluctuations in the Rand economy that took place between 1890 and 1922, as well as its structural problems, affected white workers in different ways according to their skills, income, and the composition of their families. When bad times hit, men and women developed survival strategies that ranged from putting down the breadwinner's name on the lists of the Inspector of White Labour's Office to looking for the help offered by charitable organizations to turning to crime.

Between 1890 and 1922 working class neighbourhoods were fairly multiracial and, although by the 1910s local authorities started discussing racial segregation in the city, white, black, coloured and Chinese people in Johannesburg were in close proximity and interacted quite freely. The multiracial character of these neighbourhoods had two main consequences. On the one hand, it became a constant concern for the ruling class, particularly when, after the grant of Responsible Government to the Transvaal in 1907 and the constitution of the Union of South Africa in 1910, political parties competed for the vote of the working class and poor whites. On the other hand, it generated alternatives to unemployment, mostly in the fringes of criminality, that also defied the colonial racial hierarchy.

Some features of white working class life during this period emerged with particular strength. Marriage was but one stage in the process of settlement of white workers in Johannesburg. The way in which families were formed was crucial to the development of white working class social networks. While the newness of the colonial society was a powerful reason for Afrikaner and English working men and women to step over ethnic boundaries at the time of choosing partners and godparents, life in the city also brought people together. Workplace, trade, neighbourhood, and men's as well as women's relationships had a role in fostering closer links between families and frequently they were also instrumental in the establishment of less formalized relationships.

Far from being limited to the workplace, class experience and culture were actively created in the social and physical space of the neighbourhoods. Working class daily life involved men, women and children, single and married people, the employed and unemployed, in a social continuum that included the workplace, the street where they lived, the bars, the churches and the schools they attended.

Between 1890 and 1922 Johannesburg's white working class population slowly developed a sense of community deeply embedded in their class experience which in 1922 found some political expression in the Rand Revolt.

Notes

1. Thompson, E.P., *The Making of the English Working Class* (Harmondsworth 1968), p. 13. Hereafter, *The Making*.
2. Thompson, E.P., *The Making*, pp. 9-10.
3. Buchan, J., *The African Colony: Studies in the Reconstruction* (London 1902), pp. 311-12.
4. Markham, V.H., *South Africa: Past and Present* (London 1900), pp. 114-15. Hereafter *South Africa*.
5. Leyds, G. A., *History of Johannesburg* (Johannesburg 1964), p. 30.
6. Van Onselen, C., *Studies in the Social and Economic History of the Witwatersrand, 1886-1914* (Johannesburg 1982), volume 1, *New Babylon*, 'The World the Mine Owners Made: Social Themes in the Economic Transformation of the Witwatersrand, 1886-1914', p. 2. Hereafter 'The World the Mine Owners Made'.
7. Markham, V.H, *South Africa*, p. 365.
8. Transvaal Archives Depot (TAD) Mayor of Johannesburg (MJB) 4/2/35, 1901. Report of the Medical Officer of Health on Fordsburg's water supply.
9. *Evidence of the Johannesburg Insanitary Area Improvement Scheme Commission of Enquiry, 1902-1903*, Evidence of Dr. R. Mackenzie, paras. 3511-3512. Hereafter *Evidence Insanitary Area*.
10. *Evidence Insanitary Area*, Evidence of Dr. C. Porter, paras. 866-867.
11. "A collection of low class, poor and unsightly dwellings. They are built of the very cheapest materials and the houses are dumped down promiscuously as if the owners had carried them on their backs and dropped them down when they felt tired. The streets are irregular,

[12] (TAD) (MJB) 1/1/3, 1903. *Minutes of the Johannesburg Town Council*, 25 March 1903. Interim Report of the Medical Officer of Health (M.O.H.) on enteric fever in the Jeppestown District.

[13] (TAD) (MJB) 5/1. *Medical Officer of Health Report 31st July 1902 to 30th June 1903*, p. 27.

[14] (TAD) (MJB) 5/1. *Medical Officer of Health Report 31st July 1902 to 30th June 1903*, p. 27.

[15] According to Charles Porter's report, "It is predisposed to by devitalizing influences of any kind such as irregularities and excesses of life, insanitary environment, overcrowding, and air pollution, as well as by inferior and insufficient food." (TAD) (MJB) 5/1. *Medical Officer of Health Report 31st July 1902 to 30th June 1903*, p. 26.

[16] Silicosis is an incurable and often fatal occupational disease caused by prolonged exposure to dust containing microscopic silica particles. The disease has two variants, chronic silicosis and accelerated silicosis. While chronic silicosis was somehow taken for granted as an occupational hazard by both miners and government in Britain, the accelerated silicosis that manifested itself in the miners working on the Witwatersrand and in Cornwall constituted a dramatically serious health risk, particularly amongst rock drillers. In 1902 it was found that accelerated silicosis was prevalent amongst nearly one-quarter of the Rand's white underground workforce. Katz, E., *The White Death: Silicosis on the Witwatersrand Mines, 1886-1910* (Johannesburg 1994), pp. 1-4. Hereafter *The White Death*.

[17] "In the course of my evening strolls I made the acquaintance of a number of more or less interesting scoundrels of both sexes and of all colours and nationalities. Most of these people live in veritable warrens of galvanized iron. Narrow lanes between rows of low-roofed rooms thread through blocks comprising several building lots. In one comparatively small slum warren I found Europeans of various nationalities, Indians, Chinese, Arabs, Japanese, kaffirs and miscellaneous coloured people, men, women and children seem to be mixed promiscuously", Scully, W., *The Ridge of the White Waters* (London 1912), p. 311. Hereafter *The Ridge of the White Waters*.

[18] (TAD), Colonial Secretary (CS) 316/5851/03. Combined Circulars on Canada, Australia and the South African Colonies issued by the Emigrants' Information Office, Westminster, United Kingdom, 1903.

[19] *Industrial Commission of Enquiry*, 1897, Evidence of A. Buchan Fyfe, pp. 300-3.

[20] *Industrial Commission of Enquiry*, 1897, Evidence of R. Barrow, pp. 172-6. On trade unions complaints about the high cost of living before and immediately after the South African War see Katz, E., *A Trade Union Aristocracy: A History of White Workers in the Transvaal and the General Strike of 1913* (Johannesburg 1976), pp. 16, 52 and 63. Hereafter *A Trade Union Aristocracy*.

[21] *Standard and Diggers' News*, 26 May 1896; *The Star*, 19 May 1897; 14 July 1898; 27 January 1899.

[22] *The Star*, 24 July 1897, 'Poor Benedict!'.

[23] Transvaal Archives Depot (TAD) (CS) 4/401/1901. Report from the Office of the Military Governor. Signed Colonel Mackenzie.

[24] *The Star*, 2 June 1902, 'Peace at Last'.

[25] *Johannesburg Housing Commission, 1903*, Second Day of Sitting 31 July 1903. Hereafter *Johannesburg Housing*.

[26] "In most cases the children have to be taken from school at a tender age and almost before they learned to read and write so that they may become bread-winners and help keeping the home together", *Johannesburg Housing*, Evidence of Rev. S.J. Hamilton, 31 July 1903.

27 The Vagrant, *The Star*, July 1903.
28 *Johannesburg Housing*, para. 1092.
29 "I know where there are 5 or 6 families living in Fordsburg on one stand of 200x100, and in the place where I live there is a married woman with a couple of rooms, no fireplace, and she has to do all her cooking in the outside over the fire in an old pan with holes knocked in it and that is only one instance of many." *Johannesburg Housing*, Evidence of H. Middleton, para. 1055.
30 *The Star*, 3 April 1906.
31 (TAD) Transvaal Police (TP) 91- 21/158 1908. Letter from Sub-Inspector of Pretoria Police to the Secretary to the Commissioner of Police, 18 August 1908.
32 *Evidence of the Transvaal Indigency Commission, 1906-1908* (T.G. 11-08), Evidence of Dr. J.J. Boyd, Municipal Officer of Health, Pretoria, para. 1500. Hereafter *Evidence Indigency Commission*.
33 *Evidence Indigency Commission*, Evidence of F.H. Hodgkinson, p. 67.
34 *Report of the Transvaal Indigency Commission* (T.G. 13-08), para. 159-160. Hereafter *Report Indigency Commission*.
35 *Report Indigency Commission*, para. 39.
36 Pratt, A., *The Real South Africa* (London 1913), p. 150.
37 "The sudden transition from splendour to squalor on the western side of the city is very striking. The tract opposite to the Ferreira Mine area appears to be inhabited almost exclusively by European foreigners of the poorer class and coloured people. The houses are small and badly overcrowded. There are many shops; one wonders how on earth they can all be made to pay. Treading slightly northward one reaches Fordsburg, a wilderness of mean streets. This township is much affected by Dutch people of the poorer class. Amongst these, so I am informed, a great deal of demoralisation exists. Many of their children engage in the illicit liquor traffic." Scully, W.C., *The Ridge of the White Waters*, pp. 213-14.
38 *Economic Commission, 1914* (U.G. 12-1914), para. 24. Hereafter *Economic Commission*.
39 *Economic Commission*, para. 48.
40 Van Onselen, C., *Studies in the Social and Economic History of the Witwatersrand*, volume 1, *New Babylon*; volume 2, *New Nineveh* (Johannesburg 1982).
41 Particularly amongst the first generation of British miners that came to the Witwatersrand regional origins had great importance in fostering strong solidarity in the workplace as well as a sense of cultural identity. The latter was especially evident in the creation of the Cornish and Caledonian societies in Johannesburg in the early 1890s. On the importance of this type of identity amongst white miners see, Bozzoli, B., *The Political Nature of a Ruling Class: Capital and Ideology in South Africa, 1890-1933* (London 1981), pp. 39; pp. 81-3. Katz, E., *The White Death*, pp. 64-6 and p. 81.
42 Data Base J1. Record 2733 Donovan, John and Alice.
43 Similar situations can be observed in Record 96 Duke, Robinson and Martha who lived in Roodeport and Record 504 Taylor, George and Catherine who lived in Rietfontein.
44 Another paradigmatic case was that of Walter and Johanna Hobbs and James and Minnie Bennett. Both Walter and James were bakers and both lived in Fordsburg. In 1906 when Walter and Johanna had their first child baptized, James Bennett was chosen as godparent. Data Base J1. Record 64 Hobbs, Walter and Johanna; Record 32 Bennett, James and Minnie.
45 Data Base J1. Record 1 Kirby, William and Elizabeth.
46 Data Base J1. Record 1909 van Niekerk, Stefanus and Phoebe.
47 Data Base J1. Record 185 Bentley, Edward and Margaret.

[48] Data Base J1. Record 672 Fitzgerald, Thomas and Sarah.
[49] Data Base J1. Record 2154 Truter, John and Maria.
[50] Data Base J1. Record 10 Becker, George and Letitia.
[51] Data Base J1. Record 1476 Johnson, Henry and Ada.
[52] Data Base J1. Record 27 Sharp, James and Annie.
[53] Krikler, J., 'Women, Violence and the Rand Revolt of 1922', *Journal of Southern African Studies*, 22, 3, 1996, pp. 349-72.
[54] *Evidence Indigency Commission*, Evidence of Lieut. Col. Mackey O'Brian, Acting Commissioner of Police of Johannesburg, para. 1445-1451.
[55] Van Onselen, C., 'The Main Reef Road', pp. 138-44.
[56] For a detailed account of the 1913 strike see Katz, E., *A Trade Union Aristocracy*, pp. 381-429. On the involvement of women and children see especially, p. 403 and p. 409.
[57] The Simons's analysis of the 1913 strike has pointed out the growing solidarity between English and Afrikaner workers: "Afrikaner miners, of whom some had entered the industry as strike-breakers in 1907, loyally supported the strike. The rapidity with which they 'developed a class sentiment', noted Campbell and Munro, was one of its noteworthy features. Labour leaders widened their horizon to take in the prospect of a rapprochement with Afrikaner nationalism. The *Worker* discovered that the 'Dutch temperament' had a 'remarkable leaven of what really approaches very close to Socialistic ideas'." Simons, H.J. and Simons, R.E., *Class and Colour in South Africa, 1850-1950* (Harmondsworth 1969), p. 159.
[58] White, J., *Rothschild Buildings: Life in an East End Tenement Block, 1887-1920* (London 1980).
[59] Chinese shops were very popular amongst the white working class because they sold goods cheaply, in small quantities and were prepared to offer credit. See Yap, M. and Man, D.L., *Colour, Confusion and Concessions: The History of the Chinese in South Africa* (Hong Kong 1996), pp. 82-3.
[60] Van Onselen, C. 'Randlords and Rotgut, 1886-1903', volume 1, *New Babylon*, p. 52. Hereafter 'Randlords and Rotgut'.
[61] Van Onselen, C., 'Randlords and Rotgut', p. 89.
[62] (TAD) (CS) 15/1774, 1901. Letter from the President of the Transvaal Liquor Commission to the Secretary to Transvaal Administration, 21 May 1901.
[63] (TAD) (CS) 28/ 3699/1901. Letter from Rev. John Darragh to Joseph Chamberlain, Secretary of State for the Colonies, 17 June 1901; Shall the Government become the Liquor Seller of the Transvaal? Reuter's telegram from Pretoria dated 30 April appeared in the *Cape Times*, signed by T.L. Schreiner, 12 June 1901, manuscript. (CS) 72/212/1902 Petition from Johannesburg's women to Lord Alfred Milner, 28 February 1902.
[64] The liquor industry had been flourishing in the Transvaal from the early 1890s. By 1896, nevertheless, the unruly power of the liquor syndicates, acts of violence by drunken African men and, most importantly, the fact that alcohol consumption undermined the efficiency of African workers in the mines combined to create public concern about the liquor industry. On the response of Kruger's government to these problems see van Onselen, C., 'Randlords and Rotgut', pp. 58-67.
[65] The *Longland's Transvaal Directory* for 1903 recorded 40 merchants and importers of wines and spirits in Johannesburg.
[66] (TAD) Magistrate of Johannesburg (LJB), 754-1901. Rex vs C. J. Lienbenberg; LJB 722-1901 Rex vs N. Mack alias Kitchener.
[67] *Evidence Indigency Commission*, Evidence of Lieut. Col. Mackey O'Brian, Acting Commissioner of Police, Johannesburg, para. 1437 and paras. 1445-1451. Also Evidence of S.J. Halford, Editor of 'South African Building News and Contractors', paras. 299-304 and p. 9.

68 (TAD) Law Department (LD) 1520 AG 4175/07. Report of the Criminal Investigations Department, signed T.E. Mavrogordato, 1907.
69 "Among illicit dealers are to be found a large population of indigent whites, largely South African born, who are driven by poverty to make a living by such means." *Report of the Commission of Enquiry into Assaults on Women*, 1913, para. 57.
70 *Report of the Inspector of White Labour, Mines Department Annual Report. Part IV. White Labour Department, 1911* (U.G. 51-1912), p. 1.
71 *Select Committee on European Employment and Labour Conditions, 1913* (S.C. 9-13), para. 4850. See also Evidence of J. de Villiers-Roos, para. 4856; Evidence of H. Sluyter, para. 4744.
72 South African Archives Bureau (SAB) K. 373, Assaults on Women, Evidence of Major T.E. Mavrogordato, October 25 1912.
73 Assaults on Women, Evidence of Major T.E. Mavrogordato, October 25 1912.
74 "(The chief offenders) keep in the background and employ poor whites in the active portion of the business. It is said that the principals maintain the families of their unfortunate tools when the latter are detected." *Report of the Commission of Enquiry into Assaults on Women*, para. 57.
75 *Evidence Indigency Commission*, Evidence of Sir W. St John Carr, Rand Aid Association, paras. 89-91; Evidence of J. Hale, President Unemployed Association, paras. 5720-5722; and Evidence of Lieut. Col. Mackey O'Brian, Acting Commissioner of Police, Johannesburg, pp. 62-63. *Select Committee on European Employment*, Evidence of Col. T.G. Truter, Commissioner of the South African Police, para.1232, para. 1253 and para. 1306.
76 Scully, W.C., *The Ridge of the White Waters*, pp. 208-9.
77 Van Onselen, C., 'Prostitutes and Proletarians, 1886-1914', volume 1, *New Babylon*, pp. 107-8. Hereafter 'Prostitutes and Proletarians'.
78 Van Onselen, C., 'Prostitutes and Proletarians', pp. 112-34.
79 Van Onselen, C., 'Prostitutes and Proletarians', pp. 139-43.
80 *Evidence Indigency Commission*, Evidence of Dr. T. Gilchrist, District Surgeon, Fordsburg, paras. 5702-5704.
81 White, L., *The Comforts of Home: Prostitution in Colonial Nairobi* (Chicago 1990), p. 8.
82 "Many white people will refuse to do certain kind of work altogether until they are driven to it by starvation. A conspicuous instance of this aversion occurs in the case of domestic service. Every witness whom we have interrogated has testified to the strength of the feeling amongst all classes of the South African born white population against going into domestic service." *Report Indigency Commission*, para. 36. A full discussion of the topic of manual work can be found in the *Select Committee on European Employment*, Evidence of Rev. B.P.J. Marchand, Knysna, paras. 627-749.
83 *Evidence Indigency Commission*, Evidence of Rev. D. Theron, paras.1176-1178.
84 *Select Committee on European Employment*, Evidence of Colonel T.G. Truter, Commissioner of the South African Police, paras. 1327-1328. In 1914 there were 40 Chinese laundries in Johannesburg. See, Yap, M. and Man, D.L., *Colour, Confusion and Concessions*, p. 199; and van Onselen, C., '*AmaWasha*: The Zulu Washerman's Guild of the Witwatersrand, 1890-1914', volume 2, *New Nineveh*, pp. 74-110.
85 *Select Committee on European Employment*, Evidence of Col. T.G. Truter, para. 1281.
86 "The ease with which husbands can leave their wives often induces them in times of depression to seek fresh fields leaving their wives and families dependent on charity for their support. We are anxious to see laws introduced for the affiliation of illegitimate children. Many a young woman sinks into a life of immorality owing to the great difficulty

of alone bearing the burden of supporting illegitimate children." *Evidence Indigency Commission*, Statement of the Loyal Women's League, p. 59.
87 *Select Committee on European Employment*, Evidence of P. Ross-Frames, Member of the Commission into Assaults on Women, para. 1074.
88 *Report Assaults on Women*, para. 55.
89 The word bioscope was incorporated into South African English as a synonym for cinema in 1900. By 1914 there were 19 bioscopes in Johannesburg and they constituted a major attraction for people's entertainment. *United Transvaal Directory*, 1914.
90 (TAD) (LJB) Criminal Cases 1915-1921. Inquest into the Circumstances of the Death of John McCurry, 1914.
91 Quoted in *Report of the Small Holdings Commission, 1912* (U.G. 51-13), p. 9.
92 *Evidence Indigency Commission*, Evidence of Rev. D. Theron, paras. 1193-1194.
93 *Evidence Indigency Commission*, Evidence of L. L. Playford, Chief Magistrate of Johannesburg, para. 8342.
94 The particular understanding of the magistrate as to what rape meant granted Waterboer a comparatively lenient sentence "due to the fact that no permanent injury was done to the child". (TAD) Registrar Special Criminal Court Johannesburg (SCJ) vol. 5 A2/2 133-02 Rex vs W. Waterboer.
95 (TAD) (SCJ) vol. 4, A2/2 8/1902 Rex vs J. Schrieber.
96 Assaults on Women, Evidence of T. E. Mavrogordato, Friday 21 October 1912.
97 Advertisements like this were very common in Johannesburg's newspapers: BSA and Goldfields Bicycle Club: Payments 10s a week. Club runs 25 weeks. One machine draw each week. 100 members each club. *The Star*, 1 April 1902.

Chapter 6

The Ideological Construction of the Poor White Problem, 1890-1922

Introduction

Poverty amongst the lower strata of the white population, both urban and rural, had been a fairly well known social phenomenon in the Cape of Good Hope from at least the eighteenth century.[1] By the beginning of the twentieth century, partially as a consequence of the socio-economic transformations brought about by the discovery of gold in the Transvaal, poverty amongst the white population became a specific social problem: poor whiteism. The nature, extent and definition of the poor white problem, which had its roots in the racial division of labour predominant in the colonies, was far from constant. Between the appointment of the Transvaal Indigency Commission in 1906 and that of the Unemployment Commission in 1920, the discourse on poor whites expressed different combinations of moral, social and political preoccupations on the part of the state and the ruling classes. While in the context of the 1906-8 recession it was necessary to understand who was poor because of unemployment and who because of unemployability, by 1920 the interest in poor whites was eminently political. However, what connects the understanding of poor whites in the first decade of the 1900s with that of the early 1920s is the need to know and explain poor whiteism as an aberration in the social evolution of the colony.

In this sense an analysis of the poor white problem cannot be separated from the history of racism in South Africa and its intellectual and ideological underpinnings. Because the discourse on poor whites created the ideological space to express racial anxieties that eminently defined the nature of South African colonial society,[2] it is necessary to unpack its genesis, its intersection with both definitions and perceptions of the working class, and with other social and moral discourses current at the time.

Between 1890 and 1922, official concern with poor whites generated a body of written information, mainly in the form of reports of commissions of enquiry and select committees that directly or indirectly dealt with different aspects of the poor white problem. The reports produced by each of these commissions and committees reflected the intellectual framework within which 'poor whiteism' was understood. But the reports were not only compilations of information; they were also meant to make policy recommendations to the government.

The use of commissions of enquiry in this double fact finding and policy formation function was characteristic of the workings of the British state in the first half of the nineteenth century when there was no fully formed civil service to deal with these processes and was imported into the colonies in the second half of the nineteenth century when the colonial state was still in the process of formation.[3] In the South African colonies, as much as in Britain, commissions of enquiry were far from being neutral fact-finding administrative devices. Indeed they had an important role in the construction, development and diffusion of particular discourses that both shaped reality and operated within the constraints imposed by reality.[4]

This chapter explores the construction of the discourse on poor whites between 1890 and 1922, particularly in relation to the poor white population of Johannesburg and its suburbs, and argues that until 1920, the construction of poor whiteism as a moral and ideological issue obscured the ruling class's capacity to perceive poor whites as a serious threat to the political stability of the state. Thus, this chapter looks into three related topics: the socio-economic conditions of the emergence of the discourse on poor whites; the development of the discourse on poor whites; and the tensions experienced by the state at the policy level in its attempt to find solutions to the poor white problem.

Economic Development and the Making of the Poor Whites in Greater Johannesburg, 1890-1922

The history of poor whites is intertwined with the process of proletarianization in the South African countryside and the rise of unskilled urban unemployment. Until the mid-1890s unemployment affected immigrant British skilled and semi-skilled workers thrown out of their jobs by the periodic slumps in the gold mining industry, who were compelled to seek temporary employment as barmen or waiters or, in some instances, to turn to petty crime. Afrikaner labourers with rural craft skills on the contrary avoided unemployment, at least for some time, through self-employment as brickmakers, cab drivers and transport riders.

The second half of the decade produced a dramatic change in this situation. Drought, locusts and rinderpest created acute distress in the Transvaal countryside and drove many *bywoners* from the land. The heyday of brickmaking and cab driving had passed and a new wave of Afrikaner poor drifting to the city swelled the ranks of the unemployed and the underemployed. Not only was organized charity and relief work insufficient to cope with unemployment during the second half of the 1890s, its very nature was also fundamentally inappropriate to deal with the families of the unemployed unskilled Afrikaner workers.[5]

And if as things were not bad enough at the end of the 1890s the South African War added destruction to natural disaster and the economic crisis. The war left the two Boer republics in the Free State and the Transvaal with a legacy of devastation and poverty in both the countryside and the towns. Once again distress caused the poor to flee to the towns in search of refuge and the possibility of a better life. Between 1901 and 1902 Johannesburg received the bulk of this population. But, regardless of the hopes of the returnees and the newcomers, the Rand economy had not yet recovered. By 1902 the low grade of the ore mined on the Witwatersrand was threatening the mining industry with a profitability crisis accentuated by a temporary shortage of cheap African labour, which, although effectively offset by the importation of indentured Chinese labourers, also suggested the employment of unskilled white men to do work usually done by black workers.[6]

By the end of 1901, poverty and unemployment became serious problems for the new administrators. The military authorities, and later the Milner administration (1902-5), recognized the need to organize different forms of relief for the urban population. The Refugee Aid Department and Johannesburg's nominated Town Council worked together during 1902 and 1903 to provide rations, clothing and relief work to the many ex-*burghers* who were making their way back to the city or were trying their luck in Johannesburg for the first time.[7]

Between 1901 and 1903 poverty, particularly urban poverty, was regarded as a consequence of the war, an impression reinforced by the letters asking for relief received at the office of the Colonial Secretary, George Fiddes.[8] In this context, it is hardly surprising that state aid, whether at local or central government level, had been thought of as a temporary measure. However, the war had actually intensified the general economic depression. By 1903 destitution and unemployment in Johannesburg had become more serious and enduring issues. In 1904, in a letter to the Rand Aid Association, Sir Arthur Lawley, the Lieutenant-Governor of the Transvaal, pointed out that marked economic fluctuations were characteristic of the Transvaal and that they were part of broader economic processes which the state could not and should not control.[9]

In 1903 the mining industry entered the terrain of organized charity through the establishment of the Rand Aid Association, an amalgamation of the state-run Refugee Aid Department and the Present Help League, founded in 1895 with the support of Lionel Phillips. This move not only signalled the mine owners' awareness of the potential dangers that white unemployment posed to the colonial state but also marked an alliance between the British administrators and the mine owners in addressing the problem of poverty on the Rand.[10]

By 1905 the newly created organization had had ample opportunity to deal with large-scale unemployment. A slump in the price of gold and the political and economic uncertainties surrounding the concession of Responsible Government to the Transvaal had created a full-scale recession. Unemployment affected both skilled and unskilled workers and the situation was so bad that Milner asked the British Colonial Office to temporarily discourage immigration to the Transvaal because the number of skilled artisans already in the country, waiting for an expansion of the labour market, exceeded the demand.[11]

All the work done by the Rand Aid Association to rally support from the mining houses, mainly in the form of employment for semi-skilled and unskilled white workers in the industry, was not enough to alleviate the problem. Lord Selborne, Milner's successor after 1905, readily responded to suggestions made by the elected Johannesburg Town Council and set up a commission of enquiry to investigate "the general and permanent conditions of indigency and its remedies".[12]

The Transvaal Indigency Commission of Enquiry met for the first time in November 1906. By 1908, when the commission presented its final report, the Transvaal had become a self-governing colony and Prime Minister Louis Botha and Colonial Secretary Jan Smuts were the leading politicians of the newly elected *Het Volk* government, a circumstance that partially explains why the report of this commission was not acted upon.

While the commission was still hearing evidence, mineworkers' discontent erupted in the 1907 strike. This strike, like the ones that followed it, had its roots in the vulnerability of the gold mining industry to cost increases. The fact that the price of gold was internationally fixed, that the ore mined was low grade and that capital costs were high, meant that the mining industry could maximize profits only by pressing costs down. Labour costs were reduced by modifying the labour process in such a way that skilled jobs usually performed by white workers were fragmented into semi-skilled jobs that could be done by African labourers supervized by whites.[13] The 1907 miners' strike started in May and lasted until July when the *Het Volk* used British troops to repress the strikers. The irony of the situation made Lionel Phillips comment to J. Wernher in London:

> The whole situation is really getting topsy-turvy; a Boer government calling out British troops to keep English miners in order while Dutchmen are replacing them in the mines. This must be good for the country anyhow as wages earned by such men remain here instead of being to a large extent sent to England; and the intercourse between Dutchmen and the mining population must also tend in the direction of eradicating racialism. [14]

Despite the fact that the strike aggravated unemployment, it also created an opportunity for the incorporation of growing numbers of unskilled Afrikaner workers into the mines. This development was followed with interest by the *Het Volk* government, which was especially concerned about the plight of its Afrikaner constituency. Whatever relief the governing party might have felt in this regard, unemployment in the Transvaal in general and in Johannesburg in particular was not any better. It soon became clear that under these circumstances finding relief for the unemployed was as necessary as monitoring the labour market.[15] These were precisely the functions of the Office of the Inspector of White Labour in September 1907. Administratively the office depended on the Secretary of Mines and the post became a statutory office in 1908 with the creation of the Department of Labour.[16] Information provided by the office indicated that a month after its creation the Inspector of White Labour had registered 406 unemployed males and that five months later the number had increased to 2,422. Although most of the men applying for jobs were classified under the category of 'general workers' in the records, the inclusion of 108 miners in the lists of the unemployed indicated that unskilled white men were facing serious competition from black workers on the mines.[17]

By March, 1908 the situation was so bad in most of the Witwatersrand municipalities that James Thompson, the Mayor of Johannesburg, together with the Mayors of Roodeport and Krugersdorp and representatives from the municipalities of Springs and Benoni, plus Lionel Phillips and the Inspector of White Labour constituted the Rand Unemployed Investigation Committee. This body, whose task was to provide work for the unemployed, registered applications for work and sent out applicants to the mines.[18] However, the work of the committee also focused on issues of social control, as suggested by their drawing up of lists of "lazy, undisciplined and intemperate workers".[19] In 1908 the obvious overlap between the functions of the Inspector of White Labour and the work of this committee suggested that until the creation of a labour bureau, the Office of the Inspector of White Labour should became a state department.[20]

While the Transvaal Colony's government was trying to cope with the undercurrents of social malaise which kept resurfacing obstinately, the broader political process in the four South African colonies was following a different course. Between October 1908 and May 1909 an Intercolonial Convention was held in Bloemfontein. Representatives of the four colonies gathered to discuss the unification of South Africa.[21] The creation of a national state implied the transformation of local politics into national politics, and, obviously, the transformation of local political parties into national ones. And a pre-condition for this often was the alliance of Afrikaner parties with English-speaking voters and politicians.[22] In this context of high political competition *Het Volk* attempts at solving unemployment were especially directed at a labour movement that, thoroughly alienated from the party after its handling of the 1907 miners' strike, thought that "Botha and Smuts were as capitalistic as Farrar".[23]

It took slightly more than a year for the South African Bill to be enacted in the British Parliament and then Botha formed a new government. The first national cabinet was composed of members of *Het Volk*, the Cape South African Party and *Oranje Unie*, created by James B. M. Hertzog.[24] In 1911 all three joined to create the South African Party but soon enough differences between Botha and Hertzog provoked the first split in the party. In January 1914 Hertzog created the National Party on a platform of South African self-sufficiency, dual-medium education and compulsory bilingualism in the public service. The international crisis of World War I accentuated the divisions between Hertzog and Botha/Smuts who leaned toward the pro British Unionist Party for support. This revived the anti-capitalist and anti-British feelings amongst the Afrikaner rank and file. Conflict in the government favoured the growing influence of the South African Labour Party and brought its leadership closer to Hertzog's National Party.

As these political developments were taking place the situation of the white unemployed at a national level showed no improvement. In 1913, the South African municipalities were unable to cope with the numbers of indigents and unemployed people in their cities and suggested that the matter should be in the hands of the central government.[25] Johannesburg, as the economic centre of the Union, seemed to have been receiving "all the poor of the country" who, together with its own poor, made the work of the Johannesburg Town Council rather difficult. Actually, in January it was recommended that, given the growth in the number of applicants for help, the town council should cease making grants in aid for charity.[26]

The House of Assembly took the matter in hand at the national level, appointing the Select Committee on European Employment and Labour Conditions to look into the extent of European unemployment throughout the Union. The committee was chaired by John X. Merriman, a member of the South African Party and a personal friend of Smuts, and counted amongst its members the leading Labour Party politician, F. H. P. Creswell. The report, presented in May 1913, added very little to what was already known about the causes of indigency and did not provide actual figures on the extent of poverty and unemployment in the country. In terms of its actual recommendations the *Report of the Select Committee*, like its predecessors, suggested the establishment of labour and agricultural colonies, and relief works such as irrigation and afforestation.[27]

It is noteworthy that the report thought it necessary to point to the "far from sympathetic" attitude of the mines towards the employment of unskilled white labour.[28] This, which implied a turnabout from the earlier attitude of the industry, has to be explained as a consequence of a profitability crisis that had been looming over the mining industry since the beginning of the 1910s. As the better grade ore had been mined out in the central Witwatersrand, many mines were making little or no profit. To counteract this, mining companies put pressure on their workers, both white and black, to increase productivity. By the 1910s the process of the fragmentation of skilled jobs was aided by accelerated proletarianization in the countryside which provided a constant supply of cheap African labour. To understand the full import of this, it is necessary to remember that while in 1907 the trigger of the strike had been workers' refusal to operate three instead of two drills, in 1913 it was a common occurrence that white miners supervised six to ten drilling machines.

How tense the situation was in the mines was shown towards the end of May 1913 when a minor issue at the New Kleinfontein Mine sparked other grievances. Workers demanded an eight-hour day bank-to-bank and the recognition of trade unions, which the mining companies refused. Negotiations failed and the strike began to spread. On July 4 workers voted on a general strike. By then 63 out of 67 mines on the Rand had stopped working and 18,000 men were on strike. The following day all mines had stopped working and the number of strikers had increased to 19,000. The government had proclaimed martial law on July 4 and a day later there were already five people dead. Louis Botha and Jan Smuts intervened directly in the conflict to negotiate a settlement on behalf of the mineowners that turned out poor results for the labour movement.[29]

The situation was tense not only in the mining industry. The retrenchment of railway workers at the end of 1913 showed the widening political distance between the Botha government and white workers. A general strike was declared in 1914. Once again the South African Party government proclaimed martial law and called in the Active Citizens Defence Force to control the workers. The government had not had time to fully evaluate the political consequences of its way of dealing with the strike when another sign of dissatisfaction, this time in the countryside, erupted in October 1914.[30] Interestingly, the rebellion of the rural Afrikaners was commanded by the same generals who had led the onslaught against white workers nine months before.

The results of the 1914 elections signalled white workers' and the general public's dissatisfaction with the way in which the South African Party dealt with both strikes and the rebellion. Not only did the elections show an unusually high level of participation (73 per cent as against 45.8 per cent in 1910)[31] but it also gave the Labour Party an important victory in the Transvaal, winning 23 out of 45 seats in the Provincial Council.

In terms of social and economic development the period 1913-18 was contradictory. On the one hand, industrial disturbances in 1913 and 1914 and the 1914 rebellion created a climate of economic insecurity that deepened unemployment. The 1913 strike caused widespread retrenchments on the mines. At the end of July 1914 there were 2,340 fewer men employed on the mines than in June 1913. The war itself saw a shedding of white labour on the mines at an average of 85 men per month.[32] Building operations, which had been improving constantly for four years, experienced a decline. In 1915 the estimated value of buildings approved for construction by the Transvaal Municipalities was more than £500,000 less than in 1914.[33] As the recovery of the mining industry in 1910 had attracted many workers to the Transvaal, the slump in the construction industry created an unusually high level of unemployment. On the other hand, the restrictions on international trade, imposed by the war in Europe, increased opportunities to develop local industries. This, combined with the fact that a large number of white workers had left the country as part of the Defence Force, made for a temporary upswing of the labour market for white workers.

Applications to the White Labour Bureau for all categories of work decreased between 1914 and 1916, as men left for the front, but so did the demand for workers and therefore the ability of the bureau to place workers.[34] The government's main concern was that once the men in the Defence Force were demobilized unemployment would worsen. In 1916 a report from the White Labour Superintendent pointed out that the public had been induced to take a certain measure of responsibility for the poor white problem and that this was perceived by the indigent classes themselves with the result that dissatisfaction amongst urban poor whites was gradually disappearing.[35]

Indications of diminished dissatisfaction, however, were not enough to let the matter rest and in 1917 for the first time there was a more decisive effort to quantify the number of poor whites nationally.[36]

Even were the efforts at quantifying the poor white problem not entirely successful due to budgetary constraints, the census, which was taken in the four provinces, consisted of a careful questionnaire, itself indicative of the way in which poor whiteism was defined in the late 1910s. From a quantitative perspective table 6.1 indicates the general results. In terms of geographical distribution, as expected the greatest concentration of poor whites was in the Transvaal and, within it, on the Witwatersrand.[37]

Table 6.1 Numbers of poor whites in the Union of South Africa, 1917

	HEADS	WITH FAMILIES
Extremely poor families	10,409	39,021
Poor families	16,605	67,497
Total	27,014	106,518

Interest in quantifying the poor white problem extended to the organizations dealing with it and to the forms of relief provided by them. During 1917 there was an attempt to co-ordinate the work of the institutions engaged in relief in Johannesburg, the Rand area and Pretoria and to establish how many people were receiving relief from them; their monthly expenditures; the class of people assisted; and the methods adopted for the distribution of relief.

Given the relation between cost of living, unemployment and indigency, the post war years were especially propitious for an increase in the numbers of poor whites nationwide. The cost of living had been increasing steadily since 1914 due to the inflation in international prices that followed the outbreak of World War I. The low wages received by white unskilled labourers, between 17s 6d and 25s per week, did not allow them to meet the high cost of accommodation and foodstuff.[38]

As for the mining industry, between 1913 and 1922 the rate of output of the gold mines fell by 1.9 per cent per annum.[39] This process was the result of a combination of three main economic factors: high cost of the materials and foodstuff, the shortage of African labour, and a shortage of white skilled and semi-skilled labour, which in turn raised the cost of white labour in the mines.[40] The decreasing margin of profits and dividends was felt most acutely on the low grade mines, those mines which were working at a profit of less than 2s per ton milled. By 1917 14 of 35 working mines on the Rand had fallen into this category. Two years later, in 1919, three low-grade mines had closed down and 11 more had fallen into that category.[41] Between mid-1919 and 1920 a temporary premium in the gold price helped to offset the fall in the profit margins, but the gold price started declining again in 1921. Thus by the end of that year the Chamber of Mines urgently needed to address two of the structural problems of the industry - rising costs and plummeting output - in order to weather the crisis.

In January 1917 white underground miners in the Van Ryn Deep mine at Boksburg came out spontaneously in a strike against the employment of black labour in semi-skilled work, showing the growing discontent amongst white mineworkers. The strike was solved rapidly as the government intervened, advising the company to withdraw the black workers, and promised an enquiry into the events. The enquiry, which was conducted by the South African Police, showed that amongst the Van Ryn Deep labour force there were 2,500 Afrikaners from the Orange Free State who had been laid off from the Koffiefontein mine.[42] Inspector J.M.L. Fulford, in charge of the investigation, suggested that the majority of these people were actually agriculturalists who had been forced to seek employment in the mines due to the failure of crops and drought. The Van Ryn Deep strike was a symptom of the tensions between workers and employers which had been developing in the industry during the war. Paramount amongst these was the fact that despite the agreement with trade union representations on the reservation of certain jobs for white workers, faced with a new profitability crisis in 1920-2, the Chamber of Mines was about to break the 1918 Status Quo Agreement.

Against this backdrop the South African Party appointed a new commission of enquiry into white unemployment with a brief to investigate and report on the extent and causes of unemployment; the best method of preventing the influx of white unskilled labourers into towns; the problems of white employment in the mines; and the possibilities of establishing an insurance scheme against unemployment.

The commission's report restated the seriousness of the poor white problem and proposed their resettlement on the land,[43] a view which reflected a generalized interest amongst political parties about Afrikaner rural and urban constituencies.

The South African Party had good reason to be concerned about workers' disaffection in general, and Afrikaner workers in particular. In 1913 and 1914 the strikes drew English-speaking working class votes to the South African Labour Party candidates in the Transvaal; Hertzog's National Party, on the other hand, capitalized on the nationalist discontent of the Afrikaner rural population that erupted in 1914, both in the Orange Free State and in the Transvaal, as well as on the frustration of urban railway workers. The main challenge for both parties was winning over the Afrikaner working class constituencies in Johannesburg which were still concentrated in the old working class neighbourhoods of the city like Vrededorp and Fordsburg.

Nationalistic-based parties had a better chance than Labour to capture the vote of the urbanized Afrikaner who had actually been incorporated into the mines since 1896. Although up to 1914 the Labour Party had managed to capture some of these new voters in the working class constituencies of Johannesburg, internal divisions in the party, between the pro-war, pro-British faction and the "war-on-war" faction, undermined the Labour Party's appeal to Afrikaner workers. The divisions in the party coincided with differences between socialist and non-socialist leaders, which were in turn accentuated by European political developments. The creation of the International Socialist League in 1915 and its incorporation into the newly formed Communist Party of South Africa in 1921 reflected the radicalization of working class politics during the war and post-war years. Yet, first the Socialist League and later the Communist Party found it difficult to compete for the Afrikaner workers' vote with a platform based on class rather than racial issues at a time when most workers felt their jobs threatened by the advance of African workers in the mines.[44]

The 1919 elections favoured Labour, and Hertzog's National Party won votes at the expense of the South African Party, which, however, were not enough to displace the South African Party from government since Smuts had become Prime Minister of the Union of South Africa. In December 1921 the Chamber of Mines announced the implementation of three measures aimed at solving the ongoing crisis: to lower the wages of the better paid miners; the abolition of the 1918 Status Quo Agreement; and the reorganization of underground work. The immediate and most palpable consequence of this was the retrenchment of 2,000 white workers. A strike ballot on 8 January 1922, gave overwhelming support for a strike. This marked the beginning of the Rand Revolt.

Knowledge of the Poor: The Ruling Class's and the State's Understanding of the Poor White Problem, 1906-1922

The Transvaal Indigency Commission of Enquiry was the first formalization of a discourse on poverty amongst whites. However, neither the ways in which colonial society dealt with poverty nor its production of a discourse on the matter were independent from the development of broader intellectual trends in Britain.

In the second half of the nineteenth century under the powerful influence of Darwin's theory of evolution, the emerging social sciences turned to biology in the hope of developing a science of the human condition that would encompass a knowledge of man's physiology and man's behaviour.[45] While Darwin's theories influenced the contemporary understanding of history, culture, race and society, the interest in determining laws of heredity and establishing the extent to which the social environment was a factor in evolution generated the development of theories of heredity. And both evolution and heredity informed social policy in divergent and contradictory ways as the proponents of *laissez-faire* as well as the supporters of social engineering used them to justify their positions.[46]

But it was the growing unemployment and social unrest of the 1880s that brought the "social problem" to the forefront of British political thought. In this context, Francis Galton's eugenics not only echoed the fears and pessimism about the future, characteristic of late nineteenth century Britain, but also suggested possible forms of social intervention. Galton maintained that what was perceived as the high birth rate amongst the lower classes was a threat to the evolutionary progress of the race. Thus, in order to raise the physical and mental status of the race it was necessary to control its reproduction.

None of these ideas were alien to the colonial world. On the contrary, Social Darwinism made rapid inroads in late nineteenth century South Africa. Two areas of concern concentrated the minds of English-speaking intellectuals in the colony: "racial" and cultural differences between Boers and Britons and what was called in the early twentieth century the "native question". These concerns, that were to find political and ideological expression in social policy and state-led investigations, also constituted an area of cultural interest in colonial circles. The creation of the South African Association for the Advancement of Science in 1903, the Fortnightly Club in 1906 and the Transvaal Native Affairs Society in 1908 give an idea of the importance that these issues, as well as the theories that helped in thinking of them, had for the colonial intellectuals and politicians.[47]

Social Darwinism, however, did not penetrate the discourse of the ruling classes or colonial society's common sense in an institutional manner. On the contrary, the language of Social Darwinism together with its metaphors was rapidly integrated into normal parlance and was routinely applied to the explanation of society from the nineteenth century onwards.[48]

The work of the commissions of enquiry appointed to deal with social issues directly or indirectly related to the poor white problem during the 1906-1920 period showed the pervasive influence of Social Darwinism in colonial discourse. This does not mean, however, that either the witnesses or the members of these commissions of enquiry were familiar with the technical aspects of the theories of heredity or evolution. It simply shows that Social Darwinism provided commissions of enquiry with "the kind of moral universe in which nature reflected society and vice-versa"[49] that fitted well with the moral anxieties in which white colonial society was immersed at the time.

After the South African War men like Lionel Curtis, Richard Feetham,[50] and Phillip Kerr,[51] who were part of the liberal professions that had been influential in the development of social thought and practices in Britain, became the social engineers in Milner's team, and their work influenced social thought in the colony beyond Milner's administration.

The Transvaal Indigency Commission was led by all three of them while its chairman, John W. Quinn, had been involved in the problems of Johannesburg's indigency since the constitution of the Rand Aid Association in 1903.

This commission did more than investigate the extent of indigency in the Transvaal. It established the existence of indigency as a question. And it did so through a process of classification and theorization aimed not only at explaining white poverty but at acting upon it. The commission named and classified indigents and organized a typology of the poor, distinguishing between rural and urban indigency. This typology did not use the Victorian concept of deserving and undeserving poor as it main classificatory criterion. Instead, the report recognized two broad classes of poor: those who experienced actual want of the necessaries of life and those who, having enough, were ignorant and lazy and "potentially" indigent. Poor whites were included amongst the former because their inability to perform skilled and semi-skilled and their incapacity to compete as unskilled labourers against the coloured races made them unemployable.[52]

Consistent with this view, the commissioners understood poverty as a social issue that could not be dealt with by focusing on the indigent classes alone.[53] The *Report of the Transvaal Indigency Commission* conceived poverty both as a symptom of a sick society and a sickness in itself, which therefore needed cure and prevention. The direction in which the tension between these two propositions was solved had fundamental policy consequences. If poverty were a problem of weak individuals and their lack of preparation (education) for rising in society, the solution lay with the individual and the guidance the state could give him or her.[54] But if poverty was a consequence of the historical organization of the colonial society, the solution involved the whole organism and not just the sick individual.[55]

The report grappled with these tensions through the elaboration of the much quoted theory of the "aristocratic relation" between white and black races.[56] This "aristocratic relation" was the origin of the poor whites' unwillingness to be engaged as unskilled labourers.[57] However, the actual difficulties faced by unskilled white labourers entering into the labour market were not only due to an ideology founded on racial superiority in a colonial context. There were powerful economic reasons undermining their incorporation into the labour market. The fact that native labour was cheaper made it preferable to more expensive and, generally, less efficient white labour. Moreover, when white workers were employed as unskilled labourers, the wages they earned were based on 'native' standards and were, therefore, too low to satisfy their needs.[58] This characteristic of the colonial labour market stood in contradiction with the expectations that English-speaking immigrants and the local Afrikaner population had in terms of their standard of living in the racially divided Transvaal.

The problems that derived from white workers' unwillingness to perform unskilled jobs were aggravated by the accelerated proletarianization of African labour and its use as cheap labour in all colonial industries, especially in the gold mines. The Transvaal Indigency mission saw in industrial expansion a way to create jobs for the less skilled white workers. Yet the commission was aware that the racial division of labour characteristic of the Transvaal's economy meant that industrial development would depend on the availability of cheap black migrant labour, which would in turn restrict the number of white workers any new industry would be ready to employ. Thus, in an argument that subsequent South African governments would have done well to listen to, the *Report of the Transvaal Indigency Commission* pointed out that:

> Further, as it is impossible to prevent the coloured worker by means of legislation from doing any skilled work for which he is qualified, it would undoubtedly lead to the contraction of the sphere of the white man's activities as the coloured man became more skilled. We are therefore opposed to any policy that would enable the country to draw upon an unlimited supply of coloured labour from outside South Africa on which to base its industrial expansion. Whether that labour was confined by legislation to unskilled labour and ultimately repatriated or not, the effect on the economic position of the white man would be the same. He would still remain a supervisor only. The pernicious theory that the line between white man and black man's work should coincide with the line between skilled and unskilled labour would continue to dominate the economic situation.[59]

This, however, was only one part of the problem. From a political perspective the most worrying consequence of African proletarianization, was that the more proletarianized African workers became the closer they got to the socio-economic position of white unskilled workers. The consequences of this homogenization, mainly the potential development of non-racial solidarity, needed to be counteracted ideologically. Thus, one of the fundamental problems dealt with by the Indigency Commission, and the investigations that followed it, was how to change the class position of the poor whites.

In 1908 the commission pointed to two methods of dealing with indigency: one aimed to prevent poverty through the management of its socio-economic causes; the other was aimed at "curing" existing indigency and was based on the principle of the moral and economic regeneration of the poor through education, temporary assistance and organized charitable relief. While the idea of regeneration and cure was informed by the biological treatment of the social and moral world, the actual methodologies of the cure stressed the Victorian conviction of the need to elevate charity from a sentimental feeling to a knowledge of the poor and what was best for them.[60]

In the South African context the moralization of the poor, which implied the reform every phase of working class life from infancy to old age, needed to make one further distinction between the indigent/poor whites and the unemployed.[61] Unemployment could be prevented by widening the area of employment for male white workers to include unskilled labour in the mines, the railways and road construction, and encouraging women to work in domestic service; by the encouragement of industrial activity once the depression was over; and by controlling immigration. The treatment of the indigent, on the other hand, began with the recognition of the characteristics or symptoms of this class. The commissioners established that white urban indigents tended to do casual work, live on money earned by their children and showed a strong proclivity towards criminal behaviour.[62] In order to remedy this situation it was necessary to make elementary education compulsory so as to keep white children off the streets and to prevent exploitative employment by their parents, as well as to develop technical education in elementary schools.[63] As for urban life, it was essential to remove certain features of the towns that were instrumental in the perpetuation of indigency and crime. Thus, it was necessary to watch the poorer quarters in town and to prevent the reproduction of "these squalid, unhealthy and demoralizing poor white settlements".[64]

Despite all the socio-economic explanations of poverty and their role in the construction of solutions, poverty was also seen as a pathology. Vagrants, loafers and the vicious were collectively considered a class of people at the final stage of demoralization and social degeneration. Criminalizing mendicity and locking beggars and vagrants in jail for short periods was no solution. It was agreed that these people needed to recover their capacity to work both physically and morally. The best method for this was long periods of hard labour during which these people became "the moral, physical and technical patients of the State".[65]

Social Darwinist metaphors, such as the "fall from the ranks of civilization",[66] went hand in hand with the conception of poverty as a social disease that needed appropriate treatment and the elaboration of a hierarchy of indigents that descended from the unemployed to the criminal. But whatever the hopes for a "cure" of indigency, it was fundamental to prevent its development through the control of the reproduction of the working class to avoid mental and physical hereditary diseases that were often the root of the problem.[67] Both Social Darwinism and eugenics operated in the colonial world along the lines of a racial hierarchy based on the assumption that down below this class of white indigents there was another group, i.e. blacks, who could never reach the white level of civilization.

What distinguished the Transvaal Indigency Commission was that it not only related the poor white problem to the characteristics of the colonial society, but that it saw poor whiteism largely as a rural phenomenon that eventually would reach the towns, but that was not engendered in the cities. This view of the problem helped to strengthen the link between poor whites and rural Afrikaners, and conditioned the solutions that the *Report of the Transvaal Indigency Commission* submitted to the government for its consideration: transformation of the rural economy and the rescue of the urban poor.[68]

The influx of white indigents from the countryside continued unabated between 1908 and 1912. By 1913 the growing number of poor whites in the cities, especially Johannesburg, the apparent failure of attempts at relief, and the increase of unemployment were again the subject of an official enquiry. The Select Committee on European Employment and Labour Conditions was appointed by the Union government in the context of a generalized moral panic over mounting crime and sexual assaults on women. At the time, the situation of poor whites was seen as a menace to the entire white race in South Africa:

> The importance of the question in South Africa arises from the fact that the European minority occupying, as it does, in relation to the non-European majority, the position of a dominant race, cannot allow a considerable number of its members to sink into apathetic indigency, and to fall below the level of the non-European worker. If they do, and if they manifest an indifference founded on the comfortable doctrine of

letting things find their economical level, sooner or later, notwithstanding all our material and intellectual advantages, our race is bound to perish in South Africa.[69]

In a climate of tough political competition for the vote of white workers it was not possible for the members of the select committee to endorse a *laissez-faire* approach to the poor white problem, especially when its outcome, because of the demographic realities of a colonial society, would undermine white dominance. With an Afrikaner constituency in mind, the select committee, like the Indigency Commission before it, insisted on the importance of agricultural development as a method of preventing poor whiteism.

The novelty was that, notwithstanding the need to find a way of preventing poor whiteism in the rural areas, the select committee focused its attention on the urban poor. It was the perceived decomposition of urban life, and perhaps a tacit recognition that white working class votes were becoming concentrated in urban areas, that made the problem of poor whites in towns a central issue in the evidence and report of this committee. Consistent with this, the committee developed further the identification between poor whites and Afrikaners.[70] This shift in the understanding of urban poverty has to be read against the interest that political parties, especially the Labour Party and Hertzog's National Party, were showing in co-opting the white working class electorate in Johannesburg and elsewhere along the reef. But it was also a reflection of the concern that at least some members of the South African Party had about poverty and workers' grievances.

Once again, readily available charity was singled out as first encouraging the emergence and prolonging the existence of an undesirable class. Although the presence of multiracial urban slums was not a novelty, in the context of the 1913 moral panic miscegenation, real and imagined, became a recurrent concern.[71]

The "misdirected pride" that prevented young white women from working as domestic servants, also mentioned in the Indigency Commission, was now seen more negatively since most of these women preferred to take up jobs in Chinese laundries and married Chinese men and lived in "appalling conditions" in the neighbourhoods of central Johannesburg and Fordsburg.[72]

The extent of the participation of poor whites in liquor trafficking seemed to confirm the criminal tendencies of this class. And the fact that some illicit liquor dealers not only supported the families of the white "runners" when they were in jail but that they also drew children into the traffic made the problem even less palatable.[73] All of this aggravated the perception of poor whites as lacking parental responsibility and having lost their moral sense at the same time that it confirmed the idea that life in slum areas was breaking up the family unit.

These issues came to the fore during the hearings of the Commission of Enquiry into Assaults on Women, appointed on 18 June 1912. The commission was chaired by M. de Villiers, who had been a criminal judge in the Orange Free State Supreme Court before the South African War and was an advocate at the time of the hearings. Amongst its members was General Christiaan R. de Wet, who later became a leader of the 1914 rebellion, and three women representing the two most important Afrikaner women associations in the country, the *Zuid Afrikaansche Vrouwen Federasie*, which operated in the Transvaal, and the *Afrikaansche Christelyke Vrouwen Vereeniging*, based in the Cape.

The commission regarded the existence of those white women prepared to have sexual intercourse with black men as an indication of moral perversion. According to the prevalent theories, moral perversion, which was a form of insanity, had its roots in inheritance and was bound to be reproduced in the cities. The medical opinion was that frequent intermarriage amongst poor whites had produced weak-minded people who, although technically responsible, had not developed their moral sense.[74] Poor whites' behaviour in the cities was not understood as a survival strategy for desperate men and women. Illicit activities, such as liquor selling to natives and prostitution, were seen, in the main, as indications of hereditary degeneration. Certain low status occupations, such as hawking by females[75] and the selling of flowers and newspapers by children[76] were perceived both as an indication of how low poor whites had sunk, and as potential avenues for further demoralization.

The commissioners, drawn largely from rural or small-town backgrounds themselves, viewed urban life as a seed-bed of crime and immorality in which the unemployed easily took root. If this was bad and dangerous in itself, it had a particularly pernicious influence on the black population who:

> From his contact with or observation of the white criminal classes and other experiences, the native's estimate of the European virtue has suffered, and from these experiences he probably forms an exaggerated and distorted idea of the vices of profligacy of the white man and especially of the frailty of the white woman.[77]

The demoralizing effect of poor white conduct on the black population was regarded as a social danger of even greater proportions. For what would the future of South Africa be if, as the commission would have put it, the ruling race could not command the respect of its subjects, if the well-constructed hierarchy of race and class was undermined by "the fallen classes of the white races"?

Eugenic thought explained the danger of reproducing hereditary weak traits that were related both to the lower classes' tendency to intermarry and their genetic characteristics. The idea that the environment was an important factor in the perpetuation problems of a hereditary nature accentuated the fear of urban slums. Finally, miscegenation, the practical negation of the social hierarchy sanctioned by scientific racism, was seen as the worst threat to the future of South Africa for it implied a degradation of the white race.[78]

Following this line of reasoning, F. H. P. Creswell, a member of the Select Committee on European Employment, a long-standing advocate of a white labour policy, warned the committee that the submerged European population in South Africa was "worse than the submerged European population in an European country".[79]

The Select Committee on European Unemployment and the Commission into Assaults on Women used the language of Social Darwinism to define the constitutive elements of the poor white problem. The shared language and preoccupations are hardly surprising for not only did the select committee and the commission of enquiry hear evidence from the same witnesses like, for instance Colonel T. G. Truter, Commissioner of the South African Police, but also at least one of the members of the commission, P. Ross-Frames, gave evidence before the select committee. Moreover, by 1913 the attempts to deal with poverty and unemployment and the involvement of private and public institutions in the matter had created a group of expert witnesses on the issue. This group drew on the members of the Rand Aid Association, the Salvation Army, and the medical profession, on women involved in associations such as *Zuid Afrikaansche Vrouwen Federasie* and *Afrikaansche Christelyke Vrouwen Vereeniging*,[80] and on the police, the church, state officials and politicians.

Nevertheless, despite all the concern and fear aroused by the poor white problem, neither the evidence and report of the select committee nor those of the commission of enquiry made explicit on the potentially dangerous effect of unemployment in political terms. While there was a clear perception of poor whites as a social and political danger to the state, in the sense that their very existence subverted the racial order on which South African society was based, there was no indication that the misery of the submerged classes could explode into political or social revolt.

Industrial and rural unrest in 1913 and 1914 and the results of the national election of 1914 showed that white workers were almost completely alienated from the governing South African Party. In 1915, probably influenced by his participation in the Select Committee on European Unemployment, John X. Merriman, a friend of Smuts' and member of the House of Assembly for the South African Party, let Smuts know his view on the recent events:

> I refer to the question of the Poor White. This question constitutes a great and growing evil - of the four really important questions before us it is by far - to my mind - the most important as its growth and persistence threatened the very foundations of our national existence. I need not enlarge on the magnitude of the disease - recent events both in the rebellion and the elections that followed, must have convinced even the dullest of us - and I hope neither of us is dull - of the dire possibilities that lie before us from this course.[81]

Despite the fact that at least some of the members of the government saw the warning signs, the outbreak of World War I somehow displaced the government's preoccupations. As social conflict subsided during the war years and unemployment receded temporarily, there were no more investigations into social issues related to the poor white problem until the end of World War I.

The post-World War I years brought about growing unemployment and a new profitability crisis in the mining industry. Politically the war produced important cleavages within the Labour Party that eventually gave rise to the organization of the International Socialist League as an independent party. The 1917 Bolshevik revolution seemed to justify the hopes of the more convinced and militant socialists on the Rand.

In 1920, the South African Party appointed yet another commission of enquiry into unemployment. The tone of the *Report of the Unemployment Commission*, published in 1921, was very different from that of its predecessors. It warned the government and the public in general that growing numbers of poor whites without hope of a better future in a world marked by social revolt were eminently dangerous to South African society at large because:

> Urged by specious propaganda they will in ignorance seek remedies which will prove to be merely aggravations of their trouble, but it will be difficult to restrain them. If, therefore, we wish to save them, and avoid possible disaster in the direction indicated we shall have to show them that we have something better to offer them, not only something

better than they have today, but something they can look forward to as a means to them and their families of living life upon a civilised scale.[82]

By 1921 it had become clear that poor whites making a living in illicit occupations and indigents had unemployment in common and that, aside from its alleged moral dimension, unemployment was an economic problem with potentially serious political consequences.

The socio-economic developments that took place between 1908 and 1913 created a shift in the definition of the poor white problem. While in 1908 the Indigency Commission understood the condition of poor whiteism as being largely rural in origin, in 1913, the Select Committee on European Employment and the Commission into Assaults on Women perceived poor whites mainly as a product of urban conditions. In 1913, poor whites became a social category that included urbanized men, women and children who did not have the appropriate skills to find employment and who, quite often, turned to a life of crime because of their lack of moral sense. This perception of the poor and unemployed was accompanied by a view of the cities, especially Johannesburg, as the sites where moral degradation, miscegenation and the social reproduction of poor whites took place.

In 1913 the poverty of poor whites was still seen as a moral problem while unemployment was held to be basically an economic problem which could be dealt with through relief measures. It was only in the post-war years that this view started changing. In 1921, at the time of the publication of the *Report of the Unemployment Commission*, poor whiteism had become an economic problem of ominous dimensions for the state and poor whites a social group whose political loyalty was unclear.

The State and the Poor White Problem: *Laissez-Faire* versus Social Engineering in the Transvaal, 1906-1922

Every step of the development of a discourse on poor whites was accompanied by discussions about the extent and nature of both the state and private sector interventions in alleviating or preventing poverty and unemployment. However, the issue became far more acute when economic crises accentuated unemployment. It is therefore unsurprising that the heights of the debate on state intervention had taken place in 1906-8, 1913 and 1920-2. Throughout the period two opposing views were at stake. One relied on market forces to solve unemployment. The other counted on the state's action both to prevent poverty and unemployment and to provide assistance to the unemployed. The arguments supporting both positions show that the state's involvement in the solution of poverty was faced with serious conceptual tensions and practical contradictions some of which were related to the changing perceptions and understanding of the poor white problem during this period.

Prior to 1906 churches, private organizations and the state had been involved in charity and unemployment relief without making any effective attempt at centralizing the work of the many organizations active on the Witwatersrand. The creation of the Rand Aid Association in 1903 was a move in this direction. The organizational reshuffle, however, did not take away the fact that there was great confusion about the boundaries and definition of poor relief. Thus, the delimitation of functions and tasks in relation to poverty alleviation was a recurrent topic in the discourse on the poor white problem between 1906 and 1920.

Like the commissions and committees that followed, the Transvaal Indigency Commission had, over and above its other terms of reference, to find out whose responsibility the alleviation of indigency was. Despite its socio-economic approach to the explanation of poverty and its sharp understanding of the influence of race in the labour market, the commission took a liberal approach to state intervention in these problems. In fact, the *Report of the Transvaal Indigency Commission* argued that free competition in modern industrial society implied that at times both capital and labour would be idle and no artificial provision of work could change this.[83]

The recommendations of the commission on the modality of the state's action were clearly against short-term interventions, such as labour colonies,[84] that, due to their very nature, did not attack the root causes of unemployment. In terms of charity work, the commission disapproved of state-based charity, whether this was understood as the distribution of temporary relief or as the moral rescue of the poor. The creation of a semi-public institution to centralize the distribution of charity was one of the Transvaal Indigency Commission's stronger recommendations.[85] In this institutional environment charity could become again a mechanism of social control based on the "scientific" observation of the poor.[86] This entailed the investigation of each case as well as follow-up investigations through visitation and supervision to avoid the negative effects of indiscriminate alms giving:

> Careful enquiry must be made by a competent person before assistance is given at all, and the case must be kept under constant supervision during the whole period that is being relieved. Efficient visitation is the key to success in the work of charity.[87]

Visitation not only helped to detect the existence of the poor and to classify them, it also operated simultaneously at two other levels. On the one hand, it contributed to the rescue of the poor by educating them in new and better habits of work and hygiene. On the other hand, and not less important for the state and the ruling classes, the receipt of charity developed a sense of subordination and gratitude amongst the poorer popular classes that was to neutralize deeper social dissatisfaction.

Despite the conceptual separation between the unemployed and the poor that the Transvaal Indigency Commission has so forcefully argued, both categories became subsumed under the proposed new central organization that was also to have the control of the labour bureau. This not only meant putting poverty and unemployment in the same category. It also restricted the action of the state to the provision of relief works during crises and the partial funding of charity.

The most important role assigned to the state in dealing with poverty was the provision of education, especially technical education. State intervention through education was, nevertheless, by definition directed to the new generation and not to the population already in distress. Compulsory education for white children had been introduced in the Transvaal in 1907. But the need to take children off the streets, which became more demanding after Union when the socialization between black and white children was seen as part of the process of miscegenation of poor whites,[88] implied more than simply putting children into school. Taking children off the streets was a way of punishing the parents and families who had allowed children to enter into the criminal classes as well as an opportunity for the state to reform those elements of the lower classes' culture and ideology that were contrary to the development of a disciplined white workforce.[89]

The concern with industrial education, however, was neither confined to the new generation of males nor was it an exclusive project of the state. On the contrary, organizations like *Afrikaansche Christelyke Vrouwen Vereeniging*, partially responding to the redefinition in the role of women within the Dutch Reformed Church, insisted on the need to create industrial schools for girls and stressed the fact that illiteracy and lack of education were the major components of the poor white problem.[90] The insistence and eagerness about Afrikaner education was part of a broader cultural and political process that started around 1905 with the creation of Prellers's *Afrikaansche Taal Genootskap*, which was geared to the preservation of *taal* and *volk* against both the Anglicization of education that had followed the South African War and the dissolution of the Afrikaner family caused by rapid urbanization.[91]

The debate about intervention in the poor white problem during the early 1910s focused on the issues of infancy and education. The urban environment, increasingly characterized as unhealthy and immoral in the hearings of the 1913 Select Committee on European Employment, made all the more evident the deficiencies of the poor white families in the education of their children. And that these deficiencies should be partly compensated for by the school, was a point that Rev. A. D. Luckhoff, minister of the Dutch Reformed Church in Darling, Cape Province, made abundantly clear:

> There (in the schools) you would reclaim the child of the fallen classes and the child who is reclaimed is an asset to the state, whereas if he is left to himself he is a liability and a serious liability too. I think in almost every district in the country should be an institution for the reclamation of these destitute children and children of the criminal classes.[92]

The Prisons and Reformatories Act of 1910 and the passing of the Children's Protection Act in 1913, which put white children under the protection of the state, were part of a wider movement of state intervention in the social sphere that had two main objectives. On the one hand it attempted to criminalize and racialize poverty. On the other, it aimed to prepare and train the future generations of poor whites to compete in an increasingly racially structured labour market.[93] The fact that industrial schools depended on the Administration of Prisons indicates how punishment and re-education complemented each other in the state's perception of the poor white problem. As Jacob de Villiers Roos, Secretary of Justice and Director of Prisons for the Union, put it in his evidence before the select committee:

> Other institutions which we have and which are not really criminal are the industrial schools for European juveniles, waifs and stray male and female, whom we pluck away from circumstances and surroundings which would cause them to drift into crime.[94]

The investigations of both the Select Committee on European Employment and of the Commission into Assaults of Women faced their members with the issue of the social reproduction of the white working class. By 1913, the concern that the future generations of white workers should be won over to the discipline of work, to healthy habits, to temperance and to thrift echoed the British preoccupation with separating the "residuum", casual workers with no habit of industry and with criminal tendencies, from the disciplined and healthy workers.[95]

Nevertheless, the preoccupation with the social reproduction of the working class had also a clear physical dimension that found its way into the points discussed during a Child Welfare Conference held in Cape Town in 1917. The existence of poor whites was explained through defective birth and degenerative features "because they are mentally defective and they have not the opportunities which we had".[96]

This concern gave a new point of entry to the health visitors introduced by Charles Porter in 1908. Now the early notification of birth became compulsory in order to prevent mortality and control the health of the newborn. Medical inspections also reached schools where it was necessary to detect the feebleminded, who, according to statistics handled in the conference, were five in each 1,000 poor white children.

Thus, by the late 1910s as public charity was slowly transformed into welfare in the post-war years, the science of the poor became more sophisticated. Medical doctors, health visitors, teachers, and town planners, no less than the personnel working in the prisons and reformatories, were integrated into state departments dealing with the different aspects of what was regarded as the poor white problem.

Conclusion

Urban poverty in Johannesburg was the result of historical processes in which economic forces as well as social conditions and political decisions were involved. Between 1890 and 1922 economic development in the Transvaal increased the number of the poor amongst the white population, both in rural and urban areas. Especially in the late 1890s the seriousness of unemployment and indigency amongst whites turned poor whites into a question that needed the state's attention. In 1908 the *Report of the Transvaal Indigency Commission* argued for the separation of poor whites from the unemployed and the chronically poor, at the same time that it emphasized the rural origins of poor whites as a social group, making poor whites largely synonymous with Afrikaners. In the context of the changes in the government and the organization of a greater South African state that took place in 1907 and 1910, the ethnic character of poverty added a political dimension to the poor white problem as first local and later national political parties started competing for the votes of this sector of the population.

By 1913, increasing urbanization and growing numbers of white indigents in cities like Johannesburg brought about a change in the conceptualization of the poor white problem and the perception of the pernicious effects of the urban environment. The interest in poor whites as a social category generated in the countryside shifted to the cities.

And this new understanding of the poor white problem, combined with a view of the cities as places of degeneration and demoralization, accentuated the ruling class's tendency to criminalize poverty. This, in turn, eclipsed the initial separation between poor whites, the unemployed and the chronic poor.

Before the outbreak of World War I the poor white problem was essentially understood at a social and ideological level. Its most alarming features were the criminal tendencies shown by this sector of the population and the lack of moral sense that allowed them to interact socially and to have sexual intercourse with the black population in the urban slums.

Rural and urban unrest in 1913 and 1914 served as a serious warning about discontent in the countryside, working class disaffection, and the magnitude of white unemployment on the Witwatersrand. Yet most of the proposed solutions to the poor white problem and unemployment were aimed to instil the discipline of work in new generations rather than to solve the existing unemployment problem.

The immediate post-war years were characterized by a profitability crisis in the mining industry, growing unemployment and a radicalization of the working class politics. In this context another shift took place in the discourse on the poor white problem. The Unemployment Commission argued in 1921 that poor whites were not only a menace to the survival of a racially organized society, but a political danger for the state because of the effect that the international revolutionary climate could have on this group.

Between 1890 and 1922, and especially in the aftermath of the South African War, Social Darwinism was applied in South Africa to the understanding and explanation of, and the remedies proposed to eliminate, white indigency. The concept of evolution that helped to organize race, culture and society hierarchically not only justified the ruling position of the white race, it also helped to place poor whites lower down on the scale of social evolution. Thus, within this framework, historical conditions as well as moral and biological factors located poor whites halfway between the heights of European civilization and the depths of the "uncivilized natives".

Between 1890 and 1906, consistent with the understanding of poverty and unemployment as consequences of periodic economic crises and the idea that the state should not offset market forces, political intervention in the poor white problem was restricted to the provision of relief work and to the organization of institutions to coordinate the distribution of charity. But as economic crises made it apparent that, in a racially divided society, market forces left to themselves would eventually undermine white supremacy, state intervention became more active. These changes in the discourse on poor whites were intertwined with the tough political competition that followed the constitution of the Union of South Africa in 1910.

Between 1907 and 1922, as poor whiteism acquired a fuller moral and ideological dimension, there was growing intervention by the state to change the class position of poor whites. Yet it was precisely the direction taken by the state in addressing the poor white problem - the development of an educational and penal system to discipline and punish the new generation of white workers - that prevented the South African Party government, as much as the opposition parties, from seeing that poor whites, together with the employed members of the white working class, could upset the balance of power in South Africa. When the government finally saw the warning signs in 1921 it was almost too late and the Rand Revolt was already in the making.

Notes

[1] Bundy, C., 'Vagabonds, Hollanders and Runaway Englishmen: White Poverty in the Cape before Poor Whiteism', in W. Beinhart et al. (eds.), *Putting a Plough to the Ground* (Johannesburg 1986). Illife, J., *The African Poor* (Cambridge 1987). Illife's analysis of poverty in South Africa pointed out the influence of multiracial urban poverty in the emergence of the poor white problem. Yet his analysis of the poor white problem was mostly based on the report of the 1933 Carnegie Commission, thus leaving an important gap in the history of the problem.

[2] Dubow, S., *Illicit Marriage: Scientific Racism in South Africa* (Cambridge 1995), p. 172. Hereafter *Illicit Marriage*.

[3] Burton, F. and Calen, P., *Official Discourse: On Discourse Analysis, Government Publications, Ideology and the State* (London 1979).

[4] Ashforth, A., *The Politics of Official Discourse in Twentieth Century South Africa*, (New York 1990), p. 11. Hereafter *The Politics of Official Discourse*.

[5] Van Onselen, C., *Studies in the Social and Economic History of the Witwatersrand, 1886-1914*, volume 2 *New Nineveh* (Johannesburg 1983), pp. 127-31.

[6] F.H.P Creswell, manager at the Village Main Reef Mine, was the principal proponent of this alternative. On Creswell's views see Jeeves, A., '*Het Volk* and the Gold Mines: The Debate on Labour Policy', Seminar Paper, African Studies Institute, 1982, pp. 12-16; and Ticktin, D., 'The Origins of the South African Labour Party', Ph.D. thesis, University of Cape Town, 1973, pp. 136-59. Hereafter 'The Origins of the South African Labour Party'.

[7] Transvaal Archives Depot (TAD), Colonial Secretary (CS) 282/3791/03. Letter from the Director of Public Works, Pretoria, to the Assistant Colonial Secretary, 6 April 1903.

[8] (TAD) (CS) 374/9029. Letter from J.J. Fouries to the Colonial Secretary, 21 September, 1903. (CS) 374/9030. Letter from J.A. Robbertse to the Colonial Secretary, 31 September, 1903.

[9] "If relief works were to be started now at the expense of the tax payer a precedent would be set which every government would be bound to follow whenever, as will inevitably happen, periods of depression occur in the future. Relief works tend to delay the return of prosperity. They also tend to the maintenance of a population in excess of that which

the real resources of the country are able to support." (TAD) Lieutenant Governor (LTG), 118/106/3. Letter from the Lieutenant Governor to the Rand Aid Association, 29 April 1904.

10. The Rand Aid Association had Milner as patron, and its board of trustees included, amongst others, Raymond W. Schumacher, a partner of Eckstein & Company since 1902, Carl Hanau, partner in S. Neumann & Company, and John W. Quinn, a member of the nominated town council.

11. (TAD) (GOV) 160/gen69/05. Letter from Sir A. Milner to Sir A. Lyttleton, 30 January 1905.

12. (TAD) (CS) 645/7041 A-7041 B, 1906. Letter from Lord Selborne to J. W. Quinn, 28 December 1906.

13. Johnstone, F.A., *Class, Race and Gold: A Study of Class Relations and Racial Discrimination in South Africa* (London 1976), pp. 93-4. Hereafter *Class, Race and Gold*.

14. Fraser, M. and Jeeves, A. (eds.), *All that Glittered: Selected Correspondence of Lionel Phillips*, 1890-1924 (Cape Town 1977), p. 179.

15. (TAD) Secretary for the Mines (MM) 172/1893/07. Letter from the Secretary of Mines to the Inspector of White Labour, 2 October 1907.

16. The first Inspector of White Labour was Alexander Raitt, who had been Secretary of the Amalgamated Society of Engineers in 1903 and was a member of the Transvaal Legislative Council at the time of his appointment to the new office. Raitt died two months after his appointment, and was replaced by Robert Shanks, who had been a member of the Johannesburg elected Town Council in 1903 and 1904, supported by the Witwatersrand Trades and Labour Council, an association created in 1902 with the object of representing the views of trade unions on the Rand. Yet, by 1908, Shanks was not seen as a trade union man by the workers. Katz, E., *A Trade Union Aristocracy: A History of White Workers in the Transvaal and the General Strike of 1913* (Johannesburg 1976), p. 184. Hereafter *A Trade Union Aristocracy*.

17. (TAD) (MM) 172/1893/07. Letter from the Secretary of Mines to the Inspector of White Labour, 2 October 1907.

18. The total number of applications was 3,√ ?9 of which 1,316 were sent to the Eckstein group's mines.

19. (TAD) (MM) 206/1263/08. Report of the Rand Unemployment Committee, 31 July 1908.

20. (TAD) (MM) 206/1263/08. Letter from the Secretary of Mines to the Assistant Colonial Secretary, 26 October 1908.

21. The idea of union had been growing amongst the political parties in all four colonies for some time. By 1908 these feelings were strengthened by economic depression, economic disputes, mostly related to the intercolonial trade, and the fears aroused by the 1906 Zulu rebellion in Natal. Lord Selborne thought the constitution of the Union of South Africa would reinforce the Imperial power in the colony as the High Commissioner could stop acting as an arbitrator in intercolonial conflicts. Thompson, L., *The Unification of South Africa* (London 1960) and Thompson, L., 'The Compromise of Union', in M. Wilson and L. Thompson (eds.), *Oxford History of South Africa* (Oxford 1971), vol. 2, pp. 343-9.

22. Stadler, A., 'The Party System in South Africa, 1910-1948', Ph.D. thesis, University of the Witwatersrand, 1970, p. 53. Hereafter *The Party System*.

23. Katz, E., *A Trade Union Aristocracy*, p. 134.

24. Hertzog, James Barry Munnik (1866-1942). Lawyer and soldier. Practised law in Pretoria between 1893 and 1895 and was judge of the Supreme Court of the Orange Free State 1895-99. Boer general during the South African War. Attorney General and Minister of Education of the Orange Free State in 1907-10. Attended the National Convention (1908-9) and was member of the first Union Cabinet. Excluded from the

Cabinet in 1912, established the National Party in 1914 and became Prime Minister of the Union in 1924.

25 (TAD) (CS) 970/19901/13. Letter from the Municipal Associations of South Africa to the Secretary of Interior, 9 January 1913.

26 (TAD) Mayor of Johannesburg (MJB) 1/1/23. *Minutes of the Johannesburg Town Council*, 28 January 1913.

27 *Report of the Select Committee on European Employment* (S.C. 9-13) para. 53. Hereafter *Report European Employment*. On the history of poor white woodcutters see Grundlingh, A., '"God het ons arm mense die houtjies gegee": Poor White Wood Cutters in the Southern Cape Forest Area, c. 1900-1939', in Morrell, R. (ed.), *White but Poor: Essays on the History of Poor Whites in South Africa, 1880-1949* (Pretoria 1995, pp. 40-56. Hereafter *White but Poor*.

28 *Report European Employment*, para. 35.

29 On the 1913 general strike see, Simons, H.J. and Simons, R.E., *Class and Colour in South Africa*, 1850-1950 (Harmondsworth 1969), pp. 156-60; Katz, E., *A Trade Union Aristocracy*, pp. 321-60; Davies, R.H., *Capital, State*, pp. 120-5; Ould, C. R., 'General Smuts' Attitude', pp. 70-88.

30 The causes of the 1914 rebellion are complex. South Africa aligned itself with the British government after the outbreak of World War I. At British request South Africa was to send troops to invade German South West Africa. The rebellion started when Generals Beyers and de la Rey refused their commission on 22 October. The generals found support in the Transvaal and Orange Free State. The rebels were united by nationalistic feelings. But there were also far more complex and deeper economic and social forces at play that facilitated the spread of the rebellion. See Bottomley, J., 'The Orange Free State and the Rebellion of 1914: The Influence of Industrialisation, Poverty and Poor Whiteism', in R. Morrell (ed.), *White but Poor*, pp. 29-39.

31 Stadler, A., '*The Party System*', p. 62.

32 (SAB) (MNW) MM/2997/16. Inspector of White Labour, Summarised Report for 1914-16.

33 South African Archives Bureau (SAB), Minister of Labour (MNW) 283/MM 1599/1915. Inspector of White Labour, Report for the Year ended 31 December 1914.

34 In 1914 there were 4,224 applicants while the number of positions available was 816. Yet the office only managed to place 688 workers. In 1915 there were 2,278 applicants, 308 jobs available and 237 men were sent to work. In 1916 1,325 workers applied for jobs, the positions available were 321 and 213 workers were placed. (SAB) (MNW) MM 2997/16. Inspector of White Labour, Summarised Report for 1914-16.

35 (SAB) (MNW) 354/MM 2878/16. General Report in Connection with the Poor White Question, 1916.

36 (SAB) (MNW) 386/MM 2161/17. White Labour Department, Statistics on Poor Whites.

37 Macmillan's analysis of the records of the Johannesburg Public Relief Board shows a clearer picture of the permanent influx of the countryside population into Johannesburg. According to him nearly 30 per cent of all the applicants for relief between 1916 and 1917 had not been six months on the Rand. Macmillan, W. M., *Complex South Africa: An Economic Footnote to History* (London n.d.), pp. 57-8.

38 *Economic Commission*, 1914 (U.G. 12-1914), para. 35.

39 Johnstone, F.A., *Class, Race and Gold*, 94.

40 Johnstone, F.A., *Class, Race and Gold*, pp. 98-101.

41 Johnstone, F.A., *Class, Race and Gold*, pp. 95-6.

42 (SAB) Department of Justice (JUS) 250/3/20/17. J.M. Fulford, Inspector S.A.P. to Deputy Commissioner of Police, 30 January, 1917.

43 *Second Interim Report of the Unemployment Commission*, 1921 (U.G. 34-21), paras. 3-7. Hereafter *Unemployment Commission*.
44 On these issues see Simons, H.J. and Simons, R.E., *Class and Colour in South Africa, 1850-1950* (Harmondsworth 1969), pp. 180-3, hereafter *Class and Colour*, and Johns, S., *Raising the Red Flag: The International Socialist League & the Communist Party of South Africa, 1914-1932* (Bellville 1995), pp. 101-4.
45 Jones, G., *Social Darwinism and English Thought: The Interaction between Biological and Social Theory* (Sussex 1980), p. 2. Hereafter *Social Darwinism*.
46 "Conservative adherents to *laissez-faire* principles were heartened by the notion that, in the struggle for existence, only the fittest would survive. They decried forms of state intervention which supported the weakest members of society and argued that 'mental defectives' and criminal 'types' imposed an intolerable strain on societies' resources. Nevertheless, eugenics was by no means the exclusive preserve of right-wingers. Its powerful potential as a force of social engineering attracted widespread interest within the radical and socialist intelligentsia." Dubow, S., *Illicit Union*, p. 123.
47 Dubow, S., *Illicit Union*, pp. 129-30.
48 Dubow, S., *Illicit Union*, p. 8.
49 Jones, G., *Social Darwinism*, p. 149.
50 Richard Feetham came to South Africa in 1902, became Deputy Town Clerk in that year and Town Clerk of Johannesburg's elected Town Council in 1903. He was nominated member of the Transvaal Legislative Council in 1907. At the time of the appointment of the Transvaal Indigency Commission he was practising as a lawyer in Johannesburg.
51 Phillip Kerr came to South Africa in 1904 and worked in the office of the Lieutenant-Governor of the Transvaal. Soon after his arrival in Pretoria he was appointed assistant to Robert Brand at the Intercolonial Council where he worked until June 1908.
52 *Report of the Transvaal Indigency Commission, 1906*-1908 (T. G. 13-08) Hereafter *Report Tvl. I.C.*, para. 7.
53 *Report Tvl. I.C.*, para. 10.
54 "Indigency, except where it is caused by illness, accident or old age, or by some public calamity which ruins or renders unemployed a large number of people, is almost invariably the product of lack of education or some weakness of character. The only way of effecting a permanent improvement in the conditions in which most indigents live is to correct the weakness of character or to make good the deficiency in education or training which is the real cause of their poverty, at the same time that they are afforded means to keep themselves alive." *Report Tvl. I.C.*, para. 11.
55 "The problem, however, is a far wider one than that which is concerned with the means by which the necessaries of life can best be supplied to those who are in absolute want of them. The real causes of indigency often have no apparent connection with the actual indigents themselves." *Report Tvl. I.C.*, para. 10.
56 *Report Tvl. I.C.*, paras. 40-44.
57 *Report Tvl. I.C.*, para. 47.
58 *Report Tvl. I.C.*, paras. 48-50.
59 *Report Tvl. I.C.*, para. 60.
60 *Report Tvl. I.C.*, paras. 9-11 and paras. 318-337.
61 *Report Tvl. I.C.*, para. 231.
62 *Report Tvl. I.C.*, paras. 220-223.
63 *Report Tvl. I.C.*, paras. 295-298.
64 *Report Tvl. I.C.*, para. 228.
65 *Report Tvl. I.C.*, para. 281.

66 *Report Tvl. I.C.*, para. 7.
67 On the role of the medical profession in spreading eugenic thought in South Africa from the early 1900s see Klausen, S., '"For the Sake of Race": Eugenic Discourses of Feeblemindness and Motherhood in the *South African Medical Record*, 1903-1926', *Journal of Southern African Studies*, 23, 1, 1997, pp. 27-50.
68 *Report Tvl. I.C.*, para. 217.
69 *Report of the Select Committee on European Employment and Labour Conditions*, (S.C. 9-13), para. 2. Hereafter *Report S.C.E.*
70 *Evidence of the Select Committee on European Employment and Labour Conditions*, Evidence of Col. T.G. Truter, para.1232; Evidence of J.J. Naude, Inspector of White Labour, para. 1529; Evidence of J. Quinn M L A, para. 3336. Hereafter *Evidence S.C.E.*
71 *Report S.C.E.*, para. 45.
72 *Evidence S.C.E.*, Evidence of the Minister of Native Affairs, para. 833.
73 *Evidence S.C.E.*, Evidence of P. Ross-Frames, member of the Commission into Assaults on Women, paras. 1070-1074.
74 The evidence of this commission was not published. Together with the report, it is housed in the Central Archives in Pretoria. (SAB) K. 373. *Evidence of the Commission of Enquiry into Assaults on Women*, 1913, volume 3 (evidence), 3 December 1912. Dr. T. Gilchrist, District Surgeon, Fordsburg. Hereafter *Assaults on Women*.
75 "...greatly conduces (women working as hawkers) to a low estimate being formed by the natives of the standard of womankind amongst white races." *Report of the Commission of Enquiry into Assaults on Women* (U.G. 39-13), para. 98. Hereafter *Assaults on Women*.
76 "...poor white children are becoming the dregs of the population. In this connection it is urged that the practice of young white boys and girls selling flowers and other articles late at night in the streets of large towns can only tend to their eventual demoralisation and should be prohibited." *Assaults on Women*, para. 100.
77 *Assaults on Women*, para. 88; See also Assaults on Women, Evidence of Major T.E. Mavrogordato, Commissioner of Police, 25 October 1912.
78 *Assaults on Women*, para. 128, see also paras. 55; 88; 92. *Report S.C.E.*, para. 2, and *Evidence S.C.E.*, Evidence of F.H.P. Creswell, para. 2663.
79 *Evidence S.C.E.*, para. 2664.
80 The ACV was created in 1904 in Cradock, Cape Province, under the leadership of Elizabeth Roos. It was an offshoot of the Afrikaner women's movement around the South African War, and it was connected to, though not controlled by, the Dutch Reformed Church. Since 1907-8 the association had been active in helping Afrikaner poor women and had a deep nationalist content in its ideas and policies. The ZVF was founded in 1903 and its bilingual character and its search for a South African identity brought it closer to *Het Volk* first and to the South African Party later. Yet both organisations had in common their concern about poor white women.
81 J.X. Merriman to J. Smuts, 20 December 1915, quoted in Bottomley, J., 'The South African Rebellion of 1914: The Influence of Industrialisation, Poverty and Poor Whiteism', Seminar Paper, African Studies Institute, University of the Witwatersrand, 1982, pp. 2-3. Two years earlier, in an address delivered at Stellenbosch, Merriman pointed out that what had triggered the 1913 strike was the conditions in which poor white people lived. "Like the well-to-do - I fear generally - we shrugged our shoulders and said Am I my brother's keeper? Ah, gentlemen! Our brother will soon let us know, as he has done in the past few weeks, whether we are his keeper or not. Those poor young fellows, who were incited to violent outrages, and who behaved like hooligans,

are the result of our negligence in the past, and it is our duty that that negligence is amended as soon as may be." Merriman, J.X., *The Strike and its Lessons*, Stellenbosch, 5 August 1913.

[82] *Unemployment Commission*, para. 25.
[83] *Report Tvl. I.C.*, paras. 249-251.
[84] *Report Tvl. I.C.*, paras. 249-251.
[85] *Report Tvl. I.C.*, paras. 264-266.
[86] Stedman-Jones, G., *Outcast London: A Study in the Relationship between Classes in Victorian Society* (London 1971), pp. 252-5. Hereafter *Outcast London*.
[87] *Report Tvl. I.C.*, para. 320.
[88] *Evidence S.C.E.*, Evidence of P. Ross-Frames para. 1062; Evidence of Col. T.G. Truter, para.1306; Evidence of Rev. A. Luckhoff, Dutch Reformed Church, para. 1709.
[89] Chisholm, L., 'Reformatories and Industrial Schools in South Africa. A Study in Class, Colour and Gender, 1882-1939' Ph.D. Thesis, University of the Witwatersrand, 1989 p. 75. Hereafter 'Reformatories and Industrial Schools in South Africa'.
[90] Du Toit, M., 'Women, Welfare and the Nurturing of Afrikaner Nationalism: A Social History of the Afrikaanse Christelyke Vroue Vereeniging, c. 1870-1939', Ph.D. thesis, University of Cape Town, 1996, p. 94.
[91] Hofmeyr, I., 'Building a Nation from Words: Afrikaans Language, Literature and Ethnicity, 1902-1924', in Marks, S. and Trapido, S. (eds.), *The Politics of Race, Class and Nationalism in Twentieth Century South Africa* (London 1987), pp. 95-123.
[92] *Evidence S.C.E.*, Evidence of Rev. A.D. Luckhoff, Minister of the Dutch Reformed Church, para. 1704.
[93] Chisholm, L., 'Reformatories and Industrial Schools in South Africa', p. 130.
[94] *Evidence S.C.E.*, Evidence of J. de Villiers Roos, para. 4829.
[95] Stedman-Jones, G., *Outcast London*, pp. 192-3; pp. 303-8; and pp. 309-12.
[96] (SAB) (MNW) 386/2193/17. Letter from the Juvenile Advisory Board to the Superintendent Chief Inspector of White Labour, Cape Town, 1917.

Chapter 7

The Making of the White Working Class in Johannesburg, 1890-1922

During the 32 years that constitute the focus of this study, the making of the white working class in Johannesburg was a continuous and sometimes contradictory process punctuated by five economic crises related to the mining industry (1890-1; 1896-7; 1906-8; 1913-14; 1921-22), a costly and bloody war (1899-1902), and three major political changes in 1902, 1907 and 1910.

These events had both direct and indirect consequences on the lives of Johannesburg's white workers. As we have seen, political uncertainty and profitability crises combined to aggravate some of the daily plights of the working class like the high cost of living and the scarcity of housing. At the same time the racial division of labour which characterized the economy of the colony of South Africa encouraged the employment of Black workers not only in unskilled jobs but also in more skilled occupations within and outside the mining industry.[1] This which, from an ideological perspective, fuelled racist feelings and actions among workers, one only has to remember the banners displayed during the 1922 Revolt to realize the extent of this issue, also explains worker's fear of unemployment and their anger against the Chamber of Mines and the government for allowing Black workers to perform jobs previously reserved for white miners.

But white workers' anger was not built only around racist feelings. So many workers had died of silicosis that, by the end of this period, it is correct to say that the white mineworkers who were the protagonists of this book belonged to two different generations. By 1904 the ravages of silicosis had either killed or disabled most members of the first generation of overseas mineworkers who came to the Witwatersrand.[2] The oft quoted example of the 18 members of the 1907 strike committee of whom, by 1913, 13 had died of silicosis,[3] suggests that the process of development of white workers' class consciousness was literally interrupted by the death of the first generation of white miners.

The anger was neither confined to the British section of the working class,[4] nor to the workers employed in the gold mining industry. By the 1910s the rapid urbanization of Afrikaner rural workers had brought the poor white problem to the fore in a context in which the state, as we have seen, had not developed the infrastructural or political means to deal with it.

The results of national and local elections after the formation of the Union as well as the strikes of 1913 and the rebellion of 1914, and especially the 1922 strike were expressions of white workers' anger and dissatisfaction.[5] White worker's anger, however, was not limited to working men in the workplace. It involved families as well as neighbourhoods, it was supported, sometimes actively, particularly in the case of the Rand Revolt, by men who did not work on the mines. Although the involvement of both women and children,[6] and of non-mining workers in the strikes of 1913 and 1922 has been mentioned in the literature, no substantive conclusions have been drawn in terms of its possible meanings for the analysis of the formation of class identity and class consciousness among white workers.[7] More detail studies of these two critical events are necessary to understand why a Russian tailor detained under martial law in 1922 was carrying the following letter:

> To the Right Hon. General Smuts,
>
> May the hound of hell chase him over the blue rocks of buggery, over the red rocks of hell, and may his arsehole become a festering sore, dry off and break out in his mouth and remain there a festering sore for the remainder of his bloody life. May his balls fester and drop off into his toes and cripple him for life the bloody bastard. The day he dies we shall walk a hundred miles over broken bottles and tin tacks with our bare feet just to shit in his grave.[8]

Anger and anti-government feelings such as this, had not yet crystallized in a class identity clearly articulated in political terms. On the contrary, this book has shown that white working class identity and sense of community were far from being clearly defined, homogeneous and coherently expressed. Like the white working class itself they were also in the making.

The economic, social, political and ideological processes that took place between 1890 and 1922 influenced the lives of Johannesburg's white workers creating an embryonic sense of community and identity amongst some of these men and their families. In the case of the Afrikaner workers, this identity was neither monolithic nor was it imbued of the religious nationalism that came to characterized Afrikaner politics from the 1930s onwards. It is interesting, however, that much of the literature that has dealt with Afrikaner history has treated 'Afrikanerdom' as a social category of "natural" proportions given its alleged constant historical presence.

During the 1960s and 1970s the predominant trend was to accept Afrikaner identity expressed in the 'Afrikanerdom' as a discrete identity and organic unity of the Afrikaner people which was of an almost atemporal nature.[9] Even those who acknowledged the different components of Afrikaner national identity, at least from a demographic perspective, saw the formation of this identity as a closed historical process by the nineteenth century.[10]

During the 1980s there was a more systematic and subtle exploration of the role of Afrikaner intelligentsia in interpreting Afrikaner history.[11] H. Giliomee and H. Adam, I. Hexham, and T. Dunbar Moodie on the one hand, distinguished between the culture and identity proposed in the discourse of the intellectual and political elite and ordinary people's reactions to that discourse and their day-to-day experience of their culture and identity. Yet, at times, their analyses slid into the unproblematic idea of a unified and cohesive Afrikanerdom that permeated the "collective unconsciousness" of all the Afrikaner population.[12]

A second approach saw Afrikaner identity as historically constructed. The works of D. O'Meara and I. Hofmeyr have done much to question the existence of Afrikanerdom as a discrete unity, suggesting that Afrikaner identity was in fact "a creation" of an intellectual and political elite which saw the need to protect, especially after the South African War, the Afrikaner population from the process of Anglicization proposed by Milner.[13] Similarly, A. Grundlingh has shown how social and economic cleavages within Afrikaner society were expressed in political terms during the South African War.[14] Yet there are no studies that have pursued this line of research and showed in a more comprehensive and subtle way how Afrikaner 'ethnicity' was experienced by ordinary people in their daily lives in an urban setting where cultural interactions made the preservation of identity in a "pure" state far more difficult.

In terms of the relation between 'ethnicity' and religion, it is still generally assumed, despite the research done by I. Hexham, that the large majority of Afrikaner people lived their Christianity exclusively through the Dutch Reformed Church, which in turn had a unifying function and a decisive ideological effect in the constitution of an emerging Afrikaner 'ethnic' identity. In a recent article J. Kinghorn analyzed the inner logic of Afrikanerdom and its usage of ethnicity during the second half of the twentieth century through a study of Afrikaner religion and theology.[15] Referring to the usage of the biblical story of Babel by Reverend J. D. Vorster in 1947, Kinghorn pointed out that:

> Afrikaners were entirely unprepared to deal with the experiences of relativity and insecurity that followed their bewildering exposure to social, cultural and moral plurality. For them, all known parameters had collapsed and were subjected to all kinds of insecurity that people experience as they feel the shattering of their familiar world. A crisis of self-understanding developed. In their efforts to reconstruct their social cosmos, the combination of nationalistic politics and a religiously constructed pre-modern social cosmology seemed to provide an answer.[16]

Although Kinghorn's analysis focuses on the origin of a theological explanation for apartheid, one could certainly read his deconstructionist approach to the story of Babel onto the nineteenth century and make a parallel between the "crisis of self-understanding" experienced by Afrikaner people in the late 1940s and the "shattering of the familiar world" of the Afrikaner folk in the aftermath of the South African War. Yet, in the late 1940s as in the late 1890s, ideology and discourse were not the sole arena in which Afrikaner people sought and developed a sense of identity. For not only were there competing and varied versions of Afrikaner subjectivity and identity at play during both periods[17] but ordinary people did not always, or did not necessarily, assimilate the identity constructed through these discourses. As important as discourse analysis can be in the explanation of ideology and identity, discourses are elaborated in historical contexts and, in this sense, they are embedded in a process by which particular identities are received, incorporated, discarded and transformed according to people's needs and circumstances as well as to political conditions. The outcome of the process is by no means inscribed in the process itself.

Many of the Afrikaners families who migrated to Johannesburg at different stages between the 1890s and the early 1920s showed a great deal of ingenuity in finding an economic and social niche in a rapidly transforming capitalist city. While for many Afrikaners the Dutch Reform Church must have constituted a source of spiritual strength, and cultural identity, it was not the only one.[18] The fact that some British and Afrikaner workers intermarried and in certain cases have their children baptized in the Anglican Church suggests that ethnicity and religion cannot be read off each other in a linear way, and that whatever the force of the ideologues' and politicians' plea people are sometimes more responsive to experience than to discourse.

At a time when issues of identity appear to predominate in the focus of social enquiry it seems important to reassert, against much of what has been recently written, either by commission or omission, that identity is a historical process and that as such it changes, adapts and, sometimes, disappears. The formation of Afrikaner identity is a case in point. The fluidity of the relations between some British and Afrikaner workers, the growing importance of family, neighbourhood and trade in the constitution of white working class social networks which emerges from this book, suggest the need for a more subtle and complex analysis of the process of formation of Afrikaner identity.

This study has focused mainly on social relations: relations between some men and women; Afrikaner and Briton; employed and unemployed; single and married workers; law abiding citizens and delinquents, and, last but not least, between the state in different forms and white workers. The individual protagonists of these relationships sometimes had identifiable names, addresses, trades, wives and children, friends. But biographical details that would allow William and Anna Culvert, William and Elizabeth Kirby, Stefanus and Phoebe van Niekerk, John McCurry and the scores of working class men and women recorded in the baptismal registers of the Anglican Church, in the lists of the Inspector of White Labour, in court records, or in the evidence before commissions of enquiry, to become full historical characters are not available. Methodological limits preclude this book from being a narrative of workers' class experiences in their own words. The fragments of their lives that have been possible to reconstruct are only glimpses into working class experiences mediated by the narration. What then is the validity of this narration? Had 'workers' voices' been available in the sources, would the narrative be more valid or truthful?

The problem, it seems, is the narrative itself. In his study of the role of narrative in contemporary historical theory H.White stresses that the very possibility of narrative is based on a double equivocation. One equivocation derives from the fact that 'narrative' refers to both a form and a content of discourse. The other stems from the notion of history itself which presupposes a distinction between an order of events that is historical and one that is nonhistorical.[19] Interestingly, what makes narration suspect as a manner of speaking of real events is that as a mode of discourse narration exists both in "historical" and "nonhistorical" cultures and that it predominates in mythic and fictional discourse. According to White this raises a question not so much about the truth of the narration but about the relation between narrative and imagination, and therefore, about imagination and the writing of history:

> Is it not possible that the question of narrative in any discussion of historical theory is always finally the function of imagination in the production of a specifically human truth?[20]

Thus White reasserts not only the power of imagination in the production of a historical narration but the morality of history so far as it is capable to tell specifically human truths. Yet history, in the sense of the *rerum gestarum* - the events that occurred - is not moral or immoral. It is the memory of the events, what a society remembers, that can be moral or immoral. Walter Benjamin was probably thinking about this when he suggested that only a redeemed humankind can receive the fullness of its past.[21]

Notes

1. Johnstone, F. A., *Class, Race and Gold: A Study of Class Relations and Racial Discrimination in South Africa* (London 1976), pp. 93-150.
2. Katz, E., *The White Death: Silicosis on the Witwatersrand Gold Fields, 1886-1910* (Johannesburg 1995), pp. 209-13.
3. Katz, E., *A Trade Union Aristocracy: A History of White Workers in the Transvaal and the General Strike of 1913* (Johannesburg 1976), p. 334. Hereafter *A Trade Union Aristocracy*.
4. Simons, H. J. and Simons, R. E., *Class and Colour in South Africa, 1850-1950* (Harmondsworth 1969), pp. 156-60.
5. Johns, S., *Raising the Red Flag: The International Socialist League & The Communist Party of South Africa, 1914-1932* (Bellville 1995), 132-3.
6. Katz, E., *A Trade Union Aristocracy*, p. 403 and p. 409 and Krikler, J., 'Women, Violence and the Rand Revolt of 1922', *Journal of Southern African Studies*, 22, 3, 1996, pp. 349-72.
7. Simons, H. J. and Simons, R. E., *Class and Colour in South Africa, 1850-1950* (Harmondsworth 1969); Katz, E., *A Trade Union Aristocracy: A History of White Workers in the Transvaal and the General Strike of 1913* (Johannesburg 1976); Johnstone, F. A., *Class, Race and Gold: A Study of Class Relations and Racial Discrimination in South Africa, 1900-1960: An Historical Materialist Analysis of Class Formation and Class Relations* (Brighton 1979); Johns, S., *Raising the Red Flag: The International Socialist League & the Communist Party of South Africa* (Bellville 1995); Hirson, B. and Williams, G. A., *The Delegate for Africa: David Ivon Jones, 1883-1924* (London 1995).
8. (TAD) Johannesburg Landdroste (LJB) Martial Law, 1922. The King versus Henry Glazer. March 14, 1922. Henry Glazer was a 48-year-old Russian tailor.
9. Thompson, L., 'Great Britain and the Afrikaner Republics, 1870-1899', in Wilson, M. and Thompson, L. (eds.), *Oxford History of South Africa* (Oxford 1971), p. 301.
10. De Villiers, R., 'Afrikaner Nationalism', in Wilson, M. and Thompson, L. (eds.), *Oxford History of South Africa* (Oxford 1971), p. 366.
11. Giliomee, H and Adam, H., *The Rise and Crisis of Afrikaner Power* (Cape Town 1979). Hereafter *Rise and Crisis*; Hexham, I., *The Irony of Apartheid: The Struggle for National Independence of Afrikaner Calvinism Against British Imperialism* (New York 1981). Hereafter *The Irony of Apartheid*; Moodie, Dunbar T., *The Rise of Afrikanerdom: Power, Apartheid and the Afrikaner Civil Religion* (Berkeley 1980). Hereafter *The Rise of Afrikanerdom*.
12. Moodie, Dunbar, T., *The Rise of Afrikanerdom*, p. 33.
13. O'Meara, D., *Volkskapitalisme: Class, Capital and Ideology in the Development of Afrikaner Nationalism, 1934-1948* (Cambridge 1983). Hereafter *Volkskapitalisme*; Hofmeyr, I., 'Building a Nation from Words: Afrikaans Language, Literature and Ethnicity, 1902-1924', in Marks, S. and Trapido, S. (eds.), *The Politics of Race, Class and Nationalism in Twentieth Century South Africa* (London 1987), pp. 95-123.
14. Grundlingh, A., 'Collaborators in Boer Society' in Warwick, P. (ed.), *The South African War: The Anglo-Boer War, 1899-1902* (London 1980), pp. 258-78.
15. Kinghorn, J., 'Social Cosmology, Religion and Afrikaner Ethnicity', *Journal of Southern African Studies*, 20, 3, 1994, pp. 393-404. Hereafter 'Social Cosmology'.
16. Kinghorn, J., 'Social Cosmology', p. 402.
17. On the competing ideas of Afrikanerdom during the 1930s and 1940s see O'Meara, D., *Volkskapitalisme*, especially Introduction, and chapters 5, 11 and 12. See also Giliomee, H., 'The Growth of Afrikaner Identity' in Giliomee, H., and Adam, H., *Rise and Crisis.*, especially pp. 83-4 and pp. 112-13.

[18] Fourie, J., *Afrikaners in die Goudstad. Deel 1, 1886-1924* (Pretoria 1978). See also Hexham, I., *The Irony of Apartheid*, especially pp. 70-75.
[19] White, H., *The Content of the Form. Narrative Discourse and Historical Representation* (Baltimore 1990), p. 27. Hereafter, *The Content of the Form*.
[20] White. H., *The Content of the Form*, p. 57.
[21] Benjamin, W., *Illuminations* (London 1999), p. 246.

Bibliography

Manuscript Sources

Official:
Central Archives, Pretoria (incorporating Transvaal Archives)
a)   Departmental Correspondence
        (i)   Law Department, Transvaal, 1900-1922.
        (ii)   Provincial Secretary, Transvaal, 1900-1922.
        (iii) Refugee Aid Department, 1901-1903.
        (iv) Registrar Special Criminal Court, Johannesburg, 1901-1903.
        (v)   Secretary of Mines, 1901-1908.
        (vi) Colonial Secretary, Transvaal, 1901-1910.
        (vii) Secretary of the Governor of the Transvaal, 1901-1910.
        (viii) Secretary, Transvaal Police, 1901-1922.
        (ix) Lieutenant Governor of the Transvaal Colony, 1902-1907.
        (x)   Commissioner Transvaal Town Police, 1902-1909.
        (xi) Medical Officer of Health for the Transvaal, 1902-1910.
        (xii) Attorney General, 1902-1922.
        (xiii) Registrar of the Supreme Court of South Africa, 1902-1922.
        (xiv) Prime Minister, Transvaal, 1907-1910.
        (xv) Prime Minister, 1910-1922.
b)   Local Authorities
        (i)   Mayor of Johannesburg, 1896-1922.
        (ii)   Landdroste, Johannesburg, 1900-1922 (not catalogued).
        (iii) Health Department, Johannesburg, 1910-1922.
c)   Commissions of Enquiry
        (i)   Johannesburg Housing Commission, 1903, Evidence.
        (ii)   Transvaal Liquor Commission, 1909, Evidence.
        (iii) Small Holdings Commission, 1912, Evidence.
        (iv) Commission into Assaults on Women, 1913, Evidence.
        (v)   Commission into Cost of Living, 1917-1920, Evidence.
        (vi) Unemployment Commission, 1920-1921, Evidence.
        (vii) Martial Law Commission, 1922, Evidence.

Unofficial at Various Archives and Libraries:
1.   Johannesburg Public Library.
       Strange Collection. Miscellaneous Boxes, 1886-1899.
2.   University Of The Witwatersrand.
       Church of the Province of South Africa.
       Minutes of St. Mary Parochial Council, 1895-1910.

Baptism and marriage records from the parishes of Johannesburg, Jeppe, Belgravia and Fordsburg, 1895-1922.

Printed Primary Sources

Official Records:
1. South African Republic, 1896-1899
   Census of Johannesburg 1896.
   Industrial Commission of Enquiry, 1897.
   Gold Law No. 15 1898.
2. Transvaal Colony, 1902-1906
   Report of the Gold Law Commission, 1901-1902.
   Johannesburg Insanitary Area Improvement Scheme Commission of Enquiry, 1902-1903.
   Transvaal Census 1904.
   Report of the Working of the Immigration Act 1902 for the Year 1903 (G. 63-1904).
   Report of the Officer in Charge of Immigration and Labour for the Year 1905 (G. 4-1906).
   Report on Immigration and Labour for the Year ending 31st December 1906 (G. 21-1907).
   Report of the Johannesburg Housing Commission, 1903.
   Rating Bill, 1903.
   Vrededorp Stands Commission, 1905.
   Report of the Commission on Pretoria Indigents, 1905.
   Third Report of the Financial Relations Commission, 1906.
3. Transvaal Government, 1907-1910
   Evidence of the Transvaal Indigency Commission, 1906-1908 (T. G. 11-08).
   Report of the Transvaal Indigency Commission, 1906-1908 (T. G. 13-08).
   A Bill to Amend the Township Act of 1907.
   Township Amendment Act 1908.
4. Union of South Africa, 1910-1922
   Transvaal Leasehold Commission, 1912 (U. G. 34-12).
   Local Authorities Rating Ordinance No. 6 of 1912.
   Report of the Small Holdings Commission, 1913 (U. G. 51-13).
   Report of the Commission of Enquiry into Assaults on Women, 1913 (U. G. 39-13).
   Select Committee on European Employment and Labour Conditions, 1913 (S. C. 9-13).
   Economic Commission, 1914 (U. G.12-14).
   Report of the Local Government Commission, 1915 (T. P. 3-15).
   Report of the Committee on Industrial Education, 1916 (U. G. 9-17).
   Bill to Make Provision for the Improvement of Unhealthy Areas in Urban Localities and for Matters Incidental thereto, 1919.
   Select Committee on the Public Health Bill, 1919 (S. C. 3-19).
   Act to Make Provision for Public Health, 1919.

Preliminary Report of the Kakamas Commission of Enquiry, 1919 (U. G. 55-19).
Report of the Housing Committee, 1920 (U. G. 4-20).
Act to Provide for Loans of Public Moneys for the Construction of Dwellings, 1920.
Second Interim Report of the Unemployment Commission, 1921 (U. G. 34-21).
Report of the Unemployment Commission, 1920-1921 (U.G. 17-22).

Newspapers:
The Star, 1890-1914.
Standard & Diggers' News, 1895-1900.
The Transvaal Leader, 1912, 1913, 1914.

Directories:
Longland's Johannesburg and District Directory, 1896-1899.
Longland's Transvaal Directory, 1903-1908.
United Transvaal Directory, 1908-1915.

Secondary Sources

Selected Contemporary Books and Pamphlets:
Anonymous, *The Story of a Crime Being a Vindication of the Transvaal Legal Defence Committee in Connection with the Great Strike on the Witwatersrand in 1922* (Johannesburg 1924).
Anonymous, *Unrest. (Portrayed by a Mine Dumpling)* (Johannesburg 1922).
Brutus, *Never Again: The Psychology and the Lesson of the Rand Revolt, 1922* (Johannesburg 1922).
Buchan, J., *The African Colony: Studies in the Reconstruction* (London 1902).
Bunting, S. P., *Red Revolt: The Rand Strike, January-March, 1922* (Johannesburg, n.d.).
Curtis, L., *With Milner in South Africa* (Oxford 1951).
FitzPatrick, J. P., *The Transvaal from Within* (London 1899).
Macmillan, A., *The Golden City* (London n.d.).
Macmillan, W. M., *Poverty and Post-War Problems* (Grahamstown 1916).
Markham, V. H., *South Africa: Past and Present* (London 1900).
McDonald, R. J., *What I Saw in South Africa* (London 1902).
Merriman, J. X., *The Strike and its Lessons* (Stellenbosch 1913).
Observer, *The Strike that Did Not Fail* (Johannesburg 1913).
Pratt, A., *The Real South Africa* (London 1913).
Scully, W., *The Ridge of the White Waters* (London 1912).

Selected Books and Journals:
Ally, R., *Gold and Empire: The Bank of England and South Africa's Gold Producers, 1886-1926* (Johannesburg 1994).
Anderson, M., *Family Structure in Nineteenth Century Lancashire* (Cambridge 1971).
Anderson, P., *Arguments within English Marxism* (London 1980).
Anserson, P., 'The Common and the Particular', *Journal of International Labor and*

Working Class History, 36,1989, pp. 31-8.
Aries, P., *L'Enfant et la Vie Familiale sous l'Ancien Regime* (Paris 1973).
Ashforth, A., *The Politics of Official Discourse in Twentieth Century South Africa* (New York 1990).
Beinart, W. and Dubow, S., *Segregation and Apartheid in Twentieth-Century South Africa* (London 1995).
Berger, I., *Threads of Solidarity: Women in South African Industry, 1900-1980* (London 1992).
Bickford-Smith, V., *Ethnic Pride and Racial Prejudice in Victorian Cape Town: Group Identity and Social Practice, 1875-1902* (Cambridge 1995).
Bickford-Smith, V., 'South African Urban History, Racial Segregation and the Unique Case of Cape Town?', *Journal of Southern African Studies*, 21, 1, 1995, pp. 63-78.
Bodnar, J. et al., *Lives of their Own: Blacks, Italians, and Poles in Pittsburgh, 1900-1960* (Chicago 1982).
Bottomley, J., 'The Orange Free State and the Rebellion of 1914: The Influence of Industrialisation, Poverty and Poor Whiteism', in R. Morell (ed.) *White but Poor: Essays on the History of Poor Whites in Southern Africa, 1880-1940* (Pretoria 1992).
Bozzoli, B., *The Political Nature of a Ruling Class: Capital and Ideology in South Africa, 1890-1933* (London 1981).
Bozzoli, B.,'Class, Community and Ideology in the Evolution of South African Society', in Bozzoli, B. (ed.), *Class, Community and Conflict: South African Perspectives* (Johannesburg 1987).
Brink, E., 'Maar 'n klomp "factory" meide: Afrikaner Family and Community on the Witwatersrand during the 1920s', in Bozzoli, B. (ed.), *Class, Community and Ideology: South African Perspectives* (Johannesburg 1987).
Bundy, C., 'Vagabonds, Hollanders and Runaway Englishmen: White Poverty in the Cape before Poor Whiteism', in W. Beinart, et al. (eds.), *Putting a Plough to the Ground* (Johannesburg 1986).
Burton, F. and Calen, P., *Official Discourse: On Discourse Analysis, Government Publications, Ideology and the State* (London 1979).
Cammack, D., *The Rand at War: The Witwatersrand and the Anglo-Boer War* (London 1991).
Clarke, J. et al., *Working Class Culture: Studies in History and Theory* (London 1979).
Cooper, F., Work, Class and Empire: An African Historian's Retrospective on E. P. Thompson', *Social History*, 20, 2, 1995, pp. 235-41.
Cope, R. K., *Comrade Bill: The Life and Times of W. Andrews, Workers' Leader* (Cape Town 1943).
Davies, R. H., *Capital, State and White Labour in South Africa: An Historical Materialist Analysis of Class Formation and Class Relations* (Brighton 1979).
De Kiewet, C. W., *A History of South Africa: Political and Economic* (Oxford 1957).
De Villiers, R., 'Afrikaner Nationalism' in M. Wilson and L. Thompson (eds.), *Oxford History of South Africa*, volume II (Oxford 1971).
Deacon, H., 'Racial Segregation and Medical Discourse in Nineteenth Century Cape Town', *Journal of Southern African Studies*, 22, 2, 1996, pp. 287-308.
Denoon, D., *A Grand Illusion: The Failure of Imperial Policy in the Transvaal Colony*

during the Period of Reconstruction, 1900-05 (London 1973).

Dubow, S., 'Race, Civilisation and Culture: The Elaboration of the Segregationist Discourse in the Inter-War Years', in S. Marks and S. Trapido (eds.), *The Politics of Race, Class and Nationalism in Twentieth Century South Africa* (London 1987).

Dubow, S., *Illicit Marriage: Scientific Racism in South Africa* (Cambridge 1995).

Flandrin, J., *La Moral Sexual en Occidente: Evolucion, Actitudes y Comportamientos* (Barcelona 1984).

Fourie, J., *Afrikaners in die Goudstad. Deel 1, 1886-1924* (Pretoria 1978).

Fraser, M., and Jeeves, A. (eds.), *All that Glittered: Selected Correspondence of Lionel Phillips, 1890-1924* (Cape Town 1977).

Freund, B., 'The Social Character of Secondary Industry in South Africa, 1915-1945', in A. Mabin (ed.), *Organisation and Economic Change, South African Studies*, vol. 5 (Johannesburg 1989).

Giliomee, H. and Adam, H., *The Rise and Crisis of Afrikaner Power* (Cape Town 1979).

Gordon, C., *The Growth of Boer Opposition to Kruger, 1890-1895* (London 1970).

Grundlingh, A., 'Collaborators in Boer Society' in P. Warwick (ed.), *The South African War: The Anglo-Boer War 1899-1902* (London 1980).

Headlam, C. (ed.) *The Milner Papers* (Cape Town 1966).

Hexham, I., *The Irony of Apartheid: The Struggle for National Independence of Afrikaner Calvinism Against British Imperialism* (New York 1981).

Hirson, B. and Williams, G. A., *The Delegate for Africa: David Ivon Jones, 1883- 1924* (London 1995).

Hobsbaum, E., *Industry and Empire* (London 1980).

Hobsbaum, E., *Labouring Men: Studies in the History of Labour* (London 1968).

Hofmeyr, I., 'Building a Nation from Words: Afrikaans Language, Literature and Ethnicity, 1902-1924', in S. Marks and S. Trapido (eds.), *The Politics of Race, Class and Nationalism in Twentieth Century South Africa* (London 1987).

Iliffe, J., *The African Poor* (Cambridge 1987).

Johns, S., *Raising the Red Flag: The International Socialist League & The Communist Party of South Africa* (Bellville 1995).

Johnstone, F. A., *Class, Race and Gold: A Study of Social Relations and Racial Discrimination in South Africa* (London 1976).

Jones, G., *Social Darwinism and English Thought: The Interaction between Biological and Social Theory* (Sussex 1980).

Joyce, P., *Visions of the People: Industrial England and the Question of Class* (Cambridge 1991).

Katz, E., *A Trade Union Aristocracy: A History of White Workers in the Transvaal and the General Strike of 1913* (Johannesburg 1976).

Katz, E., 'Miners by Default: Afrikaners and the Gold Mining Industry before Union', *The South African Journal of Economic History*, 6, 1, 1991, pp. 61-80.

Katz, E., *The White Death: Silicosis on the Witwatersrand Gold Mines, 1886-1910* (Johannesburg 1995).

Keegan, T., *Rural Transformations in Industrialising South Africa: The Southern Highveld to 1914* (Johannesburg 1986).

Kennedy, B., *Silver, Sin and Sixpenny Ale: A Social History of Broken Hill, 1883-1921* (Melbourne 1978).

King, A., *Colonial Urban Development: Culture, Social Power and Environment* (London 1976).

Klausen, S., '"For the Sake of Race": Eugenic Discourses of Feeblemindness and Motherhood in the *South African Medical Record*, 1903-1926', *Journal of Southern African Studies*, 23, 1, 1997, pp. 27-50.

Kleinberg, S. J., *The Shadow of the Mills: Working-Class Families in Pittsburgh, 1870-1907* (Pittsburgh 1989).

Krikler, J., 'Women, Violence and the Rand Revolt of 1922', *Journal of Southern African Studies*, 22, 3, 1996, pp. 349-72.

Krut, R., 'The Making of a South African Jewish Community in Johannesburg, 1886-1914', in Bozzoli, B. (ed.), *Class, Community and Ideology: South African Perspectives* (Johannesburg 1987).

Kubicek, R., *Economic Imperialism in Theory and Practice: The Case of South African Gold Mining Finance, 1886-1914* (Durham 1979).

La Capra, D., *History & Criticism* (London 1985).

Laslett, P. and Wall, R. (eds.) *Household and Family in Past Time* (Cambridge 1972).

Laslett, P., *The World We Have Lost - further explored -* (London 1983).

Levine, D., *Reproducing Families: The Political Economy of English Population History* (Cambridge 1987).

Leyds, G. A., *History of Johannesburg* (Johannesburg 1964).

Macmillan, W. M., *Complex South Africa: An Economic Footnote to History* (London n.d.).

Mantzaris, E. A., 'Radical Community: The Yiddish-speaking Branch of the International Socialist League, 1918-1920', in Bozzoli, B. (ed.), *Class, Community and Ideology: South African Perspectives* (Johannesburg 1987).

Marks, S. and Trapido, S., 'Lord Milner and the South African State', *History Workshop Journal*, 8, 1979, pp. 50-80.

Maud, J., *Johannesburg and the Art of Self Government* (Johannesburg 1937).

City Government: The Johannesburg Experiment (Oxford 1938).

Medick, H. and Sahean, D. (eds.), *Interest and Emotion: Essays on the Study of Family and Kingship* (Cambridge 1984).

Moodie, D. T., *The Rise of Afrikanerdom: Power, Apartheid and the Afrikaner Civil Religion* (Berkeley 1980).

Morrell, R., 'The Poor Whites in Middleburg, Transvaal, 1900-1930: Resistance, Accommodation and Class Struggle', in R. Morrell (ed.), *White but Poor: Essays on the History of Poor Whites in South Africa, 1880-1940* (Pretoria 1992).

Newbury, C., 'The March of Everyman: Mobility and the Imperial Census of 1901', *The Journal of Imperial and Commonwealth History*, XII, 2, 1984, pp. 80-101.

Nimocks, W., *Milner's Young Men: The "Kindergarten" in Edwardian Imperial Affairs* (Durham 1968).

Novick, P., *That Noble Dream: The Objectivity Question and the American Historical Profession* (New York 1988).

O'Meara, D., *Volkskapitalisme: Class, Capital and Ideology in the Development of Afrikaner Nationalism, 1932-1948* (Cambridge 1983).

Palmer, B., *Descent into Discourse: The Reification of Language and the Writing of Social History* (Philadelphia 1990).

Palmer, B., La Teoria Critica, el Materialismo Historico y el Supuesto Fin del Marxismo: Retorno a la Miseria de la Teoria', *Entrepasados*, V, 9, 1995, pp. 143-72.
Parnell, S.,'Slums, Segregation and Poor Whites in Johannesburg, 1920-1934', in R. Morrell (ed.), *White but Poor: Essays in the History of Poor Whites in Southern Africa, 1880-1940* (Pretoria 1992).
Parnell, S., 'Origins of South African Public Health and Town Planning Legislation', *Journal of Southern African Studies*, 19, 3, 1993, pp. 471-88.
Pirie, G., 'White Railway Labour in South Africa, 1873-1924', in R. Morrell (ed.), *White but Poor: Essays on the History of Poor Whites in Southern Africa, 1880-1940* (Pretoria 1992).
Poster, M., *Critical Theory of the Family* (London 1978).
Robertson, A. F., *Beyond the Family: The Social Organization of Human Reproduction* (Cambridge 1991).
Rosenzweig, R., *Eight Hours for What We Will: Workers and Leisure in an Industrial City* (Cambridge 1983).
Ross, E., 'Survival Networks: Women's Neighbourhood Sharing in London before World War I', *History Workshop Journal*, 15, 1983, pp. 4-27.
Roux, E. and Roux, W., *Rebel Pity: The Life of Eddie Roux* (London 1970).
Scott, J., *Gender and the Politics of History* (London 1988).
Seymour-Jones, C., *Beatrice Webb: Woman of Conflict* (London 1992).
Simons, H. J. and Simons, R. E., *Class and Colour in South Africa, 1850-1950* (Harmondsworth 1969).
Stedman-Jones, G., *Outcast London: A Study in the Relationship between Classes in Victorian Society* (London 1971).
Stedman-Jones, G., *Languages of Class: Studies in English Working Class History, 1832-1982* (Cambridge 1983).
Stoler, L., 'Rethinking Colonial Categories: European Communities and the Boundaries of Rule', *Comparative Studies in Society and History*, 1989, pp. 134-60.
Streak, M., *Lord Milner's Immigration Policy for the Transvaal, 1897-1905* (Rand Afrikaans University Publication 1969).
Swanson, M., 'The Sanitation Syndrome: Bubonic Plague and Urban Native Policy in the Cape Colony, 1900-1909', *Journal of African History*, XVIII, 3, 1977, pp. 387-410.
Swaisland, C., *Servants and Gentlewomen to the Golden Land: The Emigration of Single Women from Britain to South Africa, 1820-1939* (Oxford 1993).
Thompson, D., *The Chartists: Popular Politics in the Industrial Revolution* (New York 1984).
Thompson, E. P., *The Making of the English Working Class* (Harmonsdworth 1966).
Thompson, E.P., 'Eighteen-Century English Society: Class Struggle without Class?', *Social History*, 2/3, 1978, pp. 140-60.
Thompson, E. P., *Customs in Common* (London 1991).
Thompson, L., 'The Compromise of Union' in M. Wilson and L. Thompson (eds.), *Oxford History of South Africa*, vol. 2 (Oxford 1971).
Thompson, L., 'Great Britain and the Afrikaner Republics, 1870-1899' in M. Wilson and L. Thompson (eds.), *Oxford History of South Africa* (Oxford 1971).
Thompson, L., *The Unification of South Africa* (London 1960).

Van Heyningen, E., 'The Social Evil in the Cape Colony, 1868-1902: Prostitution and the Contagious Diseases Acts', *Journal of Southern African Studies*, 10, 2, 1984, pp.170-97.

Van Helten, J. and Williams, K., 'The Crying Need of South Africa: The Emigration of Single British Women to the Transvaal, 1901-1910', *Journal of Southern African Studies*, 10, 1, 1983, pp. 17-38.

Van Onselen, C., *Studies in the Social and Economic History of the Witwatersrand, 1886-1914, volume 1, New Babylon; volume 2, New Nineveh* (Johannesburg 1983).

Ward, D., *Poverty, Ethnicity and the American City, 1850-1925* (Cambridge 1985).

White, J., *The Rothschild Buildings: Life in an East End Tenement Block, 1887-1920* (London 1980).

White, L., *The Comforts of Home: Prostitution in Colonial Nairobi* (Chicago 1990).

Wilentz, S., *Chants Democratic: New York City and the Rise of the American Working Class, 1780-1850* (New York 1984).

Williams, R., *Culture and Society* (London 1958).

Williams, R., *Marxism and Literature* (Oxford 1977).

Yudelman, D., *The Emergence of Modern South Africa: State, Capital and the Incorporation of Organized Labour on the South African Gold Fields, 1902-1939* (Connecticut 1983).

Yujnovsky, O., 'Politica de Vivienda en la Ciudad de Buenos Aires, 1880-1914', *Desarrollo Economico*, 54, 14, 1974, pp. 327-72.

Zunz, O., *The Changing Face of Inequality: Urbanization, Industrial Development and Immigrants in Detroit, 1880-1920* (Chicago 1982).

Unpublished Papers and Theses

Bottomley, J., 'The South African Rebellion of 1914: The Influence of Industrialisation, Poverty and Poor Whiteism', Seminar Paper, African Studies Institute, 1982.

Chisholm, L., 'Reformatories and Industrial Schools in South Africa: A Study in Class, Colour and Gender, 1882-1939', Ph.D. thesis, University of the Witwatersrand, 1989.

Du Toit, M., 'Women, Welfare and the Nurturing of Afrikaner Nationalism: A Social History of the Afrikaanse Christelike Vroue Vereeniging, c. 1870-1939', Ph.D. thesis, University of Cape Town, 1996.

Jeeves, A., 'Het Volk and the Gold Mines: The Debate on Labour Policy, 1905-1910', Seminar Paper, African Studies Institute, University of the Witwatersrand, 1980.

Katz, E., 'The Underground Route to Mining: Afrikaners and the Witwatersrand Gold Mining Industry from 1902 to the Miners' Strike', Paper presented to the Symposium on Work, Class and Culture, History Workshop and Sociology of Work Unit, University of the Witwatersrand, June 28-30, 1993.

Krut, R., '"A Quart into a Pint Pot": The White Working Class and the "Housing Shortage" in Johannesburg, 1896-1906' Honours Dissertation, University of the Witwatersrand, 1979.

Lange, M. L., 'The Political Economy of White Working Class Housing in

Johannesburg, 1890-1906', Seminar Paper, Institute for Advanced Social Research University of the Witwatersrand, 1996.

Lever, M. R., 'Johannesburg's Adoption of Site Value Rating', Honours Dissertation, University of the Witwatersrand, 1993.

Ould, C. R., 'General Smuts' Attitude to White Labour Disputes between 1907 and 1922', M.A. thesis, University of the Witwatersrand, 1963.

Parnell, S., 'Johannesburg's Slums and Racial Segregation in South African Cities, 1910-1937', Ph.D. thesis, University of the Witwatersrand, 1993.

Shear, K., 'The 1907 Strike: A Reassessment', Seminar Paper, Institute for Advanced Social Research, University of the Witwatersrand, 1994.

Stadler, A., 'The Party System in South Africa, 1910-1948', Ph.D. thesis, University of the Witwatersrand, 1970.

Ticktin, D., 'The Origins of the South African Labour Party' Ph.D. thesis, University of Cape Town, 1973.

Wolpe, H., 'The White Working Class in South Africa: Some Theoretical Problems' Seminar Paper, Dar es Salaam, 1975.

Index

affordability, 56
African labour, 10, 13, 29, 79, 91, 135, 139, 141, 146
Afrikaner, 15, 16, 18, 19, 20, 21, 22, 24, 25, 27, 30, 31, 32, 39, 40, 52, 57, 66, 75, 76, 106, 108, 111, 112, 113, 117, 127, 134, 135, 137, 138, 142, 143, 146, 149, 150, 155, 165, 166, 167, 168
Afrikaner brickmakers, 20
Afrikaner women, 15, 18, 20, 25, 27
alcohol, 114, 115, 116, 120, 125
Alfred Milner, 11, 55, 67
Anglican Church, 17, 18, 19, 20, 22, 23, 24, 25, 31, 32, 112, 113, 168, 169
artisans, 10, 23, 29, 30, 92, 94, 136
assessment rate, 40, 46, 47

baptismal records, 17, 18, 19
bars, 9, 17, 51
Basil Williams, 27, 28
Belgravia, 9, 40, 52
black peril, 85, 116
black workers, 11, 85, 135, 137, 142, 165
boarding houses, 9, 86
booms, 9, 17, 31, 76
Braamfontein, 20, 40, 44, 51, 52, 53, 55, 61, 82, 86
Braamfontein Estate Company, 44
breadwinners, 17, 18, 19, 32, 56
Brickfields, 16, 20, 21, 22, 23, 24, 26, 31, 52, 53, 54, 58, 59, 61, 77
Brickfields-Burghersdorp, 58, 77
British, 9, 11, 13, 15, 17, 18, 20, 22, 24, 25, 26, 27, 28, 29, 30, 31, 32. 40, 45, 46, 49, 50, 55, 57, 58, 59, 60, 63, 64, 65, 66, 67, 75, 76, 85, 88, 102, 105, 107, 113, 115, 117, 118, 134, 136, 137, 138, 143, 144, 156, 165, 168
British Empire, 11
British married workers, 15
building boom, 20
Burghersdorp, 52, 55, 58, 61
business site, 61

cab driver, 19, 21, 22, 23, 52, 134
capital value of land, 46
carpenter, 15, 19, 53
census, 11, 12, 17, 21, 30, 51, 52, 53, 54, 141
central Johannesburg, 16, 18, 21, 51, 149
Chamber of Mines, 9, 32, 45, 46, 66, 80, 88, 142, 143, 165
charitable organizations, 85, 116, 126
Charles Porter, 60, 85, 95, 96, 104, 157
Chinese indentured labour, 29
Church of England, 16
City and Suburban mine, 18
claims, 39, 41, 42, 43
class consciousness, 32, 102, 113, 165, 166
class experience, 169
coachman, 18, 21, 22
Colonel T. G. Truter, 151
commercial sectors, 17
commission of enquiry, 4, 13, 15, 46, 56, 57, 67, 76, 80, 110, 117, 134, 145, 169
Commission of Enquiry into Assaults on Women, 83, 84, 85
Commissioner Street, 105, 122, 123
Communist Party of South Africa, 143
community, 47, 48, 50, 58, 60, 78, 85, 87, 94, 101, 111, 112, 113, 127, 166
construction, 1, 6, 16, 19, 21, 94, 95, 134, 140, 147
Coolie, 53, 56, 61, 118
Coolie locations, 56
cost of accommodation, 15, 79, 141
cost of living, 10, 14, 15, 31, 57, 58, 75, 88, 90, 107, 109, 110, 114, 141, 165
crisis, 9, 11, 16, 17, 20, 28, 29, 31, 53, 56, 57, 62, 63, 88, 90, 92, 93, 107, 108, 110, 135, 138, 139, 142, 143, 152, 158, 167, 168

Darwin, 144
deep level mining, 10, 11, 114
destitute, 16, 24, 47, 55, 57, 156
destitute families, 57
division of the labour market, 23

domestic servant, 28, 29, 149
Doornfontein, 43, 44, 55, 77, 87
Dr. R. Mackenzie, 104, 127
drinking, 17, 102, 111, 122, 124
Dutch Reformed Church, 155, 156, 167

Economic Commission, 88, 110
economic crises, 16, 17, 20, 28, 29, 31, 88, 107, 110, 135
estate companies, 40, 43, 44, 45, 57, 63, 66
experience, 2, 3, 5, 13, 26, 31, 41, 44, 50, 58, 60, 78, 82, 94, 101, 102, 106, 113, 117, 118, 124, 127, 167, 168
expropriation, 61, 62, 78
extension of Johannesburg's boundaries, 44, 45

family size, 15, 23
Ferreirastown, 16, 40, 51, 85, 87, 114, 117
F. H. P. Creswell, 139, 151
fictive kinship, 32, 111, 112, 113
Ford and Jeppe Estate Company, 47, 51, 52
Fordsburg, 9, 16, 18, 20, 21, 22, 23, 25, 26, 32, 41, 43, 51, 52, 53, 55, 58, 61, 82, 85, 86, 87, 103, 104, 105, 108, 109, 112, 114, 116, 117, 118, 119, 125, 127, 143, 149
freehold suburbs, 40

geography of class, 9, 41, 66, 67
gold, 9, 10, 11, 13, 15, 17, 19, 23, 26, 39, 40, 41, 42, 43, 58, 75, 103, 115, 133, 134, 136, 141, 146, 165, 169
Gold Law, 39, 41, 42, 43, 45, 66, 67, 79, 83
gold mining industry, 9, 15, 26, 165
goldfields, 9, 11, 39, 41, 42, 43

health visitors, 86, 157
Het Volk, 75, 76, 97, 118, 136, 137, 138, 159
high prices, 44, 46, 94, 107
high prices of land, 45, 46
home, 14, 16, 17, 25, 56, 58, 65, 79, 101, 106, 107, 108, 109, 111, 120, 124, 125
homeless, 46
horse-drawn tram, 19, 21, 46
housing crisis, 56, 59, 92, 93, 108
housing markets, 46
housing problem, 46, 55, 56, 57, 62, 64, 65, 66, 92, 94, 110

illicit liquor dealing, 109, 115, 116, 117, 118, 120
Immigration Act of 1902, 28
immigration of British women, 26
immigration policy, 26, 28, 30, 54, 65, 66
Immorality Ordinance of 1903, 118
Industrial Commission of Enquiry, 13, 26, 106
inner city, 52, 56, 61
Insanitary Areas, 62
Insanitary Commission of Enquiry, 59
Inspector of White Labour, 114, 116, 126, 137, 169
Intercolonial Convention, 138
International Socialist League, 143, 152

Jacob de Villiers Roos, 117, 156
Jameson Raid, 10, 13, 16, 32, 49
Jeppestown, 9, 18, 23, 25, 41, 43, 51, 52, 53, 55, 57, 104
Johannesburg Consolidated Investment, 10, 44
Johannesburg Sanitary Board, 49, 54
Johannesburg Town Council, 40, 48, 59, 63, 77, 78, 80, 81, 83, 91, 93, 136, 138
John W. Quinn, 145
John X. Merriman, 139, 152
Joseph Chamberlain, 10, 115

Kaffir, 10, 56

labour process, 64, 136, 165
laundry work, 119, 120
leasehold townships, 40, 77
legislation, 41, 59, 60, 63, 66, 86, 87, 88, 90, 91, 96, 97, 146
licence fees, 42
Lionel Curtis, 40, 44, 49, 50, 145
Lionel Phillips, 10, 16, 32, 45, 136, 137
Liquor Commission, 115
liquor traffic, 85, 115, 116
lodgers, 57, 82, 108, 114
low-grade ore, 9
low wages, 89, 141

Major T. E. Mavrogordato, 117
married miners, 15, 79
Marshallstown, 18
Medical Officer of Health, 28, 29, 60, 85, 86, 88, 90, 91, 96, 104, 127
middle classes, 5, 16, 17, 51, 109

Index

miner's wage, 15
miners, 9, 10, 13, 14, 15, 18, 23, 78, 80, 88, 106, 107, 113, 125, 126, 137, 138, 139, 142, 143, 165
mining strike, 2, 81
mining suburbs, 16
moralize, 16
multiracial population, 52, 61
municipal government, 39, 40, 44, 47, 49, 50, 59, 87

National Party, 76, 109, 138, 142, 143, 149
neighbourhoods, 2, 6, 9, 16, 25, 31, 41, 45, 50, 52, 57, 58, 60, 66, 81, 82, 85, 97, 101, 103, 104, 105, 107, 110, 111, 112, 113, 114, 118, 119, 121, 124, 125, 126, 127, 143, 149, 166
nominated council, 50, 62, 79
northern suburbs, 45

Orange Free State, 14, 142, 143, 150
overcrowding, 56, 61, 80, 81, 93, 95
overseas miners, 10

Paul Kruger, 10
poor, 6, 16, 21, 22, 24, 25, 26, 31, 32, 50, 75, 82, 83, 84, 85, 87, 92, 95, 96, 97, 104, 107, 109, 110, 115, 116, 117, 118, 119, 120, 126, 127, 133, 134, 135, 138, 139, 140, 141, 142, 145, 146, 147, 148, 149, 150, 151, 152, 153, 154, 155, 156, 157, 158, 159, 165
poor Afrikaner, 24, 48, 66
Poor White Problem, 67, 83, 85, 97, 133, 143, 153
poor whiteism, 133, 134, 141, 148, 149, 153, 159
poor whites, 51, 52, 61, 89, 116, 145, 150
population, 11, 12, 13, 15, 16, 17, 21, 22, 24, 25, 26, 27, 28, 30, 31, 39, 44, 45, 47, 48, 49, 50, 52, 53, 55, 56, 57, 60, 61, 65, 66, 76, 79, 81, 82, 83, 84, 85, 87, 89, 90, 91, 92, 93, 95, 97, 102, 105, 107, 108, 110, 111, 113, 115, 116, 119, 124, 127, 133, 134, 135, 137, 143, 146, 150, 151, 155, 157, 158, 167
prejudice against manual work, 118
Present Help League, 16, 136
private land, 42, 43
proclamation, 11, 39, 42, 44, 79, 81
profitability crisis, 135, 152

proletarianization, 21, 24, 83, 117, 134, 139, 146, 147
prostitution, 17, 29, 82, 150
public health, 60, 81, 82, 85, 86, 88, 90, 91, 93, 96, 97
Public Health Act, 82, 91, 96
Public Health Committee, 60

race, 2, 4, 27, 40, 45, 47, 66, 95, 117, 121, 144, 148, 151, 154, 158
racial segregation, 83, 88, 97, 126
racism, 4, 133, 151
Rand Aid Association, 108, 114, 135, 136, 145, 151, 154
Rand Revolt, 2, 111, 113, 127, 143, 159, 166
Rand Unemployed Investigation Committee, 137
Randlords, 13, 26
rates, 40, 45, 47, 66, 77, 80, 81, 96
Rating Bill, 44, 46, 47, 50, 65, 81, 96
Reconstruction Administration, 26, 48, 64, 65, 67, 75
reconstruction period, 11, 40, 41, 44, 59, 60, 62, 67, 93, 96, 115
Refugee Aid Committee, 28
rehousing scheme, 62, 65, 83, 88
relief work, 108, 110, 116, 135, 155, 158
rental, 46, 47, 56, 63, 106, 114
rental value, 46, 47
Report of the Johannesburg Housing Commission, 56, 65
Report of the Transvaal Indigency Commission, 82
reproduction, 6, 11, 27, 30, 144, 147, 148, 153, 156
reproduction of the white working class, 11, 26
Responsible Government, 11, 30, 75, 126, 136
Rev. John Darragh, 16

Sanitary Committee, 39
sanitary conditions, 31, 60
sanitary inspector, 60, 86
sanitation, 59, 61, 85, 88
scarcity of housing, 79
Select Committee on European Employment and Labour Conditions, 83, 85, 117, 139, 148
self-employment, 20, 21, 108, 134
semi-skilled jobs, 64, 136

service, 11, 17, 22, 53, 62, 104, 119, 120, 134, 138, 147
settlement, 9, 11, 13, 14, 20, 29, 30, 40, 41, 44, 46, 50, 52, 57, 82, 83, 97, 105, 127, 139
silicosis, 15, 58, 78, 105, 165
site value rate, 47
skilled mine workers, 13
slum area, 52, 62, 84, 150
slum conditions, 39, 61, 87
slumps, 9, 17, 31, 76, 101, 134
slumps of the mining industry, 9, 31
social control, 59, 85, 137, 154
Social Darwinism, 59, 109, 144, 145, 148, 151, 158
social engineering, 26, 59, 67, 81, 144
social mobility, 20
South African Bill, 138
South African Colonisation Society, 27
South African historiography, 2
South African Labour Party, 138, 142, 159
South African Party, 76, 80, 109, 116, 138, 139, 140, 142, 143, 149, 152, 159
South African War, 1, 15, 17, 18, 22, 24, 25, 30, 39, 43, 44, 48, 49, 54, 61, 67, 106, 107, 115, 135, 145, 150, 155, 158, 167, 168
speculative holding, 40
stand, 41, 42, 46, 48, 86, 126
state agency, 59, 66
state intervention, 85, 94, 97, 155
Status Quo Agreement, 142, 143
strategies of survival, 21, 110, 114
street clearance projects, 59

taxes, 40, 42, 45, 49, 55, 66, 80, 81, 83, 96
tenure, 47, 76, 77, 78, 96
Town Clerk, 26, 44, 47, 50, 87
town lands, 40, 44
Township Owner's Association, 79, 81
trade union, 91, 139, 142
transport, 10, 13, 16, 21, 22, 23, 49, 52, 56, 58, 59, 63, 89, 126, 134
transport industry, 21
Transvaal Indigency Commission, 82, 108, 109, 116, 133, 136, 143, 145, 146, 148, 154, 155, 157

Troyeville, 23

unemployed, 15, 16, 18, 21, 28, 66, 75, 82, 87, 110, 111, 113, 114, 116, 117, 123, 124, 127, 168
unemployment, 133, 134, 135, 136, 137, 138, 139, 140, 141, 142, 144, 148, 151, 152, 153, 154, 155, 157, 158
Unemployment Commission, 133, 152, 153, 158
Union, 64, 80, 81, 82, 85, 86, 88, 90, 91, 93, 96, 126, 138, 139, 141, 143, 148, 155, 156, 159
Union of South Africa, 5, 81, 85, 126
unskilled British, 23
unskilled labourer, 18, 141, 145, 146
urban poverty, 24, 135, 149, 157, 159
urbanized Afrikaners, 23, 25, 111

van Onselen's, 3, 32
Violet H. Markham, 102, 103
Vrededorp, 9, 20, 22, 23, 26, 32, 41, 44, 47, 48, 52, 53, 77, 82, 85, 104, 112, 116, 118, 143
Vrededorp Stands Ordinance, 44, 47, 48

wards, 52, 53, 54
whiteness, 4
Witwatersrand, 3, 6, 9, 11, 13, 15, 26, 29, 31, 32, 39, 41, 42, 43, 45, 51, 52, 58, 64, 88, 97, 116, 124, 125, 127, 135, 137, 139, 141, 154, 158, 159, 165
Witwatersrand Township Estate and Financial Corporation, 43
Witwatersrand Trades and Labour Council, 64
working class accommodation, 40, 41, 46, 54, 56, 57, 63, 79, 89, 90, 91, 105, 109
working class children, 124
working class culture, 3, 17, 111, 121
working class families, 7, 11, 15, 16, 23, 25, 32, 56, 57, 106, 107, 110, 111, 113, 114, 117
working class houses, 46, 88, 105, 108
working class organization, 2